D0948606

Modern Arabic Poetry

An Anthology

EDITED BY

Salma Khadra Jayyusi

Columbia University Press
New York   1987

The preparation of the manuscript for this anthology was supported by Dar al-Ma'mun for Translation and Publishing, a branch of the Iraqi Ministry of Information and Culture.

Library of Congress Cataloging-in-Publication Data

Modern Arabic poetry.

1. Arabic poetry—20th century—Translations into
English. 2. English poetry—Translations from Arabic.
I. Jayyusi, Salma Khadra.
PJ7694.E3M64 1987   892'.716'08   87-678
ISBN 0-231-05272-3

Columbia University Press
New York Guildford, Surrey
Copyright © 1987 Columbia University Press
All rights reserved

Printed in the United States of America

Book Design by Ken Venezio

This anthology was prepared under PROTA, PROJECT OF TRANSLATION FROM ARABIC LITERATURE, founded and directed by Salma Khadra Jayyusi

Other PROTA books to date:

The Secret Life of Saeed, the Pessoptimist, a novel by Emile Habiby. Translated by S.K. Jayyusi and Trevor LeGassick. 1982; 2d ed. 1985.

Wild Thorns, a novel by Sahar Khalifeh. Translated by Trevor LeGassick and Elizabeth Fernea. 1985.

War in the Land of Egypt, a novel by Yusuf al-Qaᶜid. 1986.

The Literature of Modern Arabia: An Anthology. Edited by Salma Khadra Jayyusi. 1987.

Modern Arabic Fiction and Drama: An Anthology. Edited by Salma Khadra Jayyusi. Forthcoming.

In Memory of my sisters,
Aida and Bouran Khadra
Salma

CONTENTS

This volume, which has been prepared at a time when Arabic poetry is still undergoing active development, is intended both to record and to anticipate—to record the major achievements of established poets who have already contributed their best to the ongoing movement of modern Arabic poetry, and to anticipate many of the talents who, in all probability, will be at the forefront of poetic activity in the near future.

This double task creates its own difficulties. To decide on established poets might seem a relatively easy undertaking: critics and literary historians agree on them, and serious anthologies include them. But reputations need to be periodically modified and put in clearer perspective so that poets can be reevaluated as to their real artistic influence and the role they played as *poets*, not simply as social and political critics. And another difficulty arises in selecting from the works of established poets, since most of their famous poems have already been translated and published. In a few cases, when I felt that a poem carried special significance artistically or thematically, I decided that just because there was an existing translation was no reason why we should not attempt our own version. But apart from such considerations, I have attempted to present hitherto untranslated poems.

The difficulty of anticipating new talents has been more laborious. Having gone passionately about this task—asking, researching, and seeking—I am very happy about the rich new talents that I am introducing here. These are poets mostly, but not always, from the younger generation of the seventies, who have never appeared in any anthology either in Arabic or in translation, and their representation gives an added dimension to this work. At the same time I want to stress that the young poets I have introduced here are by no means the only ones in the contemporary poetic field in Arabic. There are many others equally thriving who are now enriching contemporary Arabic poetry and, in fact, modifying its trends and direction. I was unable to present them in this already large volume, mainly because of lack of space or because my acquaintance with their best work came too late in the project. Let us hope that this fact will be an incentive for another anthology to be dedicated soon to the poets of the seventies and after.

A further word on selection: the corpus of contemporary Arabic poetry is rich enough for an anthologist to offer a collection targeted only to the taste and poetic assumptions of the English-speaking reader. However, I felt that to follow this path would be unrepresentative and misleading, for it was necessary, I felt, to bring out the cultural differences and the varied interests of contemporary Arab poets: their particular kinds of experience, their special emphases, their visions, and their emotional and spiritual identities. If one of the purposes of this kind of work is to open a window on the human situations and esthetic achievements of poets who belong to a different culture, then the full flavor of that culture should be brought out with single-minded faithfulness. I fully realize that much of a reader's assessment is more or less culture-bound; in fact, more than once I came face to face with this problem as I worked on the translations with some of the English-speaking poets. But from a different vantage point, it can be quite amazing how very similar poetries are, and how unprejudiced and competent poets easily assimilate and interpret the verse of other poets of a completely different language and culture. In this sense it is possible to say that poetry has many tongues but a single language.

A major consideration in the translations themselves was the attempt to bring out a "period flavor." The pre-fifties poetry, whether neoclassical or Romantic, relies strongly on the inherited idiom of Arabic poetry and resorts to many of the well-entrenched phrases and ways of expression with which the Arab reader has always been in tune. The translation of this poetry proved to be a difficult task precisely because of these rich idiomatic trammels which obstruct the free flow of a translator's work. All poetries have their own idiomatic usages which have to be interpreted in the correct way, but the problem is increased manyfold when the translation is carried out between two nonrelated languages. In the poetry which relies on rhetorical expressions, such as that of Ahmad Shauqi, the Arab world's most prominent neoclassical poet, the difficulty was enormous, because rhetoric, which is an untranslatable feature of a poem, is not merely an external decorative additive, but part of the poem's semantic signification. A poem built on a rhetorical mode of address loses much of its heat and punch when denuded of its rhetoric in translation.

By contrast, one of the interesting discoveries which this experiment has afforded me is the realization that modernist Arabic poetry (the development and main characteristics of which are detailed in the introduction) has veered away, consciously or unconsciously, from the inherited poetic idiom. The more "modern" a poet is, the further away from this traditional idiom his or her poetry is, and therefore the more easily translatable. The situation reflects the fact that the modern poetic idiom in Arabic has been influenced, more than that of any earlier phase, by Western poetry.

In the course of preparing this anthology, it became clear to me that the poetry which used simpler sentence constructions and was less metaphorically complex was more difficult to translate than the complex kind. Complexity, unless absurd and a mere distortion, carries well into another language, and, in the hands of competent translators, often keeps its compactness and density. By contrast, the poetry of simple structures and the direct approach needs translators who can imbue the target language with the same charge and tension that was achieved in the original. It was easier, for example, to translate Khalil Hawi than Nizar Qabbani, or, among the younger generation of poets, to translate Muhammad al-Ghuzzi than Qasim Haddad.

Some critics believe that since perfect equivalence in translation is not attainable, there is no point in attempting the task of translation at all. But what a loss it would be if no one could come to know the great poets of the human race who wrote in languages different from their own! In most cases, the only way to read the poetry of other cultures is through the medium of translation. This makes the task of translation not only a major esthetic undertaking, but also a crucial cultural responsibility: poetry is the main vehicle for expressing the emotional experience of a people, and for revealing their deeper consciousness of the world, and it may bring the reader into a more intimate knowledge of other people's actual life situations. If we think about it, even when poets read a foreign poetry directly in its original tongue, they tend to go through a process of translation in order to benefit from this poetry in their own work. What usually happens is that they translate this poetry in their own minds, often as they are reading it. In short, the process of translation goes on, in one way or another, all the time.

In this volume, as with all PROTA translations, the method employed is based on the idea that only poets should translate poetry. All poems are given first to bilingual translators rooted in both languages, with a genuine understanding and love for poetry, then to English-speaking poets who creatively render the translated poems into the English literary idiom. As Arabic is a language very different from English, each lot of translators had an onerous task to perform. It will be noticed, however, that a few poems carry only the names of the first translators. This indicates that the English-speaking poet has found nothing she or he would like to change in the original translation.

The names of translators have been arranged according to the order in which the work has been conducted, the bilingual translator's name usually appearing first, followed by the name of the English-speaking poet. This arrangement indicates no value judgment but is a convenient way of presentation. I have noticed that other anthologies, such as *Modern Swedish Poetry in Translation* (ed. by Gunnar Harding and Anselm Hollo, University of Minnesota Press, 1979), have followed the same method of presentation.

I have divided the anthology into two parts: poets before the fifties, and poets after the fifties. In my introduction, I have shown how poetry in the first half of this century passed rapidly through various schools—neoclassicism, Romanticism, and symbolism—in anticipation of the modern movement which took place in the fifties. The instinctive urge in Arabic poetry during the pre-fifties period was to reach contemporaneity with world poetry, and poetry after the fifties is the outcome of the active experimentation which took place through the half century. The fifties, in my opinion, is the dividing line between the period of sowing and the period of harvest. Within each part the poets are presented alphabetically.

The notes to the poems are placed after each poet's work in the order in which they appear in the poems. The names of poets are written in the way most convenient for the English-speaking reader. A transliterated list of all the poets' names, based on the system used by the *New Encyclopedia of Islam*, is found at the end of the book.

S.K.J.

ACKNOWLEDGMENTS

My deep thanks are due to the Ministry of Information and Culture in Iraq, and above all to its Minister, al-Sayyid Lateef Nusayyif Jasim, who, throughout the long tenure of his office, has demonstrated a genuine and fruitful involvement in pan-Arab culture and its dissemination abroad. His enthusiastic support for PROTA, the Project of Translation from Arabic, which I founded in 1980, has expressed itself through a generous grant and much moral support, and has resulted in two large volumes, the first of these being the present *Anthology of Modern Arabic Poetry*, and the second the *Anthology of Arab Fictional Genres*, which is due to appear soon. I am also greatly indebted to Mr. Hasan Tawalbeh, the former head of public relations at the Ministry, who shared my vision to spread Arabic culture abroad and who inspired me with the daring to try to fulfill that dream. If PROTA has been able to achieve some of its aims, it is first and foremost because of the powerful moral support of two persons, one of whom is Mr. Tawalbeh. Thanks are also due to Mr. Naji al-Hadithi, head of the Ministry's Dar al-Ma'mun for Translation and Publishing. His love of literature has been an inspiration, as has been his genuine respect for the value and importance of literary translations and cultural dissemination.

I owe a standing debt to Professor Ernest McCarus, director of the Center for Near Eastern and North African Studies at the University of Michigan. He has been the other steadfast spirit behind PROTA, and his constant faith and support have given me great encouragement and have helped me, particularly in PROTA's early years, to strive onward toward its goals. He has been instrumental in convincing many responsible people of the value and necessity of the cultural exchange that PROTA could bring about and by this he secured the establishment of the Project with its resultant anthologies (including this anthology) and other books. To Professor Gernot Windfuhr, chairman of the Department of Near Eastern Languages and Literature at the University of Michigan, I also owe many thanks. A lover of poetry and a translator himself, he showed a genuine interest in the Project when I first started it while I was a visiting scholar at the Horace Rackham School at the University of Michigan, and he generously extended all possible help and encouragement.

To Dr. Roger Allen, professor of Arabic at the University of Pennsylvania and PROTA's spokesman, I owe more thanks than I can possibly express in words. Whether as advisor, or as member of the editorial board and of the administrative committee of PROTA, he was, at all times, prepared to do his utmost to promote the Project in all its aspects. My gratitude also goes to Dr. Issa Boullata, professor of Arabic at McGill University and member of PROTA's editorial board, for many kindnesses. He was the person who undertook "impossible" translation tasks whenever the need arose, and, in cooperation with Dr. Allen, stood by me in the final decisions concerning the present form of these two anthologies.

If a person's wealth is in her friends, then I am indeed rich in having the friendship of Dr. Trevor LeGassick, professor of Arabic at the University of Michigan and my life-long friend and colleague. As always, he extended his open-handed help to me, despite his great worries at the time. To him, this volume owes a great deal for his advice, suggestions, and encouragement.

I owe warm thanks to Dr. Salih Jawad Altoma, chairman of the Department of Near Eastern Languages and Cultures at Indiana University for his enthusiasm about this work and his constant support and encouragement.

I also owe special thanks to Dr. Charles Doria, who teaches at Mason Gross School of the Arts at Rutgers University. His lively interest in Arabic poetry and his enthusiasm to cooperate with me on translations long before PROTA's inception were a constant source of inspiration and encouragement. I also thank him for the expert work he performed in translating my own poems (several of which have appeared in K. Boullata's *Women of the Fertile Crescent*) as well as for his many helpful suggestions on the introduction.

I must also warmly thank Dr. Muhammad Baqir Alwan for his great kindness in helping me, whenever the need arose, with expert information regarding several matters in this volume.

And I owe much to Patricia Alanah Rosenfield, poet, teacher of the beautiful word, and dear friend. Hers was an affectionate support, a vibrant inspiration, and a constant reminder of the crucial necessity of works like these.

It is with a deep sense of pride that I acknowledge the generous attitude of the Arab poets represented in this volume, and of the families of those poets who have passed away. If poetry is the food of the Arab spirit, then they have confirmed this many times over. Freely and with enthusiasm, they gave their permission for translation, answered my many letters without hesitation, and sent me their books from all parts of the Arab world.

This volume could not have been brought to completion without the help and advice of critics, poets, scholars, and literary friends all over the Arab homeland. They are too many to list by name here, but special thanks go to Dr. Shukri 'Ayyad, Dr. Faisal Darraj, and Mr. Ilyas Khouri, all noted critics, and to poets Muhammad al-Asʿad, Khairi Mansour, Ahmad Dah-bour, and al-Munsif al-Wahaybi for their helpful suggestions on poets and poems.

The many distinguished translators, both the bilingual translators who worked on the original texts and the English-speaking poets who modified the translated versions, form the backbone of this work. I thank them all, not only for their invaluable work on the translations, but also for the joy they imparted while working with me. Their care, their passion for poetry, and their constant patience and indulgence toward me have considerably lightened the burdens of the work. I have also been greatly impressed by their attempt, particularly in the case of the English-speaking poets, to bridge the cultural gap that exists between Arabic culture and the cultures of the English-speaking world, and by the genuine effort, especially on the part of the bilingual translators, to transcend the many well-known difficulties encountered when working on renderings between two nonrelated languages such as Arabic and English. It was a real privilege to work with them.

I should also like to thank the library staffs of the School of Oriental and African Studies of the University of London, the University of Michigan, the University of Texas at Austin, and the Widener Library at Harvard University for their courteous help over the years. Special thanks go to Dr. David Partington, head of the Middle East Library at the Widener for his help and kind appreciation. Thanks are also due to Mr. Fawzi Abd Al-Razzak and Mr. Ahmad Jebari at the Widener for their very kind assistance.

Heartfelt thanks are due to Miss Erna Hoffmann for her meticulous help in preparing the manuscript, and for many kindnesses which she often rendered at short notice.

Dr. Sharif Elmusa is one of PROTA's most enthusiastic friends, and my warm thanks and appreciation go to him for his consistent help over the years both as a reader who often assisted in the process of selection, and as sharp-eyed reviewer and literary assessor. His sensitivity, his sense of humor, and his fine literary taste made working with him a fruitful and exciting experience.

Last but not least, my own family merits my deepest gratitude. They have all shared my dream and purpose and have constantly been there to help make working conditions easier. With unstinting generosity and an intellectual and artistic appreciation for PROTA's mission, my son, Usama, made his home a haven for the Project whenever I stayed with him. To his wife, Salwa, also goes my appreciation for her enthusiasm and understanding, and for her happy companionship. My daughters, Lena and May have been indispensible to me emotionally and intellectually. I thank them both very much, particularly for the consolation and solace they gave me after the tragic death of my two younger sisters during the course of this work. To both Lena and May, also, go my thanks for many creative suggestions concerning this volume. It was my good fortune that Lena and her husband, Dr. Jeff Coulter, scholars and writers themselves, wholeheartedly shared my love and enthusiasm for the work. Jeff's abiding faith in the Project was always a source of energy and liveliness, and his good humor generated many moments of laughter amidst the avalanching mound of work. Lena herself merits mention for her professional contribution to this volume. Her sound artistic ideas and loving insight into the workings of language were always a great inspiration, and she proved to be a steadfast point of reference with whom I addictively conferred whenever the need arose, and it arose often. Especially, I want to thank her for her wonderful work on the Barakat poems, which she also selected herself after a thorough reading of the poet's complete oeuvre. This volume owes her a great debt, and I am certain that without her constant help and inspiration, PROTA would have been very difficult to achieve.

Salma Khadra Jayyusi

At the beginning of the twentieth century Arabic poetry was remote from the mainstream of world poetry; indeed, it was lagging far behind. This was a far cry from the glorious heights it had achieved in medieval times. Through countless experiments, it struggled during this century to attain contemporaneity with modern trends in world poetry, particularly in the West. The struggle for modernization was made more difficult because Arabic poetry, during its nineteenth-century renaissance, reacquired many traditional conventions: esthetic, semantic, and technical. These conventions had been part of our poetic heritage and an integral component of every poet's repertory and poetic skills. This struggle was often intense, dramatic, and sometimes painful.

This is why, when discussing modern Arabic poetry (I use "modern" here in its temporal meaning) and the many radical changes that have taken place throughout this century, I feel it is important to include an account, albeit short, of the immediate as well as the more remote aspects of the Arab poetic heritage.

At the outset of the nineteenth century, Arabic poetry suffered from many weaknesses. These were caused by the onerous social, political, and cultural conditions inflicted on the Arab world by the oppressive domination of the Ottoman Empire. The Ottomans ruled the Arab world for four long centuries until 1919, and it was the least productive period of its cultural history. This is reflected most poignantly in our literature. Creative expression was checked and often stifled. Slowly, the Arabs were cut off from their brilliant intellectual and literary past, and, with time, the art of poetry began to inhabit a cultural vacuum. It focused almost exclusively on trivial themes that utterly neglected the existential dimensions of the human condition. Mainly concerned, then, with amusement and the banal exchange of niceties, it had become repetitive, artificial, and full of useless embellishments—nothing more than an exercise of wit and almost wholly devoid of substance.

The deterioration of Arabic poetry to this state of banality was, as I have said, the massive collapse of an art form that had once reached great heights of sophistication. It had flourished even before the advent of Islam (the Islamic calendar begins in 622). The pre-Islamic poetry handed down to us is remarkably mature and boasts an artistic perfection that is at variance with the "primitive" lives led by nomadic Arabs who, rather than the urbanized inhabitants of such Arabian towns as Mecca, Medina, and Haira, should be regarded as the real originators of the poetic art. Throughout the subsequent golden epochs of the Arab-Islamic empire, which stretched from China to Spain, poetry continued to develop in harmony with changing ways of life, while it preserved its artistic splendor. Not only was poetry the first medium of expression that spoke of the human condition and the varied experiences of men and women throughout the centuries, it was also the register of the Arabs, which preserved the annals of their history: their battles, their national achievements, and the glory of their rulers, as well as their ethical attributes—their special kind of wisdom, their chivalry, hospitality, and valor. It is important to note here that, before Islam, poetry was the sole artistic expression (along with oratory to a lesser extent) that had the opportunity to develop. The pre-Islamic period was a preliterate age, when only oral expression could prevail. The Arabian Peninsula was largely desert, and offered limited opportunity for artistic development: nomads could not chisel stone or paint, they lived constantly on the move in search for new pastures and life-giving springs. Later on, after the advent of Islam, painting and sculpture were discouraged out of fear of iconography and idol worship, which are strictly prohibited in Islam. However, during the first forty years of Islam (the Orthodox years and the period of formation and confirmation) poetry as well was discouraged in favor of the memorizing of the Quran. The Quran's high literary standards and fine artistic style were regarded by knowledgeable Muslims as inimitable. Poetry regained its central importance at the beginning of the Umayyad period (660), when the caliphs felt the need for personal publicity and for solidly entrenching the Umayyad dynasty. From that time forward poetry achieved a unique status in Arabic culture. Through its fine esthetic attainments and its moving portrayal of Arab achievements and history, it has become the art most revered by Arabs down through the years.

In modern times, the Arab literary renaissance began in the nineteenth century, first in Lebanon and then in Egypt. However, the early pioneers of the literary renaissance in Lebanon experimented mainly in prose, developing a modernized language and style suitable for expressing the needs of the times. Although they also experimented in poetry, they did not achieve the same success, suggesting that the art of poetry needs a longer time to develop than prose. The first real poetic renaissance took place in the second half of the nineteenth century in Egypt. The impulse for cultural change in Egypt came with the aftermath of the Napoleonic invasion (1798–1801), which shocked people with the discovery of the great cultural and technological gap that existed between the Arab East and the European West. The enlightened rule of Muhammad Ali Pasha, who ruled from 1805 to 1849—the many students he sent to be educated in France, the schools and educational institutions he established (among them the illustrious School of Languages, which became the principal center for translation from other languages), the publication of a major newspaper, and the active utilization of the Arabic printing press introduced by Napoleon into Egypt—brought about a true cultural awakening and aroused a deeper interest in learning and reviving the literary achievements of the past. The most important aspect of this activity, as far as poetry was concerned, was the publication of many collections of classical Arabic poetry and *belles lettres*. Poets all over the Arab world were now able to read the best poetry of their ancestors and to benefit directly from its stylistic, syntactical, and technical excellence. The availability of these printed books proved providential in the extreme. At this time, poetry needed an infusion of vigor that could only be found in the best examples of verse from the more eloquent past, before it could turn to the introduction of innovations borrowed from the poetic art of other languages. The attempt to graft foreign poetry onto fragile roots would certainly have weakened Arabic poetry even more.

The work of the Egyptian Ahmad Shauqi (1869–1932), who became the major neoclassical poet in the Arab world, and that of several other leading poets in Egypt and in other Arab countries, secured for Arabic poetry the strength and rootedness it needed at the time. New linguistic and stylistic foundations were established for Arabic poetry along classical lines, characterized by a vigor and terseness of expression, a more direct approach, and a greater balance betwen emotion, imagination, and ideas, and between the subjective and the objective. Poetic diction renewed itself, making good use of the old rhetoric of the classical *qasida*, with its loud, oratorical tone. The neoclassical poets felt in harmony with the fundamental assumptions of their age. Their verse reflected a stable and well-ordered universe where all evil came from the outside, a world well understood and respected by the poets and their audience, with clearly defined ethical, moral, esthetic, and philosophical values.

The neoclassical style, however, initially vital for invigorating the weak and artificial verse of the prerenaissance era, later proved to be out of step with the times. Because of its direct links with the old poetry it was modeled on, it had opened up whole vistas of past poetic achievements dear to the Arabs, imitating classical techniques, rhythms, and syntactical constructions and evoking a similar spirit of grandeur, nostalgia, and national pride. However, the attitudes and in fact the whole world view this poetry reflected, as well as the classical method itself, were incompatible with the winds of change that had begun to blow over the Arab world from all directions. Once the advantages gained from a return to the vigor and terseness of the old poetry were assimilated, the continuing entrenchment of neoclassicism became an embarrassing liability for poetry and a stubborn hindrance to innovation and change. However, neoclassical Arabic poetry proved more tenacious than any other school of poetry which poets embraced during the first half of the twentieth century. It would require a great struggle to loosen the grip it had on the tastes and minds of its large Arab audience.

The urge for change took hold of the younger generation of poets and critics that rose to fame in the first two decades of this century. The first real impetus for a genuine break with neoclassicism came from the Arab poets who had emigrated to North America. Their leader, Gibran Kahlil Gibran (1883–1931) was the single most important influence on Arabic poetry and literature during the first half of this century. He was helped in North America by such distinguished poets as Ilya Abu Madi (1890–1957) and the poet-critic Mikha'il Nu‘aima (1889), whose critical writings, with their iconoclastic intentions and their invigorating insights into new poetic methods, helped greatly to shake the blind attachment of a *select* Arab audience to neoclassical rigidity and traditionalism. At the same time, a group of poet-critics in Egypt joined forces in the battle against neoclassicism, forging a vital link with the North American group in the early twenties. As a result of persistent criticism by these two groups, combined with the example of Gibran's writings and those of the Mahjar group in particular, a Romantic current was released that was backed by a deep need for new freedom in both art and life. By the late twenties, Romanticism had become a major trend in poetry. Several poets rose to fame on a pan-Arabic scale. Their various experiments helped foment a deep change in poetic method, style, mood, tone, imagery, and language. However, among them the central influence was Gibran.

Gibran's influence touched all aspects of the poem. The most interesting phenomenon to notice here is that Gibran was not a great poet in verse, and most of his writings in prose should not be regarded as "poetry" even in the broadest meaning of the term. However, in his prose poems and poetic prose, he released poetry from its neoclassical limitations and introduced a great courage among Arab poets to use words and images in completely unprecedented ways. Influenced by sources that had hitherto not influenced Arab poets, such as the Bible, Western literature and painting, and other fresh sources of culture and thought, East and West, Gibran displayed a completely new sensibility and a new kind of creativity; he opened windows on a different kind of world. The famous "Gibranian style" was a decisive influence on the poets and creative writers of his generation. It was characterized by a rhythm which fell on the ears like magic, intoxicating in its frequent use of interrogations, repetitions, and the vocative; by a language which was at once modern, elegant, and original; and by an imagery that was evocative and imbued with a healthy measure of emotion. His vision of a world made sterile by dead mores and conventions but redeemable through love, good will, and constructive action deepened his readers' insights and enlightened their views of life and man. The number of creative men and women who fell under the charm and potency of his experiment was great. For over two decades, the twenties and thirties, his work was the hinge around which Arabic poetry turned. Without him, the story of modern Arabic poetry would have been quite different.

Arab Romanticism did not have the same philosophical background which European Romanticism enjoyed; it stemmed rather from the realization by poets and intellectuals of the beleaguered status of an Arab world which was being challenged by a more modern, more progressive, more potent life in Europe and North America. It came about as a direct result of this spread of a new enlightenment, a new curiosity, a new sense of wonder, and the yearning toward seemingly unattainable aspirations. It gave birth to a poetry of volition, of individual longings and dreams, of a deep desire for freedom. This new Romanticism began among Arab immigrant poets in North America, where personal freedom was available. Their personal freedom allowed them to write a literature that sought wider horizons for human thought and action, that eagerly yearned to change the world for everyone, in every sphere. This new spirit launched direct incisive attacks against political inertia in the Arab homeland, and struggled against the social injustice and outmoded traditions that shackled the individual and suffocated his or her life. It spoke for change and revolution and awakened people's souls to new possibilities for freedom. In the Arab world, where no such personal freedoms yet existed, where most people felt trapped and cheated out of their youth and its legitimate joys, the new poetry at first was mostly a passive trend, sometimes full of sorrow and pain, sometimes driven by an inner need for the joys of the exotic and the search for love and beauty. It reflected a thirst for the image of woman and for the liberation of the heart. This is what we see in such major Romantic poets as the

Sudanese al-Tijani Yusuf Bashir (1912–1937), the Egyptians Ibrahim Naji (1898–1953) and ʿAli Mahmoud Taha (1901–1949), the Lebanese Ilyas Abu Shabaka (1903–1947), and the Tunisian Abu al-Qasim al-Shabbi (1909–1934). The latter, however, reflected two opposite attitudes, sometimes speaking as a herald of revolution and social change, and other times (when social and political involvement exhausted him) escaping into solitude and love.

Although Arab Romanticism in literature enjoyed but a short life span, it was a necessary phase and helped greatly to shake stultified concepts and make the poetic tools more malleable, ready for a change in another direction. It is interesting to observe that Romanticism in the Arab world did not happen all at once, but arrived gradually to this country or that whenever a deeper awakening to the social and personal shackles became manifest. Although many critics linked its rise with political failures (such as the thwarting of the Egyptian revolution of 1919, for example), it was not really the result of political involvement on the part of its protagonists. In fact, the political poets in the Arab world at this time (the twenties and thirties) were writing more in the neoclassical vein, while the Romantics were writing mainly about the personal dilemmas of people living in an age of transition still dominated by strict taboos and outmoded social mores.[1]

By expressing a will to change, however, Arab Romanticism took a great step toward modernity. It is amazing, nonetheless, to see how quickly it incorporated such typical Romantic weaknesses as sentimentalism, dilution, formlessness, and occasionally even decadence. It was now becoming increasingly clear that other methods needed to be found which could correct these flaws. Arab poets were avidly reading Western poetry, in the original as well as in translation, and absorbing Western poetic ideas. The time was ripe for experimentation.

Although it is impossible here, for lack of space, to treat in depth all the details of the poetic changes that occured in Arabic poetry in this century, the overall picture is indicative of a *pattern* that seems to govern poetic change in general. Romanticism, in the Arab world as in the West, penetrated and supplanted neoclassicism because it provided a needed antidote to neoclassicism's weaknesses. However, Romanticism itself had to be checked and its faults curbed by symbolism.

Symbolism established itself with a good measure of success in the thirties. It achieved subtlety, and evocative and connotative signification, and it conjured meaning through the musicality inherent in words. It sought to distill poetry to its purest form, incorporating the Ideal and the Beautiful in typical symbolist fashion. The directness, rationality, and traditionalism of the neoclassical school were transcended, as were the dilution, flabbiness, sentimentality, and spleen of Romanticism. The major protagonist of the new Arab symbolism was the Lebanese Saʿid ʿAql (1912). In his introduction to his best work, a long poem entitled *Al-Majdaliyya* (1937) on the meeting of Christ and Mary Magdalene, ʿAql spoke of the main tenets of such French symbolists as Mallarmé, Paul Valéry, and the critic Abbé H. Brémond.[2] ʿAql's poetry and critical writings are direct echoes of these French symbolists. However, they seemed quite original and fresh to the Arab lovers of poetry at the time, and as a result ʿAql won great fame in the thirties and forties. In *Al-Majdaliyya* and other poems, his use of symbols and the way he exploited color and music to serve meaning were a great step toward the later incorporation, when the modernist movement began in the fifties, of more sophisticated obliquities. Another important aspect of *Al-Majdaliyya* was its successful introduction of a purely Christian theme into a poetry which, while it was never deeply religious in Arabic (the mystics of Islam were an exception), was nonetheless predominantly influenced by Islamic ideas and attitudes.

ʿAql was never to achieve the success of *Al-Majdaliyya* again. It was unfortunate for him that the political climate was undergoing radicalization, and later erupted into the fury and tragedy of the post-1948 Palestine disaster, a catalytic landmark which, while changing the whole world of the Arab poet decisively and permanently, did not do much to touch Said Aql the poet. He remained ensconced in his temple of worship of the Beautiful and the Ideal. In 1950, when he published his first collection of poems, *Rindala*, it passed almost unnoticed by major critics outside Lebanon. The mood and the expectations of the age had changed, and there was little tolerance for the calm, labored, dreamy, and rather ethereal utterances of a poet still living in a world of harmony and blissful leisure, while tragedy and feelings of national shame and grief raged throughout the Arab world. It is amazing, moreover, to observe that the passage of years which brought even more severe tragedies to the Arab world, increased international aggression and internal coercion, and made the fight for freedom the major theme in modern Arabic poetry, did not change ʿAql's thematic involvements.[3]

Symbolism, a doctrine that calls for the worship of Beauty and the Ideal and cocoons itself from the heat and blizzards of life, could not possibly survive in the face of the political upheavals since 1948. It had to give way to a more realistic, a more committed poetic utterance. Modern Arab poets in the fifties would continue to exploit the new capacities poetry had acquired through romanticism and symbolism, while rejecting, often with decisive aversion, both the ivory tower position of the symbolists and the often introverted and oversentimentalized vision of the Romantics.

During the first half of the century, Arabic poetry has indeed run a fast course toward the goal of arriving at modernity and contemporaneity with world poetry. Arabic poetry, not simply through an acquired knowledge of poetic theory, but also through the internal dynamics of art, which can propel artistic growth and govern change, was led toward this goal with vigor and courage, compressing into only a few decades the evolution that took centuries to achieve in the West. In retrospect, the scene seems dazzling. By the end of the forties, Arabic poetry had gained great flexibility. Its imagery and language had undergone major transformations, its diction gained a new capacity for obliquity and mystery, its rhythms attained greater lyricism, its tone a wider expressive range. It was rich, full of nuance, pulsating with the spirit of adventure, open to everything. Experiments which would have seemed impossible before were now becoming commonplace. Everything seemed possible.

Some of the most important and conscious experiments that took place in the twentieth century were in form, that most intractable element in the inherited poem. The traditional form in Arabic poetry is characterized by a two-hemistich monorhymed arrangement and has been the only form used in traditional "formal" (as opposed to other nonelevated) poetry since time immemorial. It became, therefore, the only Arab model for the poetic revival in modern times. Other forms in classical times, such as the stanzaic *muwashshah* (introduced in Arab Spain in the tenth century A.D.) and the *dubait* (a kind of couplet) were never elevated to the status of formal poetry.[4]

In the two-hemistich form, the single line of verse which ends in the monorhyme (and rhymes are very rich in Arabic), is divided into two almost equal hemistichs. Each hemistich ends in a caesura. The one at the end of the first hemistich is arbitrary but is resorted to more often than not because of the inordinate length of the verse in many of the original sixteen meters in Arabic. However, the caesura at the end of the second hemistich, i.e., at the end of the verse, is obligatory. This division gives the old Arabic poem its permanent qualities of symmetry and equilibrium. It also determines that the verse be self-contained, i.e., that it contain its own meaning and imagery, independent technically from the other verses. In this form, enjambment from one verse to the other is very rare. This self-contained quality makes the verse, with its balanced measures and symmetrical division, the unit in the poem. Through long practice, this essentially *rhythmic* organization produced other arrangements, in many cases ordering meaning, thought, and syntax according to inner rhythmic and metrical divisions. There is no rule that prescribes any such apportioning at all; this form is not a determinant of syntactic or semantic arrangements, but it has developed its own characteristics through practice, in completely unconscious renderings. This is not to say that individual poets did not resort to the freedom that was theirs to utilize their creativity and originality by transcending any such syntactical and semantic divisions, for many writers throughout the long history of Arabic poetry have done just that. However, the majority, which includes many famous poets, often fell under the spell of these measured rhythmical parallelisms and their semantic and syntactical outcome, producing such arrangements in which one hemistich would contain a full sentence in parallel similarity, antithetical contrast, or causative relationship with the sentence in the second hemistich, etc. All verses in the old Arabic poem are equal in length, employing a fixed number of feet in each verse. Moreover, a classical poem is strictly built on one single meter.

This short description should be enough to point out the two most pervasive qualities of the old two-hemistich monorhymed form. The first is its *fixed pattern*, where the same number of feet is employed in each verse and similarly arranged in two hemistichs, and where a monorhyme is used throughout the poem. The second is the quality of symmetry and balance produced by the metrical division, through the two caesuras in the single verse.

It was in these qualities that the strength of the old form lay, and its intractability as well. For, in the first place, symmetry and balance can have such a hold on the esthetic sense and, in the case of poetry, on the auditory sensibility of the reader or hearer that it would be very difficult to induce audiences to relish a radical change from these seasoned, well-measured, age-old rhythms in favor of a free rhythmical arrangement, at first go-round. This was proven clearly by the violent controversy that ensued when the free verse movement in Arabic began at the end of the forties. In the second place, the way symmetry and balance determined to some extent the internal structure of the poem and its syntactical and semantic arrangement made the form even more resistant to radical change from old, established methods of poetic practice.

Most of the poets who rose to fame in this century had access to other literatures, either in translation or in their original languages. They discovered different poetic methods and musical arrangements and found reasons and incentives to try to invent new forms for the Arabic poem. The old two-hemistich monorhymed form for too long had gone unchallenged, the new poets thought. Additionally, in the dynamic modern age, with its windows open to cultural influences from East and West, change was of the essence. Experiments in form have taken place at least since the beginning of this century, but most of them either concentrated on developing new rhyme schemes, abandoning rhyme altogether, or creating poems with mixed meters, or poems with various stanzaic arrangements. The results, at best, were insignificant or downright unsuccessful, as was the attempt to employ blank verse in this form.[5] It never occured to these experimental poets that the intractability of the old form lay in its fixed symmetrical patterns. So long as these poets still regarded the verse as the sole unit of poetic composition and kept the caesuras which determined symmetry and balance, they were not going to create any radical change in the form of the Arabic poem. The only way to accomplish this was for the experimentalists to discover a way of breaking through the symmetrical divisions, on the one hand, and discovering new methods of flouting the rule of a fixed number of feet in each line of poetry, on the other. When, in the mid-forties, poets succeeded in creating an acceptable form of free verse (already achieved in the thirties but developed to greater maturity in the mid-forties), it was because they were now able to abandon the age-old adherence to a fixed number of feet and to the two caesuras in each verse. In free verse, a poet makes the single foot his or her basic unit, repeating it as many times as artistic instinct dictates in the single line. It is interesting to note that the first poets to successfully discover this were not great poets by any means. However, two splendid young talents in Iraq, Nazik al-Mala'ika (b. 1923) and Badr Shakir al-Sayyab (1926–1964), found in this discovery a new method for writing poetry, and they launched the movement with vigor and faith. Al-Mala'ika, moreover, supported the experiment with her critical writings.

The form of the Arabic poem was liberated at last. Symmetry and balance were overcome. The fixed number of feet was broken. The unit of the poem became the single foot, not the single verse. All caesuras became arbitrary, and rhymes were varied and sometimes successfully done away with. Many possibilities for poetry were now open. Poets experimented diligently, not simply to achieve variety and create their own original forms, but also to succeed finally in repudiating the old two-hemistich form, which now fell into disgrace and became synonymous with reaction, rigidity, and repetitiveness. Rigidity and conventionalism were the reasons avant-garde poets and critics in the fifties advanced for the permanence of this form over the centuries. It never occurred to them that the intractability of the old form for so many centuries could not have been due to a lack of creative flexibility on the part of the poets, since all the other elements of the poem—language, imagery, theme, attitude, tone, etc.—had undergone infinite changes. At the time, none of the critics realized that there must be deeper artistic reasons why the two-hemistich form had persisted so tenaciously. Over and above the ideas already expounded, the single verse in this form, which is composed of two equal hemistichs ending in a rhyme and is usually semantically self-sufficient, furnishes a closed unit in the poem which the rhyme seals. However, the repetition of this unit, which can continue as far as human capacity and intention and the availability of rhyme allow, makes the poem as a whole open and expansive. The presence of these two opposing factors, closeness and openness, at once in the poem represents the two opposing primary trends in art, which satisfy at once the need for limitation and freedom, containment and continuity, restraint and release. This is a characteristic of Arab Islamic art and can be seen in particular in arabesque designs in which the closed basic unit can be endlessly reproduced to achieve a suggestion of infiniteness, great esthetic intensity, and timeless polarity.

The truth is that the two-hemistich form is a powerful and exciting poetic form, capable of accommodating various methods and schools far more than the champions of the new movement of free verse in the fifties could admit or wanted to see. This is what its long history demonstrates. A quick look at poetic developments in this century will confirm this suggestion. Poetry changed quickly and radically, but continually observed this same form throughout these evolutionary stages: first, the calculated metrical compositions of the prerenaissance poets, with their decadent adherence to clever wording and geometric, affected design; second, the neoclassical poetry with its majestic sweep and fascinating rhetorical swell, its wealth of well-chosen words and images, its balance and stately measures rooted in Arabic culture; third, the Romantic orientation, with its flow of intoxicated rhythms, its dizzying swell, uncontrolled at times; fourth, the symbolist method, with its calm pace, gemlike selection of words, harmonious compositions, and gentle rhythms. In the forties, this same form, in the hands of a talented young poet from Syria, Nizar Qabbani (1923), who was to become the Arab world's greatest love poet and champion of feminist freedom, was able to accommodate successfully the rhythms, intonations, and idioms that approximate everyday language: the patter of Qabbani's early bourgeois heroines, their empty mannerisms and vacuous concerns; and the tone of the traditional chauvinist privileges of the male—his predatory seductions, his fascination with conquest, his pride in his own virility, his moments of anger and defeat, and his climaxes of joy and pleasure.

That the two-hemistich form has not lost its strength and immense maneuverability is clear; however, it is also clear that the new generation of poets and readers craved a change, legitimate and timely, and sought to create their own new forms. During the formative years of free verse in the Arab world, at the end of the forties and throughout the fifties, the free-verse poets and their critics displayed a fanaticism for their innovative achievements and an antagonism toward the old form that border on ideological rigidity. This is typical of the exuberant enthusiasm of many new creeds and ideologies. At the same time, however, the lovers of poetry who were mostly adherents of the old verse forms found ample ground to denounce, reject, and ridicule free verse. Thus, a violent battle ensued, perhaps the most vehement in the history of Arabic poetry. Some great poetic figures who only wrote in the old form regarded free verse as a fad and a hybrid, and predicted its early demise with a fanaticism equal to that of the free-verse champions. But fanaticism is never free of some measure of naiveté, and during this decade many arguments were offered for and against free verse which time has proven simplistic and even sometimes invalid. For free verse was there to stay and it outshined its early beginnings, developing ever greater sophistication and esthetic diversity. Continued experiments also led to the blossoming of prose poetry and prose poems (introduced by Gibran at the turn of the century) on a high artistic level, which eventually competed with metrical poetry for esthetic merit. With the years, the new verse forms became the established forms of avant-garde Arabic poetry that young poetic talents adopted instinctively, and the two-hemistich form lost much of its old status. However, with the passage of time it began to have a comeback. Avant-garde poets began to use it again occasionally, with a good measure of success, usually as part of a poem otherwise written in free verse, but sometimes as the compositional mode of the whole poem. This proved the infallibility and great potential of this verse form; indeed, unlike what the early protagonists of free verse claimed, there is no artistic reason why free verse and the two-hemistich poetry should not both be preserved as alternative ways of writing poetry.

Officially, free verse as a movement started in 1949 with the publication of Nazik al-Mala'ika's collection, *Ashes and Shrapnel*, for which the author includes an introduction that attempts to explain the advantages of the new form as opposed to the old. Naive and erroneous in many of its judgments, al-Mala'ika's introduction nevertheless helped launch free verse as a new form for avant-garde poetry, starting the long argument which was to last for over a decade and a half. At the hands of al-Mala'ika herself and other poets and critics, the form developed a greater sophistication and insightfulness.

I have already mentioned that another experiment in form also took place starting in the early decades of this century: prose poetry and the prose poem. The thesis that prose can be another medium for writing peotry was very difficult to impose on a poetry audience accustomed to the strong, balanced rhythms of the old two-hemistich form. Gibran had proven the form's viability in his many highly appreciated prose poems and poetic prose pieces. However, although experiments in prose poetry continued throughout the first half of this century, influenced by Gibran and other pioneers (such as the famous Arab-American writer, Amin al-Raihani [1876–1940], termed "the father of prose poetry"), it was only in the fifties and sixties that the experiment came to be regarded as a serious addition to the element of "form" in poetry. This happened with the rise of a few avant-garde poets who only wrote in prose, such as Tawfiq Sayigh (1923–1971), Unsi al-Haj (b. 1937), Muhammad al-Maghut (b. 1934), and Shauqi Abi Shaqra (b. 1935). The form was strengthened even more when prominent modernists such as Adunis ('Ali Ahmad Sa'id, b. 1929) and Yusuf al-Khal (1917–1987), who wrote primarily in verse, also used prose as a poetic medium. Adunis's work, in particular, reached a high level of sophistication. It was clear by the mid-sixties that the form had acquired its rightful place in contemporary poetry, and that there was much that poets and critics could learn from the many good examples of prose poetry and prose poems* that have enriched Arabic poetry. Shauqi Abi Shaqra's work possesses a delicate sensi-

---

*Prose poetry differs from the prose poem (*poème en prose*) in the following ways: prose poetry, like the prose poem, is without meter and is usually rhymeless, although it might sometimes employ rhyme for decorative reasons. It is written on the page like a poem in free verse with short lines. Often the reader pauses at the end of each line. The prose poem, on the other hand, has the appearance of prose on the page. *The Princeton Encyclopedia of Poetry and Poetics* defines it as "a composition able to have any or all features of the lyric, except that it is put on the page—though not conceived of—as prose. It differs from poetic prose in that it is short and compact, from free verse in that it has no line breaks, from a short prose passage in that it has, usually, more pronounced rhythm, sonorous effects, imagery, and density of expression. It may contain even inner rhyme and metrical runs. Its length, generally, is from half a page (one or two paragraphs) to three or free pages, i.e., that of the average lyrical poem."

tivity, with a special attention to esthetic and refined objects and experiences, and his mellifluous rhythms display a tender, harmonious flow. Unsi al-Haj's poetry broke through the barriers of traditional diction to express, sometimes surrealistically, the poet's ever deepening vision of the human condition. Al-Maghut's poetry reveals an unrivaled capacity to express human predicaments in an age of repression and great upheaval. And Tawfiq Sayigh's work exhibits extreme precision and a great ability to express anguish and conflict, while his occasional recourse to humor reflects the flip side of an extreme situation—a quality also shared by al-Maghut. These poets, and others like them, proved that for poetry to be original and powerful, it did not need to be written in meter and rhyme.

However, I should mention here that the prose medium for poetry has been only a variation, an addition to the still robust and developing metrical forms. Arabic metrics are extremely rich: there are sixteen meters, with over eighty variations. There is still a very large field for poets to explore in the metrical form itself.

The question of form is only part of the poetic revolution, the greatest in the history of Arabic poetry, which took place in the fifties. Avant-garde poets and cirtics, who had acquired a more modern knowledge of the art of poetry, found themselves involved in the many problems presented now by the condition of poetry on the one hand, and the condition of Arab life on the other. This, one should remember, is the postromantic, postsymbolist period, and this is also the period of the post-1948 Palestine disaster—perhaps the only fixed date that we can regard as a catalyst for poetic change. Substantial parts of Palestine were appropriated by the newly formed state of Israel, and the Palestinian people were dispersed, thus creating a new, non-Jewish diaspora. Most of these refugees were forced to face abominable living conditions, living in wretched tents and shacks, and trying to come to terms with new and unbearable realities. The failure of the other Arab states to restore Palestine cast doubt on the ability and sincerity of purpose of the Arab governments of the time. Arab intellectuals everywhere felt that the Arab world was hemmed in: trapped from the outside by an external enemy—Israel—whose power base lay in the industrial countries of the West that gave it support in every respect; and trapped on the inside by ruthless potentates who repressed freedom and blocked the free life of individuals in many Arab countries.

Meanwhile a new outlook on life and art, supported by great critical audacity and adventurism, was taking hold of most Arab poets. They attacked all the previous schools of poetry, none of which reflected the bleak and confused atmosphere that dominated the Arab world after 1948. Poets were drawn more and more to look for poetic inspiration outside their own literature, and to gain from the experience of foreign poets, and from the poetic theory that had developed during the last centuries in the West. Much foreign poetry and poetic criticsm were translated, mostly from French and English. The influence of such poets as Pound, Eliot, Edith Sitwell, Rilke, Lorca, Rimbaud, S.J. Perse, Eluard, Aragon, Yeats, Auden, Pablo Neruda, and Nazim Hikmat could be detected in much of the poetry written in the fifties and sixties.

The spirit of change dominated the period. Avant-garde poets recommended a change in all the tools of poetry, including outlook. They called on other poets to write about real experiences and depict in real terms the many tragic happenings around them, as well as the general emotional and spiritual atmosphere of the time and its existential malaise.

It is important to contemplate here the heroic situation of Arabic poetry in the fifties. On the one hand, it had evolved artistically, through the unceasing experimentation from 1900 to 1950, reaching a point of maturation where it was ready to reap all the fruits of previous experiments and meet the challenges of modernity. It proved able consciously to avoid the pitfalls of the three previous schools with varying degrees of success, while benefiting fully from their achievements: from the strength and terseness of the neoclassical school, the emotive involvement of the Romantics and their enhancing of the imagination, and the increased capacity of Arabic poetry to be symbolic and express the connotative aspects of language. Above all, it benefited from successful experiments in form. It is possible to look at the first half of this century as a period of preparation and gestation, in anticipation of the movement of modern poetry which began formally in the fifties and engaged the full artistic concentration of avant-garde poets.

On the other hand, the political climate made it impossible for the modern poetic movement to restrict its focus to esthetic matters. The Arab world was so disillusioned with its condition after the Palestinian disaster of 1948 that it lost confidence in many of its inherited values. This is all the more true because those who upheld traditional values with zeal usually belonged to the old hierarchies which people had come to mistrust: to either the stale religious hierarchy or the political hierarchy which had betrayed the nation and caused the breakdown of life and honor. People's psychological defenses were shattered, and there were few shields to protect them against the attacks that rained down ceaselessly on the culture itself from all sides. Reminders of past Arab glory seemed devoid of inspiration and could only stir anger and pain. In such a climate, divergent and often opposing ideas and notions found fertile ground in the breakdown of prevailing assumptions and values, whether artistic, social, or ethical.

In the field of poetry itself, the frightening Palestine debacle wiped out the innocence and naive faith of both poet and audience. Poetry, with only few exceptions (foremost of which was the erotic poetry of the Syrian Nizar Qabbani), abandoned the songs of weddings and festivals, the prayers of lovers, and the private longings of the soul, in favor of a more communal expression rife with anger and frustration. This was enhanced by loud cries for commitment, which rang in the fifties with a sonorous insistence. Poets in particular felt the need to commit themselves as, for Arabs at the time, poetry was still the most effective verbal expression. It also had a long tradition of spontaneous commitment in modern times, particularly in the works of the neoclassical poets and such preromantics as Mutran Khalil Mutran (1870–1949) and others, who voiced protest, incitement against oppression, and the celebration of national aspirations. Now the call for commitment found an atmosphere haunted by feelings of sorrow, disgust, shame, anger, frustration, apathy, and alienation.

The vision of poetry was to become more and more horrific with time, as it slowly uncovered the treachery, cruelty, and aggressiveness of a world order that had betrayed its human responsibilities. Poetry entered the long, bitter, and still unresolved struggle against both internal coercion and external aggression that reached apocalyptic dimensions after the June 1967 War. No poet can now rise to prominence in the Arab world who does not make the fight for human dignity and freedom one of the main themes of his or her poetry.

However, it is astonishing to observe that the art of poetry does not seem to have been burdened at all by this twofold, onerous task of esthetic engagement and political commitment. Yet it often turns out that the poetry written on behalf of the people, and about them, is too sophisticated, artistically, to be understood by them. Despite the attempts of a few committed writers to warn against the increasingly intricate involvement of poetry with excessively complex methods, no movement to return poetry to a new simplicity took place. I find nothing comparable, for example, to the New Simplicity Movement which took place in Sweden in the early sixties. From the fifties onwards, Arabic poetry has delved deeper and deeper into new realms of obliquity and metaphorical adventure, while at the same time reflecting an ever-widening awareness of the political and social predicaments strangling the Arab world—in particular, the problems of our freedom and liberation.

In the fifties, poetry as an art proved to have been more advanced than the knowledge the poet-pioneers had about its methods: it successfully faced the challenges of modernity, although some of its major protagonists were still unaware of the full implications of its grand adventure. Among these are such great pioneers of modern Arabic poetry as Badr Shakir al-Sayyab, whose work had a pervasive influence on the whole course of modern Arabic poetry; al-Mala'ika, who supported her sophisticated poetic creations with less sophisticated critical writings; and ʿAbd al-Wahhab al-Bayyati, whose poetry represented some of the more advanced developments in technique and promoted the spirit of socialist engagement in Arabic, but paid little attention to the theoretical implications behind such experiments. All three poets are Iraqi. In Lebanon, Khalil Hawi (1925–1982) abandoned his early method of writing simple and traditional poetry and turned to more sophisticated methods. His important collection, *River of Ashes* (1957), was a major work which combined an advanced artistic technique with a deeply committed stance.

It was the Lebanese Yusuf al-Khal who should be termed the first conscious promoter of modern poetry; he himself gave it the name of "Modern Poetry" (Al-Shiʿr al-Hadith) in 1957 and described its major attributes. He opened his collection of poetry, *The Deserted Well* (1958), with a dedication to Ezra Pound, the pioneer of modernism in English:

> We asked you for a fig leaf
> We are naked here, naked!
> We've sinned against poetry, forgive us
> return our life to us
> You have our promise: we will
> wander through the earth, building,
> with the tears of our brows,
> citadels for poetry whose keys
> are from Abqar.[6]
> If your wounds were a solace for our ancestors
> they are a road of salvation for us.
> If they have crucified you there,
> You are resurrected here.[7]

Here, the subtle analogy is between Pound and Christ and between Pound as a maligned and rejected literary pioneer and al-Khal himself. Al-Khal was determined to be a teacher and leader of poetic developments but foresaw the difficulties that would confront him, and his suspicion later proved right as his esthetic attempts became mixed with his unpopular political ideas, as described below.

It was his lecture given in Beirut in the spring of 1957 which defined in critical terms the whole attitude of the moderns and their concept of poetry, and laid the foundation for the modern movement in clear and sophisticated terms.[8] In this lecture, his first move was to attack the bulk of the poetry written during the previous half century, including most of the poetry written in his present days, completely overlooking the connectedness between the various developmental phases of poetic growth as well as the debt the poetry he was advocating owed to the previous experiments that paved the way for the implementation of modernism and made the tools of poetry malleable and ready for change.

In the lecture, al-Khal also insisted that poets should no longer resort to the same themes and outlook as their predecessors, and not allow their "cosmic experience of life" to stem from an "ancient, ruminative mentality." This was an important point to make because it established a relationship between modernity and the poet's outlook and attitude, a relationship which has not always been recognized even by some of the advocates of Arab modernism. Al-Khal, moreover, rejected romantic sentimentality and the introverted attitudes of the symbolists. The poetry of his time, he insisted, was still not modern if measured by the standards of modern poetry in the world. Some leading poets (he was referring here to Saʿid ʿAql) were living physically in one age and spiritually and intellectually in another, an inspired comment at the time. He insisted that the spirit of the age must be reflected in the poetry itself, which should be the outgrowth of lived experience as apprehended by the poet both in mind and heart. The objective of poetry is the human being, in all his joys and sorrows, a point already expounded in the second decade by the Arab-American poet and critic, Mikhaʾil Nuʿaima. Al-Khal regarded all themes not involving human experience as hollow and unreal. He believed there should be a fusion with the spirit of the people, not with nature, for people are the inexorable and limitless source of inspiration and continuity. He invited poets to explore with language, to abandon old words and phrases which have become obsolete with overuse, and to find their own living language. The use of the image should also be changed; it is the real image that poets should seek, not verbal abstractions and old rhetorical devices. He emphasized the vitality of presenting a challenge to logic, of destroying old traditional patterns. Rhythms also should be revolutionized, for "there is no sanctity surrounding the traditional meters." He issued a strong invitation for poets to benefit from the experience of poets in other languages; he called for them to reexamine with "objectivity," as he put it, the old Arab heritage and assess it without fear or compromise—a piece of advice, however, that suggested the reprehensibility of the classical Arab heritage. This clarion call would be repeated over and over again by him and a few other writers, such as the Syrian poet Adunis, sometimes with so much vehemence that it aggravated many people and undermined to some extent the self-confidence of poets and writers growing up in the devastating aftermath of 1948 and the June 1967 War. So it was that while the edifice of modern poetry was being built, another great edifice, which was the very foundation of Arab civilization and culture, was being systematically attacked and maligned. However, there should have been no ultimate contradiction between the two: modernization, even if it poses as discontinuity, is actually the proof of a vigorous continuity, of the triumph of the old poetry over itself and over the traditionalists who insist on keeping it at a standstill and stealing its lifeblood and vigor. When poetry, any poetry, develops and embraces timely changes, it only proves that it possesses enough vigor to embrace those changes and enough vitality to produce ever new forms of expression.

In the winter of 1957, al-Khal had started *Shi'r*, a quarterly review dedicated exclusively to poetry and poetic theory. On the pages of this important review, new ideas on poetry were expounded and much experimental verse was published. *Shi'r* was unique because it carried the spirit of modernity and change to its fullest limits, yet it quickly foundered on the rocks of politics, falling victim to the political views and activities of its two editors, al-Khal and Adunis. When, for example, the Civil War broke out in 1958 in Lebanon between the right-wing forces of the president of the republic, Camille Chamoun (viewed by most Arabs in Lebanon and the rest of the Arab world to be at the center of most of the harm, injustice, and disunity that befell Lebanon at the time) and the oppressed people of Lebanon, the two poet editors sided with Chamoun. This stigmatized the magazine while still in its early years. Moreover, the general attitude of the magazine's editors toward the volatile subject of Arab politics deterred many avant-garde poets from cooperating fully with the magazine, and one by one, they dropped their support. However, this must be seen in retrospect as a great loss for poetry, for the magazine itself hardly got into the game of politics and was a genuine messenger of modernity and poetic change, a platform which encouraged poets to dare to create ever new forms and methods. It was also a window on all the major poetic events of the century. Moreover, Arab poets and critics could have benefited much more from al-Khal's erudite, timely, and inspired ideas on poetry and his active demonstration of the dynamics of artistic change and progress. In addition to the review and its publishing house, dedicated to the publication of avant-garde works of literature, al-Khal conducted a poetic forum in his own home every Thursday evening, which became famous as *Khamis Majallat Shiʿr* (The *Shiʿr* Review Thursday), in which poets, critics, and lovers of literature met and discussed the problems of contemporary Arabic and world literature with candor and freedom. Although the liberal atmosphere of the *Khamis* allowed also for literary quarrels, it provided the basis for many lasting friendships among avant-garde writers of the time.

Shiʿr ceased publication at the end of 1964, the same year in which Adunis, its coeditor, aspiring to a greater role as a poet on a pan-Arab scale, broke his ties with the magazine and with al-Khal. The magazine resumed publication in 1967, only to cease publication permanently in 1969 for lack of funds and support. All in all, forty-four volumes of *Shiʿr* appeared over eleven years. However, the message of the magazine, which was one of modernity and revolutionary poetic experimentation, was established for a long time to come.

Another avant-garde magazine, the monthly *Al-Ādāb*, was able to continue with only few interruptions. It was founded in 1953 by another Lebanese, Suhail Idris, a writer of fiction and an Arab nationalist strongly versed in the Arab-Islamic tradition in both culture and politics. Idris had an instinct for sensing the major trends of Arab thought in politics and art, and was able to ride the crest of the wave. In the pages of his magazine, new trends and movements in literature were assessed, followed up, and sometimes even anticipated. The magazine led the movement of innovation, perhaps not as a guide, or as an initiator of trends, or as a teaching platform with a particular message (like that, for example, of modernity) whose specific tenets it was aggressively determined to preach. It was, rather, a watchpost for all experimental endeavors and a liberal meeting place for poetic and literary exchange. It never attained the high esthetic standards of *Shiʿr*, and might have been a little demagogic at times, but it was able to stimulate great interest in innovative techniques and new ideas and to survive the numerous stresses and pains of contemporary Arab life for over a third of a century.

The struggle of poets in the fifties to renew art and themsleves, to revolutionize their attitudes toward the past, the present, and the future, to modernize vision but also to revise memory, to search for identity and for a place in the world, and to apprehend their roles as poets in an Arab world still greatly deferential to poetry, was a more dynamic struggle than any that Arab poets had hitherto experienced during the previous half century, despite much anxiety and crucial change. One of the major stances reflected by the poet either through his or her writings or in the way he or she manipulated poetic devices was an attitude of rejection of the past, as I have already mentioned above. The immediate past, which seemed full of failure, was rejected together with the present, but the remote past was attacked and rejected, too. Faith in the old order of life seemed to have drained away from most poets' hearts, and it was easy for some writers to launch their attacks on all persisting traditions, and to demand new beginnings in all aspects of life and art. Later on, the remote past was going to be explored for its wealth, but in the fifties, it was maligned by many avant-garde poets.

However, the fifties seem now to us in retrospect to have been a more relaxed and optimistic period than the years that followed, despite the wave of rejection and alienation that swept over the decade, creating at times an alienation which some modernist poets made, in Lukacs's words, into an absolute. The poets of the fifties were still able to dream, to hold a vision of a world potentially able to rebuild itself. The ideological poets, the Marxists and the Nationalists, were the more optimistic of the avant-garde poets, reflecting a deep faith in the possibility of human struggle to bring about the final triumph of freedom and justice. The main difference between their writings and those of the more alienated poets was that the ideological poets wrote with a spirit of optimism and faith, of strength and determination. They provided a specific formula for the success of the struggle for freedom, while the alienated group, who also believed in the inevitability of a resurrection from the deathlike stupor that made defeat possible, spoke about it with the dejected attitude of men and women who have suffered a deep wound to their humanity, and could only see the seeds of life sprouting through great suffering, pain, and enormous sacrifice. Khalil Hawi's lovely poem on the subject, "The Bridge," makes the inevitable crossing to safety of the rising generation possible only by means of a bridge built from the ribs of the the victims of the catastrophe.

The modernist poets delineated this vision of suffering and final triumph, of barrenness and fecundity, of death and rebirth, by resorting to various kinds of obliquity: symbols, folklore, allusion, myth, and archetype. The greatest influence on the use of myth in the fifties was T.S. Eliot, whose use of the fertility myth in "The Wasteland" was an eye-opener for avant-garde Arab poets in the fifties. The idea of a death that leads to a new birth attracted them deeply. Fertility myths such as those of Adonis or Tammuz, which were associated with the area many centuries ago but had been submerged by monotheism, were no longer alive on the lips of people. Modern

Arab poets resurrected the myths of fertility from books, especially from Frazer's *The Golden Bough*, translated in part by Jabra Ibrahim Jabra (b. 1921). They also benefited from commentaries on Eliot's poem and other critical writings.

The first poet to use the myth of fertility with artistic skill was al-Sayyab. In his famous poem, "Song of Rain," which he wrote in the mid-fifties, he used the myth implicitly, employing the image of water as the symbol for life's renewal.[9] The poem carried the spirit of hope and faith for a people who were feeling trapped in their own helplessness, and it inflamed the imagination of other poets who saw in it an answer to their own search for new meanings and methods. They used this and other similar myths, such as Baal (Hawi) and the Phoenix (Adunis), all of which pointed to the possibility of rebirth after suffering and death. The group of poets who used these fertility myths (al-Sayyab, al-Khal, Hawi, Jabra, Adunis, etc.) came to be called "The Tammuzian Poets"[10]—a term which proved to be short-lived, since the intensity with which poets experimented with the myth of death and rebirth within the span of five or six years quickly created esthetic fatigue. It became hazardous, poetically, to employ them, particularly in 1961 in the atmosphere of growing gloom after the severing of the union between Egypt and Syria.[11]

Other myths were also used, some with a good measure of success. The myth of Sisyphus, which several poets used, was given special poignance by al-Sayyab, who inverted the myth by having Sisyphus, the symbol of eternal toil, throw away his rock and turn his face to the sun on the Atlas mountains (referring here to the gallant struggle of Algeria against the French in the War of Liberation). Prometheus was also used with success, especially by 'Abd al-Wahhab al-Bayyati (b. 1926), but these imported myths more or less remained a kind of intellectual rather than an emotional means of linking human experience with a mythical correlative. During that early period, the most interesting myths used were those that stemmed from the living tradition of Arabic culture. A case in point is Khalil Hawi's eloquent use of Sinbad the Sailor, a folk hero still living in the Arab folk memory. In his poem, "Sinbad on His Eighth Voyage," Hawi used the myth to symbolize the poet's own search as an Arab for the sources of strength within himself. Describing Sinbad's search for a region full of treasures and dangers, tortures and conflicts, he has him arrive at the glorious moment of self-discovery, of awareness of his own power to achieve great goals. Hawi then ends the poem with a prophetic vision of a new generation marching proudly on the road toward the future, of the whole Arab nation rejuvenating itself and regaining its stolen dignity.

However, most of the myths used in that early period were imported, and the suddenness and deliberateness of their use betray their acquired origin. But as Arab poets themselves gained greater authority over their tools, they instinctively began a search for the genuine communal mythic sources alive in the culture. Mainly, they found them in archetypal patterns taken from Arab history. Hawi's use of the fictional folk character of Sinbad is an authentic early example, but it was al-Sayyab's moving use of the genuine historical archetype in his lovely long poem, "In the Arab Maghrib" (1956), which offers us the first powerful example of the use of mythical time in modern poetry. Al-Sayyab wrote the poem to celebrate the Algerian revolution; and in part it is an elegy on Arab-Islamic civilization, which has reached a twilight in which faith has died and God is seen weeping in a deserted Palestinian house in Jaffa. But the Algerian revolution changes everything: a new sense of power is born which revives faith and manhood, and the Prophet Muhammad and his followers are resurrected and seen in their full splendor among the Algerian rebels—God lives again in the Arab land.

It was the link Adunis made with Arab history in his major volume, *The Songs of Mihyar, the Damascene* (1961), which was decisive for other poets. In this work, Adunis forged a permanent connection with the historical past. There are many references to this past in *The Songs of Mihyar*, some positive, some adverse, but the poet maintains a balance to some extent. Over time his poetry developed a deep mythic sense of history in which the flowing together of all periods and the immanence of the past in the present are delineated to yield a sense of the simultaneity of human experience, and the power of history to recycle itself endlessly.

The first major work Adunis produced after *The Songs* was his splendid poem on Saqr Quraish, which uses an elaborate and lengthy portrayal of the historical figure ʿAbd al-Rahman al-Dakhil, the last Umayyad survivor who was called "The Eagle of Quraish"[12] (Saqr Quraish) because of his courage and authority. The poem describes his flight from Damascus to escape the atrocious massacres of the Umayyads by the Abbasid dynasty, which took over the caliphate in the middle of the eighth century and made Baghdad their capital. "Saqr Quraish" fled westward, in circumstances of great peril, until in Arab Spain he founded the Umayyad dynasty. Unlike al-Sayyab's poem on the Arab Maghrib, which expresses communal agony and ecstasy, Adunis's poem is about individual courage, ambition, and final achievement, a glorious eulogy for the ability of the individual who, in the face of all the odds of history, seeks, and wins. In the poem, written in 1961, Adunis glorifies individual instead of collective achievement, a theme he also began in *Songs of Mihyar*, for the poem also symbolizes the poet's own flight in the fifties, as a then-Syrian Nationalist, from Arab Nationalist Damascus. In "The Eagle of Quraish," Adunis asserts his vision of himself as unrivaled hero, a vision which he would repeat over and over again in his subsequent work. However, "The Eagle of Quraish" reveals great subtlety and beauty of expression and remains one of the most eloquent poetic works of the sixties.

The historical archetypes flourished from the early sixties on. Poets found in them an answer to their need for expressing, indirectly, certain continuities in culture and human experience. I have already maintained that the modernist movement called for discontinuity and a new beginning in all aspects of art and life. The use of the historical archetype, therefore, as an outgrowth of the modernist movement itself, had to comply naturally with its basic principles, with the modernist poet's demand to reject the past and effect radical change in all spheres. Historical archetypes were therefore chosen from Arab history not to reaffirm certain positive qualities which Arabic culture in its long history provides (and there are numerous qualities to uphold), but mainly to call attention to such negative qualities as oppression, tyranny, lust, and all kinds of repressions and to spotlight their continued presence in contemporary Arab life. And although heroic figures were also selected as symbols, they were usually the lone heroes who single-handedly fought injustice and often fell victim to their own integrity and valor. The emphasis more often was on the adverse qualities that victimized the historical figures rather than on their own heroic attributes. A case in point is al-Hallaj, the famous medieval mystic who was crucified because he courageously stuck to his own convictions. The emphasis in such famous works as Salah 'Abd al-Sabur's verse play, *Al-Hallaj*, is perhaps more on the inquisitorial attitude of those who condemned Hallaj than on extolling the mystic's firm stance. Other figures were sometimes taken out of their true historical contexts and described in particular ways to symbolize some negative characteristics. Harun al-Rashid, the caliph-emperor who ruled in glory during the golden days of the vast Arab-Islamic empire that stretched from the Indian Ocean to the shores of Morocco, was used by Nizar Qabbani (and others) to symbolize tyranny and lust. This was a direct mutilation of the image of this great caliph, who is sustained in both history and the popular memory as the archetype of the great ruler. However, Qabbani used Harun al-Rashid in a negative sense immediately after the June 1967 War, when the Arab audience was ready to reject all of its past and all mention of past Arab glory, due to the devastating shock that staggered the whole Arab world.

Generations vary in their emphases. The generation of Shauqi and the neoclassical poets had found great relief from their feelings of inadequacy in the face of the colonizing West when they praised the time-honored figures of Arab history. These figures, however, were not used in their mythic sense, to emphasize the continued presence of great qualities in contemporary Arab life. On the contrary, such figures were used to emphasize the contemporary absence of these attributes which had once made them and the Arab world great and important. They were proposed as noble but *discontinued* examples that needed now to be revivied and emulated. The racial memory had to be awakened and illuminated by the pervasive poetic recounting of epic events and great deeds, of the tales of conquest and glory, of power and magnanimity, of instances of liberality and justice, which neoclassical poets saw as predominant in Arab history. Poets explored Arab history to show its more positive and glorious aspects. On the other hand, the use of a mythic sense of the historical archetypes, which was influenced greatly by modern European use of the psychological and the role of myth in the human consciousness, became unique to the moderns. They aspired to touch the core of Arab history and unify the present predicaments of Arab life by invoking similar moments of negative experience, of crisis and conflict, in the history of our people. Thus human endurance, which is much needed in present-day Arab life to counter the menace of neocolonialism on the one hand, and internal oppression in all spheres of life on the other, is highlighted, sometimes also universalized, as part of the struggle of the whole human race against similar predicaments in other parts of the world, wherever injustice and aggression prevail.

A poet who was able to strike a balance in his outlook toward Arab history is 'Abd al-Wahhab al-Bayyati. He began as a poet with a broad cosmic vision which he developed in his early collection, *Broken Pitchers* (1954). A Marxist, he could easily visualize the human struggle as a unified endeavor against what he saw as the evil forces of aggression and exploitation everywhere. At the beginning of his career, he showed a greater interest in contemporary world events, but, like many other Arab poets, he was later persuaded to make links with the history of his own people. He made a diligent search for archetypal material from Arab history. The deep historical sense he developed enabled him to weave historical events and old chronicles, side by side with mythological material, into the texture of his poetry. In his quest for originality, he sometimes extends his historical material beyond allowable limits; however, much of his work is uniquely exciting and is often invested with an original flavor.

Aside from al-Sayyab and his early poem "In the Arab Maghrib," it is perhaps correct to regard the Sudanese poet Muhammad ʿAbd al-Hayy (b. 1944) as the only modernist who is able to celebrate the past fully and express a nostalgia for Sudanese historical experience. In his beautiful long poem "Return to Sinnar" (1971), he gives us a unique example of the positive integration of historical material into poetry. The poem evokes the memory of the kingdom of Sinnar (1509–1821), which succeeded in welding the two races of the Sudan, the Arabs and the Africans, into one harmonious nation. All racial differences were transcended then, and the poet extols the harmony which he no longer finds in present-day Sudan. The poem is pervaded by a mythic sense of racial continuity and the writer's longing for renewed harmony. It is a poem of peace and serenity, of universal love; in it a rare voice of calm, confidence, and celebration is heard, quite separate from those highly disturbed voices and agitated tones too often present in much contemporary Arabic poetry.

In addition to the experiments with myths and the archetype, the modernist movement has also achieved a bold revolution in the language and imagery of poetry unequaled even by the original symbolist adventure of the *sufis*, those famous medieval Islamic mystics.[13] The contemporary adventure is bolder and wider; it has had a more pervasive influence on the majority of poets writing today than the *sufi* experiment had in its day. The mystics of the past remained restricted to *sufi* poetry, while the contemporary poets exploited the symbolist potential of language to speak of a wide range of subjects. The contemporary poets find that they are heirs to a wealth of poetic diction rich in the terseness and splendor of the neoclassical poets, the emotional appeal of the Romantics, and the evocative power of the symbolists. But they also are potentially heirs to all their predecessors' linguistic weaknesses. What is significant about the modern experiment is that poets are now able to discern and adopt the positive attributes of the poetic output of this century, while wisely attempting to avoid those undesirable qualities that could potentially militate against their absorption of modernity. The way the moderns can exploit, for example, the full symbolic potential of the Arabic language while disregarding other important symbolist tenets such as the emphasis on the music of words as a semantic value in itself, is only one indication of the level of sophistication and authority they have arrived at.

As the fifties progressed, two trends began to appear in the language of poetry. The first, a trend led by Nizar Qabbani and, to a significant extent, by ʿAbd al-Wahhab al-Bayyati, was the use of simple language free of laborious ambiguities, which, without shedding its well-knit constructions, was akin to the language of everyday speech. Qabbani's choice of vocabulary, and his syntactical structure and rhythmic constructions, echoes the colloquial—a singular achievement, since he managed this at the beginning of his poetic career, when he still employed the two-hemistich form.

A language that simulates the rhythms and intonations as well as the syntax of common speech would appear normal in a poetry that was in the process of modernizing itself. This also agrees with T.S. Eliot's dictum in *The Music of Poetry* that "every revolution in poetry is apt to be, and sometimes to announce itself to be a return to common speech." However, contemporary avant-garde poetry in Arabic has proven that while this is one way in which poetic language may revolutionize itself, a radically different method can be adopted. Some of the major Arab poets of this period never approximated common speech. Al-Sayyab's apt, terse, and sensitive diction can only be described as a modernized version of the best of the classical diction. The same can be said about Khalil Hawi, whose language is well-knit and intense, but also highly fluent and malleable.

The poet whose influence is paramount on the younger poets writing in the sixties and after is Adunis. His adventure with language defies comparison. It arises from the very heart of the classical tradition at its best, and it exhibits great affinity with the diction of the Islamic mystics whom he had had ample opportunity to study while he was growing up in the religious climate of the Alawite Mountains in northern Syria. Writing in a diction as far removed from common speech as possible, he shunned direct statement and invested his language with mystery, obliquity, and connotativeness, always creating new combinations of words that contravened the conventional, logical sentence order. Al-Khal, in his poetry, had attempted to remain true to his call for poets to defy the logical order and inherited sentence constructions of the old poetry, but it was Adunis who carried this recommendation through to its intended goal. Influenced by such great French poets as Rimbaud and particularly St. John Perse, he "broke the neck of logic" and produced highly original words and phrases derived from all aspects of the poetic experience, as well as from philosophy, religion, and politics. There are times when he is too difficult, and resorts to exaggerated ambiguity, often sounding esoteric and pretentious. However, his unrivaled waywardness of imagery and his authentic abhorrence of traditional vocabulary and conventional sentence structure have rendered a great service to modern Arabic poetry. He introduced freshness and audacity and drew a sharp line between modern and traditional diction and imagery, so that no ambiguity remained in the minds of younger poets as to what was new and what was old-fashioned and outworn.

Modernists made the image the central element in poetry; this led to the revolutionizing of metaphor, as the old inherited ways of coining metaphors had become unpopular. A great adventure in metaphorical variety was launched, and the image became the subject of constant poetic experimentation by writers who aimed at inventing a new tradition in Arabic for the image.

Contemporary Arab poets, like other contemporary poets in the world today, are aware of the complexity of life around them. They are able to transfer their sense of complexity to poetry. The forces in the contemporary world that make for incoherence and even chaos affect the way they deal with art. Contemporary Arab poets try to "catch the irregular rhythms of life" around them. Because they live in oppressive times and suffer from reactionary social and political conditions, they cannot always resort to direct statement; they often employ ambiguity, various kinds of obliquity, and complex systems of imagery to express their visions. Most poets have been assisted by their study of foreign poets, either in translation or in the original, particularly the works of French and English modernists.

It is clear that many young talents find this adventure with the language and imagery of poetry a great challenge. But where the older and more seasoned poets usually succeeded in their experiments, some promising young talents foundered. Mixed metaphors, images lacking "an *interior* significance," particularly those where the relationship between image and subject is untenably remote, can be found in much of this poetry, particularly in the seventies.* However, fortunately for Arabic poetry, this is a fertile and potent period, and bound, therefore, to transcend such limitations.

---

*This is not due to the perpetuation of an oral tradition in Arabic, as some have proposed. Formal Arabic poetry lost its ties with the oral tradition many centuries ago, and became a faithful mirror of the urbanity and polish of the vast Arab Islamic civilization, of its decorum and even, later on, of its mannerisms. The trend is due, I suspect, to the fact that today young poets have found in the metaphorical adventure a challenge which they feel they can meet, as the way has already been paved for them by more established poets who linked the experiment with modernity and change. It is not the result of unchallenged desert traditions from which poets can find no escape—contemporary Arab poets would certainly reject with courage and willfulness any such restraint on their creativity—but the influence of literary fashions which appear suddenly for artistic and possibly psychological reasons and affect the output of the poets of a whole generation before they disappear. The problem originally lies in the fact that these young poets acquired this deep urge for more and more originality

It is a phenomenon of great significance to see this major esthetic involvement take hold of poets who are now fully involved, heart, mind, and soul, in the great issues of our times, in the tragedy and despair, as well as in the occasional moments of hope and faith, of contemporary Arab experience. The Arab political disasters in recent times were, of course, resonant and alarming in their dimensions. The 1948 Palestine catastrophe, the June 1967 War, the 1970 Civil War in Jordan, the Lebanese Civil War which began in 1975, the outbreak of war in 1980 between Iraq and Iran which still rages on, the 1982 Israeli invasion of Lebanon—punctuated by the episodes of mass murder of innocent Palestinian and Lebanese civilians: Dayr Yasin in Palestine in 1948 and Kufr Qasim in Israel in 1956; Tel al-Za'tar in 1976, and Sabra and Shatila in Lebanon in 1982—are just some of the more infamous examples that have often been delineated in searing and original images.

A highly metaphorical style of poetry was also adopted by some poets of the Arab resistance, such as Samih al-Qasim (b. 1939), and particularly by Mahmoud Darwish (b. 1939). Darwish grew up in Palestine under Israeli domination and, like other Arab poets there, such as Tawfiq Zayyad (b. 1932), Samih al-Qasim, Khalil Touma (b. 1945), and others, he suffered much repression from the Israeli authorities, who often imprison Palestinian poets, put them under house arrest, or suppress their works. In 1970, he left Israel and chose to join his people in the diaspora, quickly becoming part of the active literary movement in Beirut, where he lived most of the time until the third Palestinian exodus, this time from Beirut in 1982.

When Darwish began writing in Palestine, his poetry was more prone to simple structures and direct statement, but it was also greatly appealing because of its capacity to invoke his audience's sympathy and bring out into the open the full dimensions of the tragedy perpetuated on the Palestinians under Israeli occupation. However, after he moved to the Arab world, his

---

before they had had time to become thoroughly grounded in the critical knowledge of the nature of metaphorical creation and the principle of esthetic fatigue, and before they were able to discover their own poetic powers and methods. Some poets among the younger generation, however, are enabled, thanks to their sound poetic instincts, to avoid the pitfalls of misunderstood complexity and to resort to the most complex style without falling into metaphorical imprecision. Examples are the Iraqi Hasab al-Shaikh Ja'far (b. 1942); in their best works the Syrians Saleem Barakat (b. 1951) and Mamduh 'Udwan (b. 1941); and the Egyptian Muhammad 'Afifi Matar (b. 1935), among others. Such poets have demonstrated that metaphorical waywardness in the hands of capable poets can be a source of great esthetic pleasure for the reader.

poetry began to gain in complexity, and he participated in the metaphorical adventure with full strength. His poetry, however, never lost its basic tenderness and rapture, nor its capacity to recount the predicament of the Palestinian experience in telling images and statements. His images remain rich and luminous; they are often unique and intimately connected to the heart of the experience which he delineates, as those of few poets are. His poetry is saved from the spleen and gloom that emanate from his dominant themes by a shimmering lyrical flow, a tender appeal to the heart, a vibrant diction, and above all a metaphorical originality. His poems are the most important and influential among all those influenced by the Palestine tragedy.

While all these experiments in language and imagery were taking place, another type of poetry which resorted to simpler, more lucid and immediate linguistic structures was also developing steadily. Al-Bayyati's deepening experimentation with poetic technique, Qabbani's evolution from the playboy of the Arab world in his early career to the champion of feminism who urged women to take control of their lives, their bodies, and their destiny, and ʿAbd al-Sabur's deepening involvement with universal themes, all reflected a growing sophistication in poetic technique, without however indulging in the other group's metaphoric complexities and its attendant vulnerabilities.

It was Salah ʿAbd al-Sabur who seemed to embrace modernity more than any other poet of the period. He wrote in a language that sprang right from the heart of everyday experience. His work, to use an expression of Frank Kermode's, "denies the consolations of predictable forms." It is sparse in its invocation of overt emotion, it defies all the reader's expectations. He speaks in a tone completely stripped of all traces of the old rhetoric and of the heroic strain which still permeates much of the verse of his contemporaries, full of defiance and assertiveness. His rhythms break away from the bouncing, impassioned, and staccato rhythms of the poetry that celebrates heroism and struggle, which became particularly dominant after the rise of the Palestine Resistance in the late sixties and seventies, the time when he created his best work. Unlike the grand sweep of Resistance verse and of such poets as Adunis, ʿAbd al-Sabur's more subdued rhythms remind the reader of the condition of men and women around him who are the victims of a social and political order that tyrannizes and wastes their lives. His whole attitude is that of a poet who sees the world through the eyes of the new victims of the twentieth century, whose predicament is compounded by the lingering maladies of present-day Arab life. He demonstrates that modernity for the Arab poet has to involve a deep change in spirit and outlook, a leap by the poet into the sensibility of the twentieth century. For while the greatest adventure in poetic technique had been going on constantly since the early fifties, poets have only to a limited degree assimilated a modernity of spirit. The poetic audience itself exhibits greater affinity with the poetry that provides a strong challenge to the internal or external enemy, or with the poetry that upholds the attributes which Arabs have always found endearing, and which are now endowed with greater esteem because of the necessities of the times: valor, chivalry, endurance, self-sacrifice. This is why the poetry of the Resistance, with its assertion of these attributes and its vision of hope and human potential, has an immediate currency and is imitated and emulated by poets all over the Arab world. The adulation of the hero, so prevalent in the old poetry, remains alive today whether the hero is a valiant freedom fighter and seeker of justice who continually faces death, or the poet himself who speaks as teacher, leader, and prophet, as one who bears a great and sacred responsibility on his shoulders and who suffers and is roused to anger because of other people's wickedness or sloth. There is some of this in Hawi's work and in Qabbani's political verse. However, it is in the poetry of Adunis that the worship of the hero and the sage is directed toward the poet himself to a marked degree. Adunis shows that despite the powerful and impassioned campaign in his prose writings for a complete break with the past, he nonetheless displays a manifest continuity in his poetry, an index of an enduring cultural sensibility that still pervades the spirit of most contemporary poets. Although, as I have said before, Adunis's diction is new and fresh, his metaphorical adventures revolutionary and effective, and his syntax original, unique, and commanding, many of his affinities remain familiar and close to the reader's heart. His stance, his tone, his choice of vocabulary, his "rhétorique profonde" are not a break from, but a magnificent continuation of the Arab poetic heritage. These qualities have earned him a greater appeal among Arab poets and critics than 'Abd al-Sabur's comparatively lackluster poetry.

'Abd al-Sabur, who achieved the greatest discontinuity with the past in modern Arabic poetry, has had few imitators. His tone is subdued, and he allows his words to ring discordantly at times, often to emerge suffocated, angular, unvarnished, and even at times prosaic. His poetry resides in the many hidden signals, the attitudes, and the unmasking of contemporary human predicaments. The struggle of hundreds of contemporary poets in the Arab world to prove that they were writing original poetry by an over-inventiveness of imagery and excessive use of neologisms and new phrases is in stark contrast to ʿAbd al-Sabur's almost ascetic avoidance of ornament and overstylization. His work is not a jewel box that spontaneously opens when you read him, but a Pandora's box. His technique combines a profound break from inherited rhetoric, style, and diction, with a modern consciousness of the world. In his poetry, the "heroic" hero, no matter how tragic a mask he may wear, is not an authentic representative of the contemporary human predicament in the Arab world. Rather, the hero is transformed into what the poet finds is the true representative of the present age: the tragic *victim*.

Muhammad al-Maghut is also able to portray man as victim. His prose poetry concentrates on describing the condition of the victims of the repressive *internal* establishment. It is important to note here that all contemporary poets voice a loud protest against the repressive political order that stretches like a dark cloud over the Arab world. However, al-Maghut speaks as the trapped victim whose wings have been clipped by the grinding political machine and who has been left wounded and bleeding, alongside a dusty road. Hawi, Adunis, and scores of other poets who attack the political establishment do so from the point of view of the poets who stand above evil and claim to fight it, or at least challenge it. Al-Maghut's voice is the voice of terror; when he changes his tone a little, his deep-rooted fright is mixed with disdain and sometimes with a sarcasm that enables him to advance a comic representation of contemporary evil in the Arab world.

Another modernist dimension of contemporary poetry is the frequent use of the theme of the *City*, the center of exploitation and misery, of social injustice and political intrigue. And the concept of City versus Village is well-rooted in twentieth-century Arabic poetry. Numerous poets, including Gibran, Ilyas Abu Shabaka (1903–1947), Ilya Abu Madi (1890–1957), Abu al-Qasim al-Shabbi (1909–1934), Muhammad Mahdi al-Jawahiri (b. 1900), and later Nazik al-Mala'ika during her Romantic phase in the forties, have drawn on the differences between the two, expressing their hatred of city life and their sometimes utopian, sometimes purely arcadian longings for Nature and the country.

In post-1950 poetry, it was al-Sayyab who provided a central contribution to this theme when he set the symbols of the lost village of innocence, peace, and love (his own village, Jaikur) in tragic opposition to the barren city of corruption and cruelty where love dies and only impotency and cruelty prevail. Al-Sayyab was a country boy who came to Baghdad from his village in the south of Iraq to study and seek a job. All over the Arab world, this emigration became frequent among aspiring rural youths after World War II, when decolonization brought independence, the setting up of national governments, and the founding of many universities in the Arab metropolises. The city provided fertile ground for nurturing feelings of awe and anomie among these young men, as they faced the complexities and alienation of city life.

The poets' reactions to this situation differ widely. Al-Sayyab's complex poetic personality and his modern poetic education transform the village and the city into archetypal symbols of universal dimension. Other poets, such as the Egyptian ʿAbd al-Muʿti Hijazi, do not share this kind of complexity; Hijazi finds in city life a personal predicament. His first collection, *City Without Heart* (1959), centers mainly on his experience as a young man from the country who faces the forbidding city for the first time. In telling and poignant terms, this volume portrays the young poet's anguish at his loneliness in Cairo. This forlorn attitude persists within him and we see him in his last collection, *Beings of the Kingdom of Night*, as still an unreconciled stranger now living in Paris, the European metropolis which reveals itself to him as a place where a mercantile and mechanized way of life seals the fate of millions and imposes on them that very dilemma which has always frightened him most: alienation and anonymity within a vast and heartless city.

However, it is al-Sayyab's treatment of the city theme which provides the example that other poets have followed. He is deeply aware of the problems of the modern city. His adoption of Marxism early in life revealed to him in sharp relief the nature of class distinctions, the degradation of human life in city slums, and the struggle of the poor and the downtrodden to survive. As a young intellectual, he was deeply enraged by the political repression which prevailed in the metropolis, the seat of government, where informers and brutal police control people's destiny. He has enriched modern Arabic poetry with many haunting images, and he is joined in this by several other poets such as Buland al-Haydari (b. 1926), a city man but nevertheless a great hater of the city and its attendant corruption. Haydari's unnamed city and Khalil Hawi's Beirut, Paris, and London are variously described as the belly of a whale, a human mill, a great prison, a wilderness, and a dehumanized enclave dominated by tyrants and their stooges during the day, and by pimps and whores at night.

However, Hawi's inspired attack on the city is also an assault on Arab and European civilizations; he represents the city as the dark destiny of both. Each of these two civilizations suffers from a different kind of evil—Western greed and adventurism and Eastern lethargy and dependency—and both have contributed to the downfall of modern humanity. Beirut, the poet's city, for example, is a false meeting place of East and West, where everything, including language, is borrowed and adulterated.

Hawi's universal vision of the city is a fresh and sophisticated introduction to modern Arabic poetry. Unlike al-Sayyab, who is the ultimate victim of the city of impenetrable walls, Hawi refuses to become its victim, stressing once again the stance of the hero and sage who suffers for humanity without himself being dragged into the gutter. Adunis emphasizes this position even more when he declares that he is, in typical manner, the self-proclaimed master of the city. But Adunis's broad vision and unique creativity reach their most universal expression in his great poem, "A Grave for New York," which he wrote in 1972 after his first visit to the United States. In this poem, he attacks the capital of the industrial world for its global exploitation, as the poet sees it, of the rest of the world. This exploitation, he reiterates in many images and statements, is predatory, aggressive, devoid of human feeling. New York is the archetypal city of lust and imperial domination, which controls the whole world from Wall Street, even as it underwrites and profits from the tragedy in the city's black areas. New York infiltrates people's lives everywhere. Arab cities, the poet asserts with resentful anguish, are New York's willing victims. They are crippled by sloth and impotence, betrayed by their native tyrannical patriarchs, and defiled by lust and cravings for trivia. In this long poem, one of the most majestic and moving works in Arabic literature, the poet's vision is prophetic and apocalyptic, and it reaches cosmic dimensions. However, it still betrays the poet's preindustrial stance. Adunis may be thinking of Vietnam and perhaps Cuba when he asserts, speaking of the Arab world, that *grass*, symbol of preindustrial simplicity, will conquer the electronic brain. This position, reiterated by him in other poems [14] (and expressed by other poets as well),[15] reflects an uncertain vision in Adunis as he fails to reconcile the theoretical concept of modernity which he so persuasively preaches in his prose writings, with his hatred, fear, and mistrust of the greatest determinant of the modern age: technology. The whole corpus of contemporary Arabic poetry, with only few exceptions, points to the fact that the poets have not yet fully entered the machine age, and still resist any reconciliation with technological reality in their lives. This has to be seen as the last bastion of resistance against the dehumanizing influence of the modern world's technology, a gallant fight for innocence and universal brotherhood. However, a certain perplexity arises due to the many contradictions in the attitudes of the poets themselves, for, side by side with these atavistic attitudes, they harbor other thoughts which condemn any residual lapses that pull contemporary Arabic culture backward to older periods, or impose upon it any inherited assumptions. In contemporary Arabic poetry, the question of modernity is still problematic.

The treatment of the city in Palestinian poetry reflects a radical difference from the rest of Arab poetry. To the Palestinians, the power of place is of the ultimate value. It is their homeland that they have lost, and there are numerous Palestinians who lack any roots. The longing for a place is eternal in their poetry, unquenchable, unlimited, and it can never be diminished because it has acquired the quality of an absolute. The land, its flora and fauna, its villages and cities, are all integral parts of their lost and ever-sought-after dream. It is interesting to note that the symbol of Palestine lost and Palestine regained, of innocence lost and innocence regained, however, is the city, mainly the city of Jaffa or "Yafa" as it is called in Arabic. For although Jerusalem, and sometimes Haifa, Acca (Acre in English) Safad, and other cities are evoked every now and then, in Palestinian and, in fact, in Arabic poetry in general, Jaffa remains the central symbol of the greatest potency. This, I suspect, may be due, among other reasons, to the fact that the orange, one of Palestine's most inspiring flora symbols, is connected to Jaffa, where so many Arab orange groves flourished in Palestine prior to 1948.

Neither in Palestinian, nor in other Arabic poetry is the Palestinian city delineated as a menace. It cannot instill any hatred or rancor. The menace it suffers is not caused by its own people, but comes instead from an external source, imposed upon the Palestinian city by strangers, Israeli settlers armed with Uzi machine guns. Innocent of the native evil and inbred tyranny of other cities in the Arab world, the Palestinian city is both a victim and a place of noble heroism, the seed-bed of resistance and valiant struggle against the usurper.

Place, therefore, as archetype and point of reference, is in Palestinian poetry a constant and stable anchor to which the Palestinian poet clings with profound faith. In Palestinian poetry written in exile, the dichotomy between constant movement and uprooting, and the deepest rootedness, between volatile mutability and serene and immutable faith, is a unique experience in contemporary Arabic verse.

Among the major poets, Mahmoud Darwish is the greatest wanderer in his personal life; he follows the path of the Palestinians in their diaspora, wherever the winds of politics drive them. Yet, among the major poets, he is the most rooted in his belief, which revolves around his people's continually worsening situation. His eyes are fixed on an unchangeable goal: the return to Palestine and the eventual triumph of justice. However, in his latest poetry, which he wrote following the exodus from Beirut after the Israeli invasion in 1982, he celebrates his people's heroic struggle to sustain their faith in an eventual triumph over the treacherous world surrounding them. He depicts a slippery world, and his greatest fear is that the dream that has sustained him and his people may vanish as a result of this unending tragedy. Yet his hero, the nameless Palestinian who has now become also the noble victim in his poetry, alone has the capacity to liberate the world around him, a world full of treachery and hypocrisy. This nameless Palestinian is being destroyed all the time, yet as he falls, he can only fall as a hero. If he were to acquiesce to a state of complete victimization, as Maghut does, it would mean announcing the end of all resistance and the disappearance of the dream.

Contemporary Arabic poetry is a poetry of longing, a longing that permeates the poetic impulse, though it is camouflaged by anger, alienation, or rejection. It is perhaps possible to say that Palestinian poetry is the poetry of longing par excellence, of an eternal dream of return and rebirth. And it is certain that the whole of contemporary Arabic poetry embodies a deep nostalgia, but one skillfully controlled and artistically freed of traditional sentimentalism by the well-sharpened tools of the modernist poet. The prime object of this longing is *freedom*, the lost love of Arab intellectuals everywhere, and the obsessive quest of the Arab creative genius. It has indeed been an elusive quest; whether it is directed toward internal or external aggression, it has always been fraught with danger, death, and prison, with loss and exile. The curtailment of freedom is a constant source of frustration and rage in contemporary Arabic poetry, and it comes as no surprise that a great number of our poets now live in exile.

Because the political scene has become increasingly merciless year after year and has represented an ever-deepening challenge to human endurance, Arab poets have to summon an ever greater faith in human possibility, in the capacity of the Arab spirit to face all the horror that springs from the inside with the same unrelenting force as that launched from the outside. What place can there be for love, beatitude, and joy in this living nightmare? The theme of love, one of the most enduring in Arabic poetry, has greatly receded. At its best, love has become unimportant, irrelevant in present circumstances—with one great and brilliant exception: Nizar Qabbani. His abundant love poetry is the major source of hope that the human heart can finally transcend pain and fear and dare to assert its capacity to summon joy and engage passion. His poetry brings freedom from tension, liberation from gloom, a refreshing release of laughter and gaiety. Above all, it proudly proclaims a new reverence for the body; it washes away the traditional embarrassment, now many centuries old, which was linked to woman's physical passion. In his political verse, loud-toned and angry, he asserts the need for freedom and liberty, but strengthens it significantly when he shows, in his erotic verse, that the freedom of the body is a path to the freedom of the spirit. After a more traditional attitude in his early verse, he was able eventually to champion feminine liberation, transcending centuries of male chauvinism and predatory attitudes. And in his later, more mature verse, which he wrote during the last twenty years, he has come to see in woman a great life force and a complete human being. Together with other writers, mainly authors of fiction,[16] he has helped to bring about a revolution in women's attitudes toward their own sexuality and erotic freedom, and their right to celebrate ecstasy and joy.

While this silent revolution has been taking place, the struggle of the Arab poet for other kinds of freedom has remained deadlocked. Not one step toward the achievement of political freedom has been successfully taken, as aggression from the outside and repression on the inside have continued unabated.

I have concentrated my discussion mainly on the achievements of earlier generations of modernist poets, those who are now called in Arab literary circles the generation of the pioneers. They have, however, been more than pioneers. They have been movers and shakers. Their literary output has been fundamentally radical and permanently profound.

The major attainments of modernist Arabic poetry have been toward complexity and coherence, esthetic sophistication and originality, together with a deep commitment to the cause of human justice and freedom. This has always been poetry's greatest aspiration, its most arduous task. The success of some major experiments must be seen as phenomenal in view of the fact that it comes on two levels which are not mutually compatible: esthetic complexity and social commitment.

Perhaps the most positive aspect of all this experimentation has been the creation of a new courage, a boldness which defies the sanctimoniousness of inherited poetic values. However, modernist poetry, as I have already explained, has also acquired some grave defects, the most serious of which are in the realms of diction and image. Critics and readers in the seventies often speak of this as a crisis in contemporary Arabic poetry.

A change is in order, a change dictated by the robust vitality of contemporary Arabic poetry and its great flexibility. It is clear to me now that it is the mission of the younger poets, those who rose to fame in the seventies and eighties, to create a new sensibility which will put an end to metaphorical chaos and modify the language of violence in poetry. Violence stems, unfortunately, from the harsh realities of contemporary Arab life: repressive, unstable, and besieged by internal anxieties and external dangers. It did seem natural for poetry to simulate this violence by verbal and metaphorical equivalents. However, this has gone on far too long and has now become a fashion which has produced great esthetic fatigue. Many contemporary poets must have sensed poetry's deep need for a radical change, and they have begun to prune acquired fashionable defects from their verse. They have demonstrated that poetry can speak of violence without itself becoming violent, and that it can be esthetically complex without becoming chaotic. This is demonstrated clearly in much of the contemporary poetry written now in Iraq under the black cloud of a protracted war—the Iraq-Iran War—that has raged since 1980. Poets such as Hameed Sa'id (b. 1941), Yusuf Sa'igh (b. 1933), 'Abd al-Razzaq 'Abd al-Wahid (b. 1932), Sami Mahdi (b. 1940), Yasin Taha Hafiz (b. 1938), Sa'di Yusuf (b. 1943), and several others, many of whom are committed to Iraq's struggle, hopes, and endeavor, have demonstrated poetry's capacity, even in violent times, to maintain its balance and contain itself within the boundaries of what is artistically viable. A number of poets outside Iraq are also writing in a more modernized manner, transcending the language of violence and pervasive heroics which has permeated Arabic poetry, particularly in the seventies. These new poets opt for the quieter, more subdued utterances of a more modern art. A sensitivity to everyday life and to personal experience illuminates their poetry, reflecting the constant urge in modern Arabic poetry to overcome the allure of fashion. Yet the same poets who speak of life's simple matters, such as a town awakening to the morning, or a tree hewn down at sunset, also speak of the deadliest contemporary conspiracies against human freedom and dignity in the Arab world. Aside from the above mentioned poets, such modernist poets as the Bahraini poet Qasim Haddad (b. 1948), and, to an extent, the late Egyptian poet Amal Dunqul (1940–1982), have also been able to use and communicate, skillfully and effectively, the new methods of the modernist poet. These new methods require a voice more subdued and less heroic, more overtly simple and direct, yet subtly complex and highly suggestive, which transforms collective anguish into private anguish while shunning the sentimental, the hyperbolic, and the consistently high-pitched and intense.

Contemporary literary reviews and many recent collections of poetry show that this trend is slowly taking hold of a new generation of poets in the Arab world. However, there is still room for more variety. Al-Munsif al-Wahaybi (b. 1949) and Muhammad Ghuzzi (b. 1949), two poets from Tunisia, for example, have furnished yet another experiment which has benefited from the riches, obliquity, complexity, and mystical fervor of classical *sufi* poetry as well as from some modernist poetry before them, while they avoid the metaphorical jumbles and fashionable heroic themes still rampant in the poetry of many of their contemporaries.

Since poets like these now appear steadily on the poetic scene all over the Arab world, the ongoing modernist experiment seems sure to prevail, and with a good measure of originality it seems certain to overcome its greatest pitfalls.

The reader of this volume, which presents selections from poetry all over the Arab world, cannot help but comprehend the coherent esthetic and social experience of this vast region, the unified spirit that dominates the poets, and the common causes they share, no matter what individual country the poet may come from. This volume is a testament to the basic unity of Arabic culture, and of the Arab spirit, and a witness to the force which a common heritage and culture can exert. The hopes, dreams, adversities, and failures that afflict one Arab country are shared by the rest of the Arab world, which stretches from the Arabian Gulf to the Atlantic Ocean. The Algerian War of Independence, the Palestine debacle, as well as the Lebanese tragedy have all been Arab issues, central to the poetry of the whole Arab world. This explains why we find so many poets from the Arabian Peninsula, the children of the new affluence, grieving over Beirut and taking up the Palestine cause.[17] Tel al-Za'tar, Sabra and Shatila, have become general Arab symbols for the treachery and brutality of evil, hostile forces bent on the destruction of the unity and integrity of the Arab world. Most importantly, the struggle for freedom is universal; the contempt and anger shown toward those who use coercion to terrorize the individual and the nation are shared by all enlightened Arabs. From every part of the Arab world, the invincible voice of poetry rises again to proclaim and extol the Arab nation in its struggle and agony, its strength and wounded pride, its patience and determination, its wisdom and exuberance, its hopes and despair. On the esthetic level, every successful experiment is immediately assimilated, and every poetic achievement becomes the possession of all. Contemporary Arabic poetry has certainly demonstrated the deep roots, unity and richness not only of the old, but also of the new Arab poetic heritage.

Salma Khadra Jayyusi

1. For more on Arab Romanticism and its causes, see Salma Khadra Jayyusi, *Trends and Movements in Modern Arabic Poetry*, Leiden: E.J. Brill, 1978), vol. 2, pp. 361–69.
2. For more on this, see *ibid.*, pp. 475–81 and 489–92.
3. See his second collection, *More Beautiful Than You? No!* (1960), and *The Book of Roses* (1972), particularly section II, entitled "The Worries of the Rose."
4. For more of these experiments in form, see S.K. Jayyusi, vol. 2, pp. 534–60 and Appendix II, pp. 756–60.
5. See *ibid.*, pp. 536–42.
6. ʿAbqar is the valley of the muses in classical Arabic.
7. Translated by Salma Khadra Jayyusi. The line before the last has been slightly modified.
8. The lecture was entitled "The Future of Lebanese Poetry" given at al-Nudwa al-Lubnaniyya in Beirut in 1957 and republished in *Shiʿr* quarterly, no. 2, Spring 1957. While he concentrated on Lebanese poetry, his analysis covered the whole poetic contribution in Arabic at the time. The ideas expostulated in this important lecture were later repeated many times in other articles he published in *Shiʿr*.
9. This was a highly inspired use of the fertility myth, easily acceptable to the Arab poetry audience. The image of water permeates classical Arabic poetry and folk usage, since in desert surroundings the scarcity of water poses great problems for people.
10. This is in reference to "Tammuz," the god of fertility in the Middle East known to the Greeks as "Adonis."
11. Khalil Hawi's long poem "Lazarus, 1962," which employs the Biblical story as an inverted symbol, is, in fact, an elegy on the severing of this union between Egypt and Syria, the first of its kind in modern Arab history. To the poet, who spoke in the words of many Arab poets and intellectuals, the severing of the union was a harbinger of death-in-life. Lazarus is seen rising from the dead, but still remaining a dead man, with no spirit left in him to bring joy and life to his world.
12. Quraish is the tribe of the prophet Muhammad. It was also the tribe of the Umayyad dynasty. The word *"al-dākhil"* means "the one who has entered," and here means the eagle of Quraish, who has entered Spain and established the rule of the Umayyads there.
13. For more on this, see S.K. Jayyusi, pp. 494–95n.
14. Such as the following short poem:

   The minaret wept
   When the stranger came and bought it
   and built a chimney over it.

15. Such as al-Maghut in his poem, "The Plateau":

   I shall return to my village even if I have to walk
   and shall throw myself on the grass and river banks
   like a horseman after an exhausting battle.

16. These were mainly women writers, foremost among whom is the Syrian writer of fiction, Ghada al-Samman. The feminist trend, however, was launched in 1958 with the publication of Laila Ba'albaki's novel, *I Live!*

17. This has been demonstrated clearly in the large anthology edited by Salma Khadra Jayyusi, *The Literature of Modern Arabia*, forthcoming, May 1987.

PART I

Poets Before the Fifties

Ilya Abu Madi (1890–1957)

Lebanese-American poet. Born in Lebanon, he spent part of his childhood in Egypt before he emigrated to the United States in 1911. He moved to New York in 1916, and was one of the most important members of the Literary Society, *Al-Rabita al-Qalamiyya*, formed in New York in 1920. Abu Madi was the most famous poet among Arab men of letters in the Americas, and has enjoyed a rare popularity in the Arab world. He introduced many innovations, writing a poetry as original and eloquent as it was balanced and imbued with the wisdom and emotionalism that appealed to his Arab readers. He has written five collections, of which the most famous is *The Streams* (1927).

THE HUMAN CLAY

The human clay forgot for a while that it was mere despicable clay, so it
    swaggered haughtily and boisterously.
Body covered with silk, it became proud; purse full of money, it grew
    arrogant.
Brother, don't turn your face away from me. I am not a piece of coal, nor
    are you a chip of a star.
You have not invented the silk you wear nor the necklace you sport.
You do not eat gold when hungry, nor do you drink strings of well-
    ordered pearls.
In your brocaded cloak, you are still like me in my tattered garments, ex-
    periencing happiness and misery.
In the light of day, you have hopes, and when darkness stretches over
    you, visions awaken.
My heart, like yours, sees similar beautiful dreams. It is not made of rock.
Are all my wishes dust and yours are golden?
Are my aspirations destined to vanish, and yours to stay for eternity?
O conceited one! If visited by illness, don't you complain, don't you sigh?
If your sweetheart abandons you and memory calls, don't you languish,
    don't you pine?

Are my tears vinegar and yours honey? Is my weeping humiliation, your
   moaning dominion?

Only one moon peers down on both of us, I say, on the hut as well as on
   the fort.

If it appears shining in your sight, I do not see it dark from my small
   window.

We both witness the stars as they disappear and glow;

In your wealth, you are not nearer to them, nor am I more distant with
   my poverty.

Is yours the well-guarded palace surrounded by sturdy walls?

Forbid the night, then, from pitching its tent over you and the clouds
   from gathering above your land.

Look how the light enters your palace without permission, why is it not
   expelled?

One bed is all you need, but do you know how many beds worms will
   make in you when you die?

You drove me away from your palace when the storm raged and the sky
   broke

While the dog was given shelter and food, and the cat equally well-
   treated.

Is yours the elegant garden with water, aloes, blossoms, and birds?

Prevent the wind, then, from shaking and twisting the garden trees,

Harness the water in the brook and command its stillness unless you are
   watching.

The birds in the trees don't care whether it is you or I who listen when
   they sing.

The flowers do not mock my poverty, nor do they flatter your wealth.

Do you think the river is yours? It is rather the gentle breeze's path and
   the birds' drinking place;

It is the stars' to bathe in, to cool themselves on summer nights.

You claim it is yours: does it run at your behest in the veins of trees, does
   it ripple when you speak?

Before you came, it was, and it will remain ebbing and flowing on the
   earth after you go.

Do you think you are handsome? You are not as resplendent as the rose,
   nor as generous.

Do you think you are strong, while the mosquito feeds on your cheeks
   ignoring the sword in your hand?

Are you powerful? Then command sleep as it overcomes you to withdraw
    from your eyelids at night;

Forbid gray hair to assail your temples, order youthfulness to linger in
    your skin.

O human clay, you are not purer or more sublime than the soil on which
    you tread and sleep.

The high palace you built will collapse, the garment you wove will un-
    ravel.

Let not your heart be a dwelling-place for hostility; mine has become a
    temple of love.

And I am more worthy of your love than the clothing that wears out or
    wealth that is exhaustible.

Translated by Issa Boullata and Naomi Shihab Nye

THE PHOENIX

I am not the first one infatuated with the glorious maiden, for she is the
    dream of all mankind.

I searched for her in the folds of dawn and darkness, I stretched my
    hands out even to the stars.

I was told, "Be pious, for she evades all but the pious ascetic."

So I buried my joys, divorced my desires, and silenced all signs of passion
    in my heart.

I smashed my flask before I was quenched, and refrained from eating
    when I was still hungry.

I thought I was approaching her speedily, but found that I had ap-
    proached only my ruin.

Like a garden denying itself its wealth of flora

To feel the sunlight in its soil and meet the breeze unmasked,

Only to find autumn creeping on it like night pitching a tent over a waste-
    land;

I was like a bird that stripped itself of its shiny plumage

To become lighter, only to fall to the ground and be attacked by ants.

I lay me down to sleep hoping she was the daughter of dreams; but I
    woke up mocking those who slept

For the world of slumber was not all joy, fearful things abounded in it.

When I dreamt of her I dreamt of a flower that could not be plucked, and
    a star that did not rise

On waking I saw nothing around me but my error, my bed, and my
    room,

For he who drinks of the rivers of his fancy travels life with an insatiable
    thirst.

Spring passed and she was not in the singing river or the fertile garden.

Winter came and she was not in its weeping clouds or crying thunder.

I glimpsed the flash of lightning and thought she was in it, but she was
    not there.

Empty-handed, led astray by youth and conniving,

I felt my hopes to find her were dashed, my sturdy moorings cut off.

Sorrow pressed upon my soul, and it tearfully flowed. It was then that I
    caught a glimpse of her and perceived her in my tears.

I learned, when learning was late, that she whom I had lost was always
    here with me.

Translated by Issa Boullata and Naomi Shihab Nye

ʿUmar Abu Risha (b.1908)

Syrian poet. He can be credited with having helped change the prevailing poetic sensibility, winning pan-Arab fame in the thirties for his poetic innovations as well as for his fiery political verse. He is well read in English, American, and French poetry, which has left a strong influence on his own work. His themes range from nationalism, to love, to descriptive verse. His poetry was recently collected in a single volume but his first book, *Poetry from Umar Abu Risha* (1947), published at the height of his fame, is his most popular work.

A ROMAN TEMPLE

Wait. This seems to be the kind of place
where I could lose myself in a trance . . .
the ruins of a palace fallen in the sand . . .
its heights have come in search of
its foundations . . .

Stunned, I gaze around
and ask the present about its past.
Did life really flow here?
Did eyelids close on happy times
and nightingales sing good fortune?
Did Fate decree its destiny and doom?
Shall I question the dumb rock
about those who carved it?
Can I summon up spectres from the grave?
The hooves of Time's dispersing horses
tell the sad destiny of this place:
here thorns are suckling at its breast
and there owls perch hooting atop it;
frightened spiders strain to free themselves
from the prison of its cobwebs.

The Hand of Destruction, sated with it,
fears the harm its touch might spread.

Here, Illusion shatters his own phantoms
and Death in desperation kills himself.

Translated by Issa Boullata and Thomas G. Ezzy

AN EAGLE

The Eagle has moved down to the foot of the mountain.
Seethe then, mountain peaks, and rage!
Your wound's scream, let it ring
throughout the world like crack of fire!
Fling your pride like a bloodied limb
at the feet of the foundering days

Peaks, gather up the Eagle's remains
and cast them at the chest of Time.
No longer does he brush the eyelids of the stars
proudly with his tousled feathers.
He has abándoned his nest, distraught,
his eyes moist with last farewell.
He has left behind him the cortege of clouds
that billowed down from their enchanted spheres
to enfold him in a dewy, dazzling kiss . . .

Now he has come down to the foot of the mountain,
has folded his wings on submerged ambitions.
Whole flocks once raced each other to flee
in fear of his strength,
but now you need not fly away, bird of the valley.
If you should know him in his present state
you would not fly away.
Weakness has pulled out his claws,
the storms of Fate have mangled his wings;
and that solemn wonder of his face
is but a vestige of a distant past . . .

Squirming with hunger, the Eagle perches
on a piece of carcass in the sand;

small and scrawny birds are pushing at it
with their stubby wings and tender claws . . .
But now, a tremor of mad pride sweeps over his body!
He shudders as though storm-tossed, and flies,
drags his crumbling bones upward
on the dusty horizon.
When he reaches the realm of dusky space
he squawks out a mighty shriek
and drops, dead, onto a lofty summit
into his old abandoned nest.

Eagle, will I ever return as you did
or has the mountain foot deadened my senses?

Translated by Issa Boullata and Thomas G. Ezzy

Ilyas Abu Shabaka (1903–1947)

Lebanese poet who led the Romantic current in Lebanon in the thirties and forties and greatly liberated "emotion" in poetry. He lived a life constrained by financial difficulties and personal conflicts. A poet with a fine poetic gift, he was influenced by classical Arabic poetry, by the Bible, by the North Mahjar Romantics and by the French Romantic poets. He wrote eight volumes of poetry, the last of which was published posthumously. His best known work is *Snakes of Paradise* (1938), but his two other volumes, *The Cry of the Heart* (1944) and *Forever* (1945), contain some of the best love poetry in the prefifties era.

YOU OR I?

This beauty, is it yours or is it mine?
In you I see a person beautiful in love
Like me. And which of us has given me life?
Is it your shape or mine that I love so?
When in my dream I see love's images
Is it your shadow in my soul or mine?
Love, all of love, dwells in all I see
Whence all this light? Your universal soul?

Did I create you in the world of fancy
Or are you my creator?
Am I the first whom inspiration blessed
Or was it you? Who writes this verse?
Did I write it for you or you for me?
And who in love can be dictated to
And who dictates? Our imaginations blend,
Your soul within my soul, your mind in mine
When things appear obscure to me I see
A doubting shadow dawning in your eyes
When we met first I found my beginning
As if you were a lost part of my being.

Translated by Adnan Haydar and Michael Beard

THIS IS MY WINE

This is my wine, companion, sample it,
for in my vineyard it has a new taste.
New faith is there for me inside that cup
Old doubts have vanished with old dying love.
Now joy wells up in my beloved's eyes
distilling hope and fragrance in my heart.
How distant now is that anxiety!
that poured its viper's venom on my wounds
which my beloved's hand healed with a touch
and from her heart the soothing balsam flowed.
Since then my heart feels mercy and compassion
for all the sick and wretched on this earth.
My old love was a purgatory. That love is dead
and to this heaven that old hell has led.

Translated by Adnan Haydar and Michael Beard

I LOVE YOU

I love you more than human heart can bear
More than a poet dreams or lover feels
You are the perfumed cloud from heaven sent
To rain upon me your enchanted dew;
I feel your heart, your veins flow into mine,
No gap to let the impure world creep in;
My heart confronts your heart, finding its twin,
As two cups meet in one ethereal vow;
In us when wine is made to mix with wine,
A blend of perfume, breeze, and dew combine;
My inspiration dwells within your eyes,
And swells when lip on lip instructs my art;
For us the fire rages, though unfed,
Though we are calm, a storm erupts within.

Translated by Adnan Haydar and Michael Beard

Al-Akhtal al-Saghir
(pseud. for Bishara 'Abdallah al-Khuri, 1884–1968)

Lebanese poet. He can be credited with having introduced Romantic notions into Arabic poetry in the first few decades of this century. His lyrical verses have great emotionalism and a vivid imagery borrowed from nature. He enhanced poetic development also through his periodical, *Al-Barq* (The Lightning) which he founded in 1908 and where he published translations from French Romantic literature, as well as some Mahjar poetry. He was hailed as "Prince of Poets" at a grand celebration in Beirut in 1961. His first *diwan*, *Love and Youth*, appeared in 1953, and a full collection of his poetry appeared in 1961.

THE WISDOM OF LIFE

Life's wisdom is best found in living drunk;
Pass me then my winecups and my lute.

Strip the world down to its delicious beauty
As you would unveil a virgin bride.

We are all in love with Life and aspire
To reap its unsoiled pleasures.

Grab on to life then, damn you,
And throw away the mask your face has hardened into.

However long you live, you're but a bird,
Tree-bound one moment, soaring high the next.

Translated by Issa Boullata and Thomas G. Ezzy

HIND AND HER MOTHER

High in the esteem of He
Who brought together

Sun and Moon,
Hind came wailing to her mother.

"Morning came to me,"
Cried she,
"And kissed me
Two kisses!

"Then he ran away . . .
When Darkness saw me
He bestowed
Two locks of his hair.

"He was bold, Mother!
He even took me to his bosom
And dimpled my cheeks
With two stars.

"Then his color melted
Into liquid mascara
That stained my
Eyelashes black.

"In the morning
I came to the garden
To hide myself
From all eyes.

"The garden cried out to me,
'Oh, my Garden!'
And was about to do
As all the others had done.

"And so I hid my face,
Mother. But the garden
Stretched its hands out
To my chest,

"And when I looked,
To my surprise,
I saw there
Two pomegranates!

"A branch continued
To follow me

Then bowed at my feet,
Making two prostrations.

"It had two roses
On its stem
And to me it gave
The roses.

"I went to the sea
To cool myself,
But then it gave me
Two waves.

"And when I walked away
They quivered in my hips
Like the sea
In undulating motions . . .

"Like the sea, Mother!
You know it! So many
Boys have drowned in it,
Or nearly . . .

"But all these things
Have made me fretful.
By God, Mother,
What do you think?"

Her mother swayed
In pride
And double self-assurance.
She laughed and said:

"I have known them
Every one.
I have tasted what you have,
Now for the second time."

Translated by Issa Boullata and Thomas G. Ezzy

Saʿid ʿAql (b. 1912)

Lebanese poet. He rose to fame in the thirties with his championship of the French Symbolist movement and his attempt to introduce a Symbolist trend into Arabic poetry. His slim volume, *Al-Majdaliyya* (1937), on the meeting of Christ and Mary Magdalene, was one of the major works of poetry to appear in the thirties. He can be rightly described as the poet who influenced modern Arabic poetry toward Symbolism. Over the years he continued to write in the same vein but did not join the modernist movement of Arabic poetry. His books include *Rindala* (1950); *More Beautiful Than You, No!* (1960); and *The Book of Roses* (1972).

DO NOT SHOW YOUR LOVE

Mirkayan, don't show your love, simply relish
the veiled passion that lures the lover.

It's enough if your marvelous eyes make me
drink a full-cupped draught from life.

Hide your love from morning dew,
from brilliant sun and searing wind

Be stingy! Till that day arrives
when the eyes stay shut and play has ceased

Leave me infatuated with your love
not knowing if you're mine, or illusion's vapor

When night overwhelms, I say, "A dream!"
and fear the fading of the awesome dark

Everything there is, is hard on beauty,
like a bee draining a flower. Lovely lover, disappear!

Translated by Matthew Sorenson and Naomi Shihab Nye

MORE BEAUTIFUL THAN YOUR EYES

More beautiful than your eyes is my love
for your eyes. When you sing, all being sings.

Are you there above me, star of my longing,
or are you just a phantom dream?

When I think of you, fragrances enter me—
Can it be you were created by a rose?

Perhaps the longing for beauty made you,
raised and hopeful hands designed your form.

Do the strings of the passionately fingered lute
imagine those who yearn for melody?

We meet in moments truant from time,
free from boundaries, dissolving all bounds.

The beckoning universe swings us into the heavens
on an endless flight.

The most beautiful aspect of our land
is the vision that you have lived here.

Translated by Matthew Sorenson and Naomi Shibab Nye

DARK BEAUTY

Dark Beauty, childhood dream!
Resistance of the stingy lips—

Do not approach me, but remain
an alluring idea for the future

When you pass, earth awakens
from its heavy slumbering dream

The tiny window of her hope
illuminated by your gleaming smile

Dark Beauty, remain for me
the most remote of pleasures

Remain a longing on my lips,
a wisp of vision in my eyes

Remain elusive, like tomorrow
to which death will beat us all.

Translated by Matthew Sorenson and Naomi Shihab Nye

FROM: THE BOOK OF ROSES

My ecstasy is that I have met you
and my golden eyes closed around you.
Say that you enjoy your prison!

*

Love, when you crossed my mind,
it became a garden of roses.
I wished I could cross your mind
to inhabit what inhabits me . . .
the reason new roses keep being invented.

*

To love you is to invent myself.
Before you, darling, I was a wisp,
the delicate closing of petals,
a chirp no bird had heard.

*

This morning a rose and a jasmine tree
winked at each other and said that I have faded.
Come back to me, my love, before they say it louder
and the neighbors hear!

*

You promised to meet me—
I know you will not come.
But I shall preserve my kisses,
adding them to the kisses of other rendezvous,
and spring will pile upon spring.

*

She is more beautiful than I?
Don't deceive yourself!
I am the song, and she but an echo,
I am embraces, she is a sigh.

*

You bring the moon to me,
You bring the sun!
Such words!
I only care
that you transport me from me to you!

Translated by Matthew Sorenson and Naomi Shihab Nye

Badawi al-Jabal
(pseud. for Muhammad Sulaiman al-Ahmad, 1907–1981)

Syrian poet. One of the greatest poets of the old school. He came from a distinguished Alawite family in Northern Syria and served many times as a member of Parliament and, in the fifties, as Minister of Health. But he also knew exile and destitution when the political climate in Syria changed. His style is a direct continuation of the classical mode, modernized to some extent by the poet's own experience but retaining much of the best in classical poetry. Since he was deeply influenced by the mystical tradition, his own poetry manifests a mystical approach and imagery. A full collection of his poetry appeared in 1978, entitled *Diwan Badawi al-Jabal*.

DARK MIRAGE

A mirage has offered its solace to my heart
Leading me on with a promise to end my drought.

How is it that I, who know of its dissembling,
Love this mirage, desire it, seek it out?

Pity the desert mirage which the dark sands,
From wilderness to wilderness, pass by.

It deceives with the promise of water, and yet it thirsts
For a fountain to love it, to make its soil less dry.

It offers the glittering ghost of a pure spring,
But its heart is ever unwatered, nonetheless.

By day it smiles, to cheat poor travelers;
Each night it spends in bitter nothingness.

If its victims knew of its secret, they would grieve
Not for themselves but for its cruel plight.

Must not this lush mirage be weary of solitude?
Does it not yearn for the waters of delight?

Lovesick, lonely, its heart longs for a haven,
And I, who embrace all things, shall receive it in mine.

Tender, forgiving, I weep for its great distress;
My sorrow for it is infinite and divine.

Though cheated, I have rewarded its deceit
With pardons, with reproaches never made.

I summon the mirage to join my soul
Where, far from deserts, there is greenest shade.

My heart laments that Fate should hold it captive,
Killing it nightly, reviving it with the sun.

All its abundance vanishes in an eye-blink:
Has its heart grown arid, its springhead ceased to run?

It wears the semblance of water, but like sweet words
That are empty of meaning, it does not meet desire.

Beauties it has in plenty; and yet the beauty
Of love has not yet touched its soul with fire.

Behold its pastures, barren of delight:
Oh, how they yearn for the shepherd's pipe to sound!

If only my sorrowing flute had leave to play,
A blooming grass would cover its desert ground.

Why did it come so close to me, this mirage,
Bringing its tantalizing presence near,

Filling my eyes with radiance, only to drift
Far, far beyond my reach, and disappear?

It is you, this mirage. And yet, for all my thirst,
No rivers of wine could take the place of you.

You have made my heart oblivious to the world.
Only the phantoms of our love are true.

Translated by Christopher Tingley with the help of the editor, and Richard Wilbur

THE VISIT

I purged my sins in a blaze of kisses
Sweet as the dreams of paradise.
Give me to drink the choice wine of your lips
And grant this good friend the grape's good wine
Do not sleep, indulge in your sinful desires, fear not—
Tomorrow my pious penance will protect you.
I will not weary of carrying your sins
If the Day of Judgment should blaze forth red
Oh, Lord, forgive me, I am intoxicated
Leave me to my error, my debauchery and my drink!
Here's to pleasure's minion, you coy, merry minx
May your memory never be laid aside.
Beauty has laid your chastity low—
Drunk with love and dizzy with youth.
Hurray for you! Even if poverty was the winepress
That pressed the wine of your cheeks into cups of sin
Hurray for you! In your eyes I see unnumbered
Ghosts of love and the dreams of lovers.
I stood before the altar of your beauty
And knelt adoring you, the idol of that altar.
The glory of beauty is revealed in your eyes
And I perceived it on your ruby lips.
I recognized love in the chamber of lust
A thousand masks could not conceal him.
That naked night, possessed of passion
Shall be ever treasured in my memory.

Translated by Matthew Sorenson and John Heath-Stubbs

IMMORTALITY

Immortality and the vaunted joys
Of eternity cannot be reconciled.
All who dwell there weary of their bliss
Just as the sick man tires of his sick bed.
The eons pass over them one like the other
Each day the same, filled with facile laughter.

They look for nothing new in their immortality
Night and day worn down by eternity's tedium.
No more dear hope is nursed in their dreams;
There is no more distinction between faith and denial.
You wretched soul, after fulfillment
Emptied now of desire, regret and bitterness!
All these immortals made stale by eternity—
Even angels' solicitude could not stir them.
They recline among houris, but without joy;
They drink the wine, though they do not thirst.
They would trade the bounteous honey and wine,
They would trade blessings of diamonds and rubies
For one moment of anguish assuring them
Of their communion with pain.

Translated by Matthew Sorenson and John Heath-Stubbs

BEAUTY

Sickness is upon me, it will not leave!
It weaves my shroud before I am old.
It has quenched all my soul's wild follies
Only my drunken heart still beats for beauty.
All beauty bewitches and exalts me to love
I pass not a fountain but I am athirst.

Translated by Matthew Sorenson and John Heath-Stubbs

Al-Tijani Yusuf Bashir (1912–1937)

Sudanese poet. He led the Romantic movement in his country and was deeply influenced by Sudanese and Arab mysticism, as well as by the strong classical traditions alive in the Sudan. His poetry expresses great love of beauty, and reflects a metaphysical vision of depth and conflict. It has diversity, color, and a strong religious and moral tone. His untimely death put an end to a career which might have secured for him and for the Sudan a leading place in the poetry of the period. A single *diwan*, *Illuminations*, which contains all his poetry, has been reprinted in many editions.

TORMENTED MYSTIC

How much mystery this atom bears in the universe.
I stand reflecting, and merge in its essence.
How profound is this air, encompassing pious faith.
Let loose, I, an atom, move freely among God's creations,
Large and small.
I envision all the universe as incessant praise,
an invocation to God. True existence, how
ubiquitous in the soul, its serenity in communion,
how steadfast in the spirit!
All that Is, flows in God's bosom.

> This ant, so delicate, is God's echo,
> He dwells in her limbs, she lives in His soil,
> Surrendering herself, His Hands receive her spirit.
> Her spirit-in-God won't end in her mortal death.

If you can see, see
In the first glow of Adam's clay, God.
If you can see, see
An unseen world of teeming nations
In the clay: souls bustling and spirits
Swarming in the water.

Creation praised, the created believed, as did I . . .
So, I escaped the void, proclaiming and proclaimed.
We see the great revealings of Your Self's Semblance in
Your rich and overflowing Sublimity. Your everflowing
Life, clear, resplendent with compassion, the nobler,
Higher Wholeness is Your praise.

With submission I guarded Your Sanctity
My soul consumed, I poured it into prayer . . .
I was pure, sincere,
                                    what happened?
I've stopped seeing what I could once see.
My spirit darkened, motes of dust clouded
my serene sky. My dreams are bound
to black fate, my hopes to death.
Oh fated end! O tyrant madness, stop
and take provisions from my food and water!

                              Come close, my heart is heavy with torment!

Only moaning, today, pierces my ear; all that is small or
Great fails my vision. Gone is the resplendent light
Out of my soul, the brilliance of dawn
The water is changed and turned to stone in every stream.
The tune is taken back quickly by the lute.
The ill and weary disappear between gloom and glory.

Translated by Matthew Sorenson and Patricia Alanah Byrne

MEMORIES OF THE VILLAGE SCHOOL

He woke from slumber rubbing his eyes,
    vexed, he cursed this adult world and all its ghosts.
The cool shades of trees spread in the village morning;
    plains with their open spaces led him on.
And images of terror ran frenzied through his mind;
    the impulse to rebel and run away recurred.
He walked resentfully, dragging his feet;
    his heart within him silently wept.

His clothes smelt of ink,
>   his head was drenched with its "fragrant" odor.
Revolt was brewing like a gale
>   silently in the heart of the little boy.

>   • • • •

He threw a glance at his teacher, that tyrannical elder.
>   What frenzied passion was hidden in his breast?
Around him his schoolmates, bright flowers,
>   lilies of the valley, wild daisies,
That take pleasure in the sun, there were a thousand temptations
>   to break away and be joyful.
But now drowsiness dwelt in their souls
>   and slumber crept over their spirits.
They grew leaden-eyed, nodding their heads
>   still bowed over their slates.
Every time sleep enfolded them round,
>   and spread its dewy wing above them
Thunder would roar overhead
>   a lofty and tumultuous echo.
They would wake and murmur a few words
>   then fall asleep again, and again the wind would roar.

Translated by Issa Boullata and John Heath-Stubbs

Ilyas Farhat (1893–1980)

Lebanese poet who emigrated to Brazil as a young man. He had begun his poetic career writing Lebanese *zajal*. In Brazil he developed his great talent as a formal poet, writing a poetry which, although it broke with no traditions, was spontaneous and pure, reflecting the dimensions of the human condition in all its aspects. Farhat's greatest claim for the Arab reader, however, was the nationalism of his poetry, which reflected the anguish and sometimes the rage against the ills he saw rampant in political life at home. He published several volumes of poetry, the first of which was his *Ruba'iyyat Farhat* (Quatrains) (1925), followed later by *Diwan Farhat*, in four volumes entitled *Spring*, *Summer*, *Autumn*, and *Winter*, respectively.

QUATRAINS

Just life and death make up our worldly state
So lose no sleep about it, early or late
Whatever firm assurances are given,
It is mere foolishness to trust a fate.
Building a house, he's wise as well as brave
Who when he does so also plans his grave
The carpenter who knows both wakes and bridals
Bits of a coffin for a crib will save.

*

Seekers of peace, enough hypocrisy!
Your words are all deceit and trickery
There's nothing but thick darkness in your hearts
In which no ray of light can ever be.
Your conference is a market where the rout
sell justice and buy perfidy. No doubt
Peace-making should be easy, but I ask
When did the tigers pull their own claws out?

*

I saw that thieves had burgled as they do
Every house but yours. I noticed too
That priests would come and visit everybody
With one exception, they'd no time for you.
I marveled then how souls their greed reveal
Good luck to the poor man, he'll not appeal
To priests who hover round and seek to fleece him
As he is free from thieves who come to steal.

*

O gold, a deep contempt for you I own
Like every foolishness to which man's prone
All those who jostle round you in contention
Are just like dogs who squabble for a bone.
In every place of them we have our fill
By word or sword they strive to work their will
You, gold, are like salt water of the sea
Who drinks of you is the more thirsty still.

*

Time promises, should I in that confide?
As for its threats, I am not terrified
Time sometimes makes a cripple walk again
Sometimes cuts down a strong man in his pride.
Not apt to curse the times of our disasters
Nor to applaud when fate brings happiness,
It's like the wayward wind that either brings
Sorrow or joy still blowing purposeless.

*

I've learnt to laugh now at adversity
Though once if but its shadow fell on me,
I wept. I'm friends with fate, not out of fear
For in my heart I am its enemy
My freedom's a veneer, I entered life
But not of my own choice, shall be at strife
With fate upon my deathbed. You who call me
Free, do you not know I've got a wife?

*

My foolish heart keeps beckoning to me
Portending hopes despite catastrophe
It does not know that my life's sun is setting—
No brief eclipse—but for eternity.
For those drawing near to death I said to them
To nurse delusive hopes is no wise fit
My springtime's done, and it was dark and clouded
Why should my autumn be by sunshine lit?

Translated by Salma Khadra Jayyusi and John Heath-Stubbs

MY BURNED SUIT

I put on my new suit, the wind and fire
Observing this, maliciously conspire
And then the wind, just for a merry lark,
Picks up from the train smoke one small spark,
A little spark, hot from the engine's coal,
And casts it on my suit and burns a hole
In that fine serge in which I took such pride
And like a tunnel's entrance it gaped wide.
Pointing this out to God I thus made free:
"You liberally clothe the forest tree
Yet you allow my new suit to be burned
If I had been a bough, when spring returned,
You would renew me. But I'll have to sweat
And moil and toil another suit to get."

Translated by Salma Khadra Jayyusi and John Heath-Stubbs

SALMA

How is it, Salma, that when you are near me
My heart must put this question to my eye:
"Is this a butterfly with roses' fragrance,
Or else a rose winged like a butterfly?"

Translated by Salma Khadra Jayyusi and John Heath-Stubbs

WILDERNESS

Have pity, God, on one you cast down here
You granted some delight, more often care.
He weeps—for he is ever on the move—
Sometimes to greet, sometimes to part from love.
Always his enemy, the treacherous night
Has hoodwinked him, depriving him of light
And given him a bitter draught to drain
A draught of black despair time and again
For forty years he's suffered this distress
Still hurled from wilderness to wilderness.

Translated by Salma Khadra Jayyusi and John Heath-Stubbs

Gibran Kahlil Gibran (1883–1931)

Lebanese-American poet and writer. Born in Bshirri, Lebanon, to a poor family, he emigrated with his family to the United States, returning home only to pursue his study of Arabic language and literature. He first wrote in Arabic, heading a productive Romantic movement that sought renewal in all aspects of literature and life, then switched to English, writing such books as *The Prophet*, which have guaranteed his immortality among generations of readers in America. His work in Arabic is central to the development of modern Arabic literature. Although his best works were written in poetic prose and sometimes in prose poetry, he was able, singlehandedly, to revolutionize the language of poetry in the twenties and thirties with his famous "Gibranian style" and a new set of attitudes and concepts. Without his contribution the story of modern Arabic poetry would have been a very different one.

VEILED LAND

Lo it is dawn, so rise and let us part;
We're barely rooted here, unwelcome guests.
What hope is there for one neglected plant,
In bloom, in color so unlike the rest?
How could the new in heart blend with the chant
Of ancient hearts that beat in ancient breasts?
Lo, there the morning calls, beloved, hear!
Let's trace its steps as it shakes off the night;
We've suffered long enough the evening's claim
That it has ushered forth the morning's light.

We spent this life confined within a vale,
Along whose ribs cascades of worry flow,
Upon its shoulders creatures of despair
We witnessed, perched like vultures, flocks of crows;
We drank but sickness from the winding stream;
We ate the poison of unripened groves;

We clothed ourselves in patience but it blazed
And left us ashes for a new attire;
And so we bedded in our ashen robes,
Which while we slept rekindled into fire.

O land veiled to our sight from ages past,
Which way to you? Which path? How long? How wide?
What wasteland hems you in? What mountain range
Enfolds your realm? Which one of us the guide?
Are you our hope? Or are you a mirage
In hearts where none but fruitless quests reside?
Are you a dream that sways within our souls
Until they wake, chasing that dream to flight?
Or traveling clouds that race the setting sun
Before they drown within the seas of night?

O source of knowledge where our forbears dwelt,
Where Truth they worshipped, Beauty was their creed:
Uncharted source, unknown, unreachable
Whether by crested wave or racing steed,
Neither in East nor West can you be found,
In southern reaches nor in northern field,
Not in the skies we find you, nor the seas,
Nor pathless deserts which beguile our art:
Deep in the soul you burst, like light, like fire,
You are within my chest my pounding heart.

Translated by Adnan Haydar and Michael Beard

EARTH

Earth issues forth from Earth forcibly, reluctantly,
Then earth struts on Earth arrogantly, proudly.
And earth fashions from Earth palaces, towers, temples.
And earth founds upon the Earth legends, dogmas, laws.

Then earth gets tired of the deeds of earth, and so it weaves from
Earth's own haloes ghosts, illusions, dreams.

Then Earth's drowsiness beguiles the eyelid of earth, and so earth too
sleeps solemnly, soundly, eternally.

Then Earth calls out to earth saying: I am the womb and the grave, and I shall remain so until the stars fade and the sun settles to ashes.

Translated by Adnan Haydar and Michael Beard

THE SEVEN STAGES

My soul grieved seven times: the first time when it tried to attain dignity by way of lowliness; the second when it limped before the crippled; the third when it was given a choice between the easy path and the rough one and chose the former; the fourth when it transgressed and consoled itself with the transgressions of others; the fifth when it feigned patience, despite its weakness, and attributed its endurance to strength; the sixth when it lifted its train from the mud of life; and the seventh when it chanted hymns before the Almighty and believed its chanting an innate virtue.

Translated by Adnan Haydar and Michael Beard

FAME

During the ebb I wrote words in the sand,
Poured all my soul in them and all my mind.

Then with the tide I sought to read and learn,
Found on the shore only my ignorance.

Translated by Adnan Haydar and Michael Beard

THE POET

I am a stranger in this world.

I am a stranger. Estrangement may be fraught with bitter loneliness and painful desolation, but it has made me think endlessly of a magic country, a country I do not know, and has filled my dream with the ghosts of a faraway land my eyes have never seen.

I am a stranger to my family and friends. I meet one of them; in my heart I say: Who is this? How have I come to know him? What law brings us together? Why am I seeking to be close to him, and why am I keeping him company?

I am a stranger to myself. I hear my tongue speak, but my ears find that voice strange. I may see my hidden self laughing, crying, defiant, frightened, and thus does my being become enamored of my being and thus my soul begs my soul for explanation. But I remain unknown, hidden, shrouded in fog, veiled in silence.

I am a stranger to my body. Every time I stand before the mirror, I see in my face what my soul cannot feel. I find in my eyes something which my depths do not contain.

I walk in the city's streets. The young men follow me shouting: "There goes the blind man; let us give him a stick to lean on." I quickly run away. Then I meet a bevy of young women who clutch my garments saying: "This man is stone-deaf; let us fill his ears with love's music." I flee. I come upon a group of middle-aged men who gather around me saying: "He is speechless as the grave; let us straighten the crookedness of his tongue." I am too frightened to stay with them. I meet a group of old men who point their trembling fingers at me and say: "He is mad; he lost his wits in the pleasure gardens of ghouls and jinns."

I am a stranger in this world.

I am a stranger. I have traversed this earth, both east and west, and never found my place of birth. Nor did I meet anyone who either knew me or had heard of me.

I wake up in the morning and I find myself inside a dark cave, serpents uncoiling from its ceiling, insects crawling along its sides. I go forth to face the light and my body's shadow follows me. As for my soul's shadows, they walk ahead to where I know not, searching for things I do not comprehend, clutching at what I do not feel I need. When evening comes I return. I recline upon my bed of ostrich down and thorns. Strange thoughts entice me, and I am swayed by strange inclinations—annoying, joyful, painful, delicious. At midnight the ghosts of bygone times and the souls of forgotten nations peer upon me through the cracks in the cave's wall. I stare at them and they at me; I talk and seek to understand, and smiling they answer. Then I try to catch them, but like smoke they melt into air.

• • • •

I am a stranger in this world.

I am a stranger. There is not one man who grasps so much as one word of my soul's knowledge.

I walk in empty wastes. I see little streams flowing upward from the deep recesses of the valley to the mountain top. I see naked trees luxuriate in flower and fruit and scatter their leaves in one brief moment. Then their branches fall to the foot of the mountain and are transformed into quivering, spotted snakes. I see birds rise and swoop down, chirping, screeching, then stop, spread their wings, and change into naked women with long necks and loose hair, looking at me from behind eyelids kohled with love, smiling with honey-dipped red lips, stretching toward me white, tender arms perfumed with myrrh and frankincense. Then they shudder and disappear into fog, leaving behind in the vast expanse the echoes of their laughter and their mockery.

I am a stranger in this world.

I am a poet. I versify life's prose; I render in prose what life has versified. For this reason I am a stranger, and so I shall remain, until death snatches me away and carries me home.

Translated by Adnan Haydar and Michael Beard

———Jinns: spiritual beings of the middle kind (between angels and devils) among whom there are good and evil. Unlike the other two, they figure greatly in folk stories and legends in both their destructive and their constructive capacities.

Hafiz Ibrahim (1871–1932)

Egyptian poet whose name was always linked with that of Shauqi. A neo-classical like him, Ibrahim was more concerned with social problems, and wrote on poverty and failure, subjects which the affluent Shauqi was not concerned about. Unlike Shauqi, he was capable of writing ironic and sarcastic verse of real appeal, but his tone was often wistful. His greatest concern, however, was with public occasions.

DESCRIBING A SUIT

I have a suit, blessings upon it.
I strut around in it, a superman.

As it swathes my body, I feel myself
Arrayed in splendor and loftiness.

People who see me think I'm grand!
My standing is that of a mayor or prince.

People haunt my tracks, like poor people
Who haunt the sun in winter time.

O beautiful suit, O fountainhead
Of all my vanity, my adorment!

I hope that nothing will change your color,
That the wild wearing winds will pass you over,

That the threadbareness will never spot you,
That the tailor's needle will pass you by.

Before your time my company was a long-worn suit,
A chameleon suit of changing colors:

Time had tamed its color, meeting people
Had turned it the shade of a liar's face.

When I wore it, people I visited
Shunned me like someone quarantined for the plague.

O new suit, you have outfitted me among my people
With a status higher than I strove for!

New clothes are pleasing to my people.
A gracious appearance is all they love.

A person to them is as valuable as the splendid
Rig he wears, as a brand new pair of shoes.

Translated by Christopher Tingley with the help of the editor, and Christopher Middleton

Muhammad Mahdi al-Jawahiri (b. 1900)

Iraqi poet and one of the greatest poets to rise to fame in the thirties and forties. He played an important role through his poetry in the political scene of his time, inciting public emotions against political decadence and compromise, and subsequently suffering oppression and exile. However, he has been honored in his old age by the present Iraqi government, and lived, for some time, in Czechoslovakia. His best poetry, much along classical lines, has an ardent tone, vivid imagery, a grand rhythmic sway, intensity, and compression. The bulk of his verse appeared in several volumes, together entitled *Diwan al-Jawahiri*.

COME DOWN, DARKNESS

Come down, darkness, on all sides, fog, come down
Come down, barren clouds
Come down, fiery smoke from conscience
Torment, come down
Ruin, come down on all who defend their ruin
Perdition, come down
Come down, judgment, on all who dig their own graves
Come down, punishment
Come down, croaking sound, let the owl of destruction
Respond to your echo!

Come down, demolisher!
Come down on sluggards whose indolence even flies disdain
They have never seen what color the sky is
So long have they bowed their necks
So long have their heads been trampled like the earth
. . . .

Night come down, may morning light
Never shine, stars never sparkle
. . . .

Come down, till doomsday
Till justice has made all things straight
Come down, night, until the forest sicks up the sloth
Of its slow people
Night, come down, until the crow is tired of his black color

Come down, night, until the eagle soars in the sky
Angry because the angry birds
Have not protected their nests
                          .   .   .   .
Come down, for you conceal these naked vices
Come down, for you are a sheath for these sharpened fangs
                          .   .   .   .
Veil them. May morning light
Never shine, stars never sparkle
Come down, night, fog, come down
Come down, you barren clouds

Translated by Christopher Tingley with the help of the editor, and Christopher Middleton

LULLABY FOR THE HUNGRY

Sleep, You hungry people, sleep!
The gods of food watch over you.
Sleep, if you are not satiated
By wakefulness, then sleep shall fill you.
Sleep, with thoughts of smooth-as butter-promises,
Mingled with words as sweet as honey.
Sleep, and enjoy the best of health.
What a fine thing is sleep for the wretched!
Sleep till the resurrection morning
Then it will be time enough to rise.
Sleep in the swamps
Surging with silty waters.
Sleep to the tune of mosquitoes humming
As if it were the crooning of doves.
Sleep to the echo of long speechifyings
By great and eminent power politicians.
Sleep, You hungry people sleep!

For sleep is one of the blessings of peace.
It is stupid for you to rise,
Sowing discord where harmony reigns.
Sleep, for the reform of corruption
Simply consists in your sleeping on.
Sleep, You hungry people, sleep!
Don't cut off others' livelihood.
Sleep, your skin cannot endure
The shower of sharp arrows when you wake.
Sleep, for the yards of jail houses
Are all teeming with violent death,
And you are the more in need of rest
After the harshness of oppression.
Sleep, and the leaders will find ease
From a sickness that has no cure.
Sleep, You hungry people, sleep!
For sleep is more likely to protect your rights
And it is sleep that is most conducive
To stability and discipline.
Sleep, I send my greetings to you;
I send you peace, as you sleep on.
Sleep, You hungry people, sleep!
The gods of food watch over you.
Sleep, You hungry people, sleep!
The gods of food watch over you.

Translated by Issa Boullata and John Heath-Stubbs

Mutran Khalil Mutran (1872–1949)

Syrian poet who lived most of his life in Egypt, having fled there from Ottoman oppression. Mutran was well versed in classical Arabic and in French, and is regarded as a precursor of the Romantic movement in Arabic poetry. His verse reflects a real attempt at forging a serious change of approach, and he experimented, quite early in his career, in modes hitherto largely unknown to Arabic poetry, such as narrative verse, which he used as a vehicle for expressing social and political dissent. However, he later devoted much of his time to the poetry of occasion, a common practice during his time. His poetry is published in four volumes under the title *Dīwān al-Khalīl*.

BOYCOTT

(Composed at the beginning of repression in Ottoman times, when the Publication Law was imposed on free thought in the Arab World.)

By sea, by land, harass us:
Scatter our best
And kill our free
One by one.

In the long run
Good will remain good
And evil,
Evil.

Smash our pens!
Will smashing them
Prevent our hands
From carving on the stones?

Cut off our hands!
Will cutting them off
Prevent our eyes
From flashing out our anger?

Put out our eyes!
Will putting them out
Prevent our chests
From heaving deep sighs?

Stop our breathing . . . !
And that's the limit of your power.
It puts us far beyond your reach.
Thank you.

Translated by Issa Boullata and Thomas G. Ezzy

EVENING

When sickness struck me I had thoughts that
It would cure me of my passion for you.
All it did was amplify my pain.
In hope I came to stay here, far from home,
In this place they said would help restore me.

If its good air can heal my body
Will any air relieve the fires of my love?
My trip across the land has been in vain;
My exile's search for cure is just more illness.

Alone with my passion, alone with my sorrow
I fling my turbulent thoughts to the sea,
It answers back with howling winds.
I sit on this hard rock and wish
I had a heart as hard as this rock.
Waves break against it like the sorrows
That have lashed my weakened body.
The wide, unquiet ocean as it heaves
Is like my heart at sunset,
A mist, like my heart's grief, rises and fills the world
And blurs the horizon to a smear of blood.

Sunset . . . How many lessons it holds
for the downcast lover
Day's death-throe, when the sun becomes its own
Funeral taper . . . it blots out certainty

And raises doubts behind dark veils;
It liquidates existence for a while,
Eradicates the contours of all things
Until daylight renews them.

I remembered you in daylight's valediction.
My heart hovered between hope and fear.
The sun's gold was dissolving into twilight
Over the dark, flesh-colored summits.
Between two clouds hung the sun
As though the universe, in sympathy,
Were shedding one final vermilion teardrop
To mingle with my own.
I felt that my life, too, was setting.
I saw my own evening in a mirror.

Translated by Issa Boullata and T. G. Ezzy

Ahmad al-Safi al-Najafi (1895–1978)

Iraqi poet. He devoted his life to poetry, and lived in a self-imposed exile in Syria and Lebanon, suffering great poverty. His original and diversified poetic experiment was also characterized by simplicity, a direct approach, and a poetic diction often approximating ordinary speech. He was also a social critic, and throughout his career he carried on an open war with the social ills and moral defects of life around him. His poetry sometimes reflects a dry humor and an interest in the ordinary things of daily life, which is rare in Arabic poetry. He has published ten *diwans* during his lifetime, but his first, *The Waves* (1932), remains one of his most popular collections.

WHERE IS THE GUARD?

When alarm bells rang
    we did not hear their clanging.
We trusted the guard, we were sleeping,
    but the guard fell asleep too.
Wide awake as night came on, he dozed off
    when thieves went on their rampage.
In our name he had gathered wealth
    but sold us cheap when he ran short of cash.
So generous, he never rejected exploiters,
    he granted everyone's request.

Don't be deceived by our grand leaders
    there is no pulp beneath the outer rind;
You've lost sight of that galloping horse
    that threw you down, then ran away.
Your mouth is shackled shut, and you
    can only pantomime your misery.
A free man's freedom lies in silence:
    if he should speak, prison will be his reward.

Breeze of Freedom, blow our way!
    We're running short of breath. . . .
Over the West, sunny days prevail,
    while in our East only a flicker flashes.
Even this flicker will die down soon:
    When will we reclaim our sun's rays?

Translated by Sharif Elmusa and Thomas G. Ezzy

THE PLEASURES OF DARKNESS

While daylight lasts, I'm reading in my books
But when I would compose, it's my own light
Illuminates me. When the sun has set,
It goes on shining still, intense and bright.

Then every meaning is transparent now,
For there is one long lucid day with me
I would not be beholden through the night
To either moon or electricity.

Often at night I will switch off my lamp
So that in darkness I may see more clear
For that which I possess is inner light
If real light shines, then it will disappear.

How often do I look away from things
And sights appear which eye has never seen
What lovely images my fancy views
As in a cinema thrown on the screen.

Some of these things I paint for you in verse
Though I employ no colors in my art
It is a dim nocturnal light I love
Lest phantom forms of happiness depart

From which all inspiration I derive
That's why in evening I such pleasure find
Those who demand a strong and powerful light
Do so because deep in their souls they're blind.

And they when darkness gathers round about them
Being of shallow mind and empty head
Suppose that they're enclosed within the tomb
And in their terror think that they are dead.

I never needed moonlight for itself
But it reminds me of my love's soft grace
As those by thirst afflicted may desire
The mirage glimmering on the desert's face.

Translated by Salma Khadra Jayyusi and John Heath-Stubbs

THE SHIP OF LIFE

Pilotless in youth was my life's ship
And she went sailing on the ocean main
Now I've a pilot who's without a ship
Both of us ache to set to sea again.

The ship's decayed, can just be dragged along
Even to a river she dares not draw near
By waves afrighted, and by winds made anxious
She dwells, being weak, within a world of fear.

She's broken spars, she's a thin, empty shell
Crumpled by Time's hand, by wind and weather
And so decrepit, only a thin thread
Of hope can hold her shattered frame together.

She fears lest water's touch should break her up
Only on Judgment Day to be restored
This pilot cannot any longer save her
Her pilot at the last must be her Lord.

Translated by Salma Khadra Jayyusi and John Heath-Stubbs

THE MOTH

I've suffered bitterness from tyrant fate
And cares that in an endless line proceed

The longer we go on the more disasters
It is all ups and downs, this life we lead.

How often have I found both joy and sorrow,
Encountered love and hate. In evening skies
How fortunate must be the moth that flutters
Just for a little while, and then it dies!

Translated by Salma Khadra Jayyusi and John Heath-Stubbs

Ibrahim Naji (1898–1953)

Egyptian poet. A physician, he also had a sound literary upbringing and knew English, French, and German. He was an important part of the Romantic movement in Egyptian poetry. His poetry revolved mainly around the experience of love, and he was able to express a great tenderness and a deep compassion unrivaled by other poets of his generation. He has three collections: *Behind the Clouds* (1934); *Cairian Days* (1943); and *The Wounded Bird* (published posthumously in 1953).

FAREWELL

Leave me, my love, it's time to part
    this paradise is not my portion.
I had to cross a bridge of flame whenever
    I visited this land of bliss.
Yet I've been your life-long companion
    since earliest youth and our tender years.
But now I come like a transient guest,
    and go away like a bird of passage.

Has anyone drunken with love like us,
    seen love as we have seen it?
We built a thousand castles on our way,
    Walked together on a moon-drenched road,
Where joy danced and leapt before us,
    we gazed at the stars that fell, and we possessed them.
And we laughed like two children together,
    ran and raced with our own shadows.

After this nectar's sweetness we awoke—
    how I wished it had never been so!
Night's dreams had vanished, the night was ended—
    the night that used to be our friend.
The light of morning was an ominous herald;
    dawn loomed up like a wall of fire.

The world was a place of horror once more, as we'd known it,
    and lovers went their way, each his own road!

Translated by Issa Boullata and John Heath-Stubbs

OBLIVION

At last the cure, I bid farewell to pain,
    and welcome with a smile the days to come.
Oblivion comes to me a kingly guest,
    with hands compassionate and blessed steps.
My guest comes strongly on,
    folding the distances, the dark unknown.
Proffering a cup that takes away
    old pain, and banishes all regrets.
So drain it to the dregs and have no fear—
    For long you've suffered, your thirst your only drink.
Oblivion now envelops me, and I
    thank God for its overwhelming flood,
Surrendering to the waves which engulf me,
    happy to embrace a void without memories.

Translated by Issa Boullata and John Heath-Stubbs

Amin Nakhla (1901–1976)

Lebanese poet and essayist. Lawyer, journalist, politician, and member of Parliament, he was also a prominent literary figure. He was noted for his deep appreciation of the subtleties of the Arabic language and held a life-long reverence for it. In both his poetry and his prose he demonstrated a tendency toward classical perfectionism, insisting on balance, emotional restraint, a selective vocabulary, and a sculptured style, and revealing a mild Symbolist streak. He published three *diwans: Book of Love* (1952), *The New Diwan* (1962), and *Nights of the Raqmatain* (1966).

TO THE BELOVED GROWN PAST YOUTH

You. You dwell in this old house
Of spent nights and twice-told tales.
You buried beauty with a fine funeral,
Such sad tidings the earth wails.
The fount that roused your hair and cheek
Is now abandoned, dry and bleak.
The wine of the lovely now matured
has vintage flavor, but the punch is weak.

You. You share with me this garden.
We're richer far than these green trees.
In a field of wheat the swaying stalk
Does well without a flowery frock.
After spring's abundant showers,
This summer refuge needs no rain.
Out of your open book of beauty
You are an abridged version.

Don't frown on spring and don't forget
The secrets lurking in the fruit.
The musk in empty bottles will
still smell of fragrant days.

Translated by Matthew R. Sorenson

BLACK SONG

Stand back, bright morning
Beauty this moist night is black.

My night a pair, the darkness dewy
One wing flown and one wing . . . well . . .

I lie in soft and supple limbs
The fruit sways, the breasts shake.

Such fragrant air, and pleasant breath,
Your fine and musklike sweetness sighs.

Lady, slaves in your black majesty,
We, the white, have our joys and sorrows.

Your hair framed about your brow
It cascades, challenges and defies.

Your gown falls to the waist,
It opens up my agony.

Your smooth and supple flesh,
Proclaims my bed in ecstasy.

A body vibrant, like a thousand branches swaying
And mine follows in throes of passion.

I would take your dainty waist
But for fear my hand would harm

The waist that sinks beneath my burden,
The waist that bends in my embrace.

Make long this night on your soft marble
In the glint of emerald blackness.

Bring your ebony to the feast of fronds
Oh how full your rich favors.

Our own festival, a chance for joy
Under the veil of night, rich provisions.

Translated by Matthew R. Sorenson

Mikha'il Nu'aima (b. 1889)

Lebanese-American poet, critic, biographer, and essayist. He studied first in Nazareth, Palestine, then at the University of Poltava in Russia. In 1911 he emigrated to America, where he studied law. He finally settled in New York, where in 1920, along with other Arab emigré poets, he founded the Society of *al-Rabita al-Qalamiyya*, whose avant-garde principles he formulated. His poetry, which is of a limited quantity, is of a contemplative nature and has achieved a departure from neoclassical tone and thematic approach. But it was in his literary criticism that Nu'aima wielded the greatest influence on the direction of Arabic poetry with his revolutionary ideas on innovation versus traditionalism. His book, *The Sieve* (1923) was a central contribution to poetry criticism in the earlier decades of this century.

SEEK OUT ANOTHER HEART

You lie down in terror of the darkness,
even your bones are trembling, your heart
longs to still itself in one final sleep.

Dawn finds you always anguished as it breaks,
seeks out others who might better make out
the meaning of what it says.

You have plunged unarmed into strife,
at noon you moan and stagger, wounded;
no one comes to see to you.

Beneath a cloud of dust you wander
alone in the desert. You are the traveler
who seeks his home but has lost his way.

Your heart is ripping apart,
you can neither get away nor turn back.
Until another heart wants to light your way
you shall stumble through the dark.

Translated by Sargon Boulus and Thomas G. Ezzy

TO A WORM

While I incessantly pursue
my death-shroud and my hearse
you crawl, like perdition,
through my mortal body.

To occupy my time
always in a hurry
I stumble into ruins of hope,
phantoms of my sorrow

And I erect in protest
palaces of nothing
whenever the hand of Time
thwarts my designs.

Every day I bring forward
a new life for myself
while Death's course surges through me.

But for the fog of my doubt
I might have found my faith
in your unflagging crawl.
O Worm of Earth!

Then, I would have let my thought
proclaim its own vanity,
my sorrow shroud my sorrow.

Translated by Sargon Boulus and Thomas G. Ezzy

Ma'ruf al-Rasafi (1875–1945)

Iraqi poet. One of the major poets of his time, who, like other contemporary poets, was deeply involved in the political life of the Arab world. He brought poetry to the heat of life around him, exemplifying the aspirations of all Arabs. He was also concerned with social problems and dedicated some of his poetry to the description of the hard lot of women and workers. His best poems attain a purity of style, a passionate appeal, and a rhetorical grandeur well suited to his role as a poet for the public. His poetry is collected in one large volume entitled *Diwan al-Rasafi*.

POEM TO AL-RAIHANI

Amin, you came to Iraq, wanting to see
How grand it was,
And how unique:

Forgive me, but the star has been put out;
After its darkening, the people seek
Only contention.

You must know:
Iraq, though beautiful, has emptinesses
And they invade places where people live—

Old fertilizing rains
Are still the same, but nothing now can thrive
For the rains flow in different directions,

And every Spring is what it was
But now, each time it comes, it complains
Of barrenness, and people are

Captives of ignorance.
Amin, do not be angry:
For all my words I can find evidence—

How can you hope
for progress, if the road our rulers
Take deranges

The real Iraqi road? Who can find any
Good in a land where swords
Are in the grip of cowards, misers

Manipulate the moneybags, and wisdom
Is minded only
By folk in exile, knowledge belongs

To strangers and the power
To interlopers, where from the few
Who tyrannize

The many,
The scraping, bowing many
Claim no due?

Translated by Issa Boullata and Christopher Middleton

THE ABYSS OF DEATH

A mountain our life is, overlooking
An abyss of death.
                    Along the ridge
We walk, blind: always, walking,
Off we fall.
            This universe,
A sea it is, created things
Surge in it. We, when they undulate,
Are the bubbles. They
Appear, vanish,
                    Are seen, not seen,
Always to scatter
Fated, fated to disperse.

Translated by Issa Boullata and Christopher Middleton

Abu al-Qasim al-Shabbi (1909–1934)

Tunisian poet whose rise to poetic eminence in the twenties immediately ushered Tunisian poetry into the current of avant-garde Arabic poetry of the time. He was influenced by North Mahjar poetry and by translations from the French Romantics, and was himself a true Romantic. He combined the two opposing trends—the one positive, strongly rejecting traditional social and political shackles and seeking to awaken people to progress and revolution, and the other negative, seeking seclusion in Nature, away from people's ignorance and submissiveness. His only volume, *Songs of Life*, appeared in 1955, many years after his death. A volume of selections of his poetry in English, prepared by PROTA and translated by Lena Jayyusi and Naomi Shihab Nye, is forthcoming.

LIFE'S WILL

When people choose
To live by life's will,
Fate can do nothing but give in;
The night discards its veil,
All shackles are undone.

Whoever never felt
Life celebrating him
Must vanish like the mist;
Whoever never felt
Sweeping through him
The glow of life
Succumbs to nothingness.

This I was told by the secret
Voice of All-Being:
Wind roared in the mountains,
Roared through valleys, under trees:
"My goal, once I have set it,

And put aside all caution,
I must pursue to the end.
Whoever shrinks from scaling the mountain
Lives out his life in potholes."

Then it was earth I questioned:
"Mother, do you detest mankind?"
And earth responded:
"I bless people with high ambition,
Who do not flinch at danger.

I curse people out of step with time,
People content to live like stone.
No horizon nurtures a dead bird.
A bee will choose to kiss a living flower.

If my mothering heart
Were not so tender,
The dead would have no hiding place
In those graves yonder."

Translated by Sargon Boulus and Christopher Middleton

QUATRAINS FROM "SONG OF ECSTASY"

Cupbearer, take your wine away,
We need nothing, drunk with love,
Pour it out for the bees and birds,
Give to the earth that bride of yours.

Why look into a cup to find
Love's ecstasy, when here it is?
Leave us be, served by Spring
This is our cup—the air we breathe.

In a quiet space like birds we float,
Like bees that answer to the lure,
Spellbound, of the quiet world
Where roses, fresh, grow from the ground.

Or we are children, two, who play,
Innocent, on slopes above
A lovely rock; of perils deep
Down in the valley, ignorant.

At noon and in the waning light
We sing with winds that cruise through fields;
Revealed to us her spirit now,
To nature's chant we are listening.

Let others be as they might wish,
And welcome: we extract the core,
For we are spirit, out of mind—
Behind us, left for them, the shell.

The rose whose fragrance we inhale,
The wine we have—enough is ours:
Nectar celestial on our lips,
Blooms of Springtime in our heart.

O time that flows, time fathomless,
Without direction, restless world,
O sky without repose that turns
The burning dawns and night about.

O death, O fate that has no eyes,
Stop where you are! Or turn aside,
Let love and dream sing out for us
With vast existence for their theme.

If not, then make away with us
With love still flaming on our lips,
The magic roses fragrant still,
And youth still at our fingertips.

Translated by Sargon Boulus and Christopher Middleton

Ahmad Shauqi (1869–1932)

Egyptian poet and the greatest poetic figure during the first thirty years of this century. At his hands, poetry regained its classical vigor and its robust spirit. Through a well-knit verse that was versatile and expressive of the deep emotional traits of the Arabs and their kind of inherited wisdom and outlook on life, he was able to win a popularity so immense that he was named "Prince of Poets" at the huge pan-Arab celebrations in Egypt in 1927. His poetry is collected in two volumes, entitled *Diwan Ahmad Shauqi*.

BOIS DE BOULOGNE

O Bois de Boulogne, don't you remember
When the whole world was at our command,
When, under the cover of darkness, my love and I
At night hurried to you.
How we lingered there talking as we pleased
With no one at all to overhear us,
When we quenched our passion, the words of my darling
Were sweet as the melody of a lute.
How we roamed freely in your open spaces,
While there was no motion in the wind,
The birds were asleep, the whole world in deep slumber.
We passed the night in pleasures, watched only
By one solitary envious star.
How we paused at each corner, dallied at each spot,
Drunk as we gazed in each other's eyes,
Our love—it was a child newborn,
Our breasts his cradle, his charm in our hearts,
The branches bowed down in seemly homage;
The star looked on with unwinking eye,
Till, at the call for parting, our sweet bond was severed,
Now seas divide me from her, and beyond them desert upon desert

My night's now in Egypt and hers in the West.
How blessed is the night that has her company!

Translated by M. Mustafa Badawi and John Heath-Stubbs

THOUGHTS ON SCHOOLCHILDREN

Lovely companionship of school, lovely those days.
Lovely the children, so full of fun, life's reins restrain
Them for they are tender and young.
Smiles of the world they are, the fragrant scent
That breathes from the flowers of its sweet basil.
At sunrise, at sunset to and from school,
Taken like a flock to strange pastures
To an unknown shepherd with an unfamiliar crook,
To a future that binds the fetters of life,
Too strict for them and hard to bear.

        • • • •

Little birds in a thicket they are, some take flight
To try out their wings, and some are unfledged;
They ride on Time's wings, not knowing the danger.
Sparrows at spelling lessons, frisky colts in the playground.
Free from all the cares of life—
These they have left to their fathers and mothers.
Around them gallops the folly of youth,
Too strong to be curbed, it has ceased the child's mind
And now has infected the teacher, till he, himself
Has become once more like a child.

Cheerful is the bell that rings for their release,
But not so cheerful when it calls them to work.
Soon that bell will be buried in a clock
Whose wheels always turn for us mortal men
Like a scorpion that lifts its sting to menace the young,
And to inject its poison into the old.
With its twin hammers Destiny
Strikes and the Fates revolve.
The satchels the children carry in their hands

Are repositories of the hidden future
In them is the man who, whether he lives or dies,
Will not be reckoned among men,
And the general, the leader, the disciple, the prophet,
He who lags at the crowd's tail, he who heads the procession.
They are dressed in a garment youth's hands have woven,
Which is more precious than gold braided velvet;
Time scratches their faces with its claws,
And makes their winsome bloom diminish,
Childhood is robbed by the prime of youth,
And youth vanishes in hoary age.
Greyness spreads slowly through the hair, as in a grass patch
Fire, encroaching the thread of life.
From book learning they turn at length
To another learning that is not recorded,
A world in which man seeks adventure,
With the armory of tooth and claw.
The rich man's son becomes a pauper;
the poor man's child attains to riches.
The child full of good health departs;
The sickly one recovers and lives.
Many a bright scholar at school
has not done so well in the lesson of life.
And gone are his schoolmates, as if he had never
Known them at all, nor yet their company,
Till they all disappear, one flock then another,
and fade like a mirage in the desert.

Translated by M. Mustafa Badawi and John Heath-Stubbs

AN ANDALUSIAN EXILE

O bird crying on the acacia tree, alike are our sorrows
Should I grieve for your troubles or lament my own?
What tale have you to tell me?—only that the self-same hand
That laid my heart waste has pinioned your wing.
Exile has cast us both, fellow strangers,
In a grove not our own, where our kind never meet
Parting has struck us—you with a knife, me with a barbed arrow.

Roused by longing, neither of us can move,
our broken wings too weak to answer our will.
Child of the valley, nature has set us apart,
and yet affliction has brought us together.
You have not forsaken your drink for unquenched longing,
Sad memory, or countless similar sorrows,
Dragging your feet on the boughs, and your tail behind you,
You go in search of one who might heal you.
There are many to heal the body if we but seek them,
But where, O where the skillful healer of the soul?

Translated by M. Mustafa Badawi and John Heath-Stubbs

'Ali Mahmud Taha (1901–1949)

Egyptian poet. He was a Romantic who rose to be Egypt's most famous poet, on a pan-Arab scale, in the thirties and forties. He introduced thematic variations and released a liberating current of emotion, confirming the Romantic movement in Egypt and the Arab world, and expressing the yearning of people toward the exotic, the past, the unavailable, or the unexperienced. His style is well-knit, highly picturesque, and often luxuriously lyrical. Taha has published seven collections of poetry, but his most famous is *Nights of the Wayward Sailor* (1940).

THE BLIND MUSICIAN

(A Dalmatian guitarist and band leader in a Cairo restaurant, 1935.)

When the moon wraps the earth in silvery light,
When the wind moans or raging lightning flashes,
When dawn opens the eyes of the tender narcissi,
I weep for the Flower who weeps with unshed tears.

Beautiful Lady, show Fate the bleeding place
Where the Archer's arrow hit the mark.
Let the sunrise touch a parched star
And soak up light from the well of your sublimity.

Let Dawn's tears kiss your sunset.
Do not lose yourself in sorrow for all the days you've lost.
All around you is the universe: see it with your touch.
Take the flowers in your hands, leave the thorns for my soul.

When night falls and silence spreads over the valley
Take your guitar. Seek your inspiration from the sorrowing clouds,
And move the stars to pity for a star without light.
Perhaps your song will draw down rays of mercy.

When birds in their humming nests
Pierce the branches in the garden with their warbling,
The fluttering music of my thoughts comes to you,
Sings out my poems, pays tribute to your beauty.

When the dew melts on the tender leaves
And the Golden Cruet pours its fragrance into flowers' cups,
I pray the Dream-Nymphs in their magic realm
To melt their tune into your eyelids, melt the sorrow in my heart.

Translated by Issa Boullata and Thomas G. Ezzy

EGYPTIAN SERENADE

Night has come. Let us go then, Goddess of my dreams.
The Angel of Love has called us to the glory of his altar.
Darkness stirs up hymns and songs,
Its joy pervades the water, trees and clouds.
Let us dream now, for this is our night of love.

Let us stand along the Nile, where moonlight, lustrous as a baby's skin,
Floods the green bank beyond its water and its shade.
Let us play as it plays, kissing the roses and the dew.
There on the hillside, grass will be our cradle,
Silence will enfold our souls, Love's nightingale will trill.

There, a sail shimmers on a sea of light, and sways us along banks
Of bright enchantment; night stars murmur like beautiful eyes,
While you are at my lips, and in my arms,
A sylph whose heart is throbbing.
Let us dream now, for this is our night of love.

Summer nights are dreams, and only lovers can perceive them,
The rapture dwells within us when the wine is gone,
The glowing cup we hold still sings and sparkles.
So let us drink our fill tonight from the sweet well of passion:
Let us dream now, for this is our night of love.

Translated by Issa Boullata and Thomas G. Ezzy

Ibrahim Tuqan (1905–1941)

Palestinian poet. He was the foremost poet of his generation in Palestine, and devoted much of his poetic energy to the Palestine cause. He employed a terse and poignant phraseology and his themes ranged from the strictly personal to the broadly national. His tone could be ardent and gentle when delineating a personal experience, grand and ceremonial when speaking of the national struggle, and sarcastic and ironic when attacking national ills. His poetry was published in Arab newspapers and was widely quoted. After his death it was collected in a single volume, *Dīwān Ibrāhīm Ṭūqān*.

THE MARTYR

Disaster frowned;
But he was smiling.
Terror surged up;
He plunged into it.
Serene in spirit and mind
Steadfast of heart and stride.
Reckless of injury,
Undeterred by pain
His soul was possessed
By high endeavor
Nobler than all
Its elements: flame and tempests.
Combining the turbulent sea
With the steadfast heights
It stems from the nature of sacrifice
From the essence of noble giving
A torch of justice whose scorching heat
Many times has set nations free.

Along the path of greatness he walks,
Seeking eternity as a dwelling place,
Indifferent whether to chains
Or to death he comes at last,
Pledged to his resolution.

Perhaps death took him
While still confined in prison
And neither a tear from a loved one
or family bade him farewell.
Perhaps he was lowered into the ground
Without even a shroud.
Who knows whether it is the plain
That hides his body, or the mountain peak.
Do not ask where his body lies—
His name is on the lips of time.
He was the guiding star that shone through
The darkness of trial.
Bringer of light to eyes so that they should
Not know slumber.
Casting flame into hearts,
So they do not know rancor.

What face glowed with joy,
Going willingly into death
Singing forth before the world
As his soul ascended to heaven
"I am for God and Country!"

Translated by Lena Jayyusi and John Heath-Stubbs

PERPLEXITY

I had no wish to be stone-hearted
    and drive the dreams from her eyes.
Desire urged me to wake her
    but my hand shrank from reaching out to her.
Sleep seemed to find joy in her eyelids
    and would not depart from them.
Woe to my heart! How was it not destroyed
    by the sight of her, as she tossed in sleep
Sighing from what was in her heart;
    Desire! Do not perturb her breasts!
There is sorrow enough for me when I see
    her hair fall about her cheeks, kissing their softness
I envy it as she rests in sleep;
    it excites me as it nestles on her arms.

I watch with a lover's yearning,
    all patience at an end. I lean over her,
Delicacy of feeling holds me back. I move away
    in awe, longing to kneel at her feet.
My soul is torn between reverence and desire.
    I remain perplexed between the two!
Did my desire reach its utmost bounds?
    For I fell enraptured upon her lips.

Translated by Christopher Tingley with the help of the editor, and John Heath-Stubbs

Jamil Sidqi al-Zahawi (1862–1936)

Iraqi poet. His role in the turn-of-the-century poetry scene was that of a radical iconoclast whose verse was a vehicle for expressing his many ideas on politics and society. He stood for modernism and progress, for the emancipation of women, for personal and national freedom, and for scientific experiment. At his hands poetic language was greatly simplified to suit his novel thematic involvements. He published five *diwans* during his lifetime, and two others were published posthumously.

BOTH STRANGERS

Down one of Baghdad's lanes I went,
Met there a man, his back was bent
With age, shuffling along, I saw
Tattered but clean the clothes he wore.

Wide his brow, in the deep furrows
I could see the mark of sorrows
Such as old folk undergo.
On he plodded, very slow.

People cursed him, right and left,
He never answered, but he'd shift
His weight, and pause, and then he'd sigh
To melt your heart with pity. I

Asked who he was and someone said:
"Truth, he has never visited
This town before: a stranger." So
Not stopping for my tears to flow

I went to him, gave him my arm
To hold him up and fend off harm,
And said: "Stranger, me and you,
We're strangers both, so kinsmen too."

Translated by Issa Boullata and Christopher Middleton

PART II

Poets After the Fifties

Hasan 'Abdallah (b. 1945)

Lebanese poet, and one of the group of young poets from Southern Lebanon called "Poets of the South," who became particularly famous during the Lebanese Civil War, but whose rebellion against the faults of the Lebanese and Arab establishment dates from even earlier. He completed his higher studies in Beirut, where he teaches now at one of its secondary schools. Like the other poets of the group, Hasan 'Abdallah wrote heatedly, often with anguish, in defense of the rights of the oppressed Southerners and other downtrodden minority groups living in Lebanon. His first collection, *I Remember that I Loved* (1978), drew the immediate attention of avant-garde writers in Lebanon with its powerful delineation of a situation at the point of crisis. It belongs to the modernist movement of poetry in Lebanon, which relies on a complex structure and an original vocabulary and use of imagery. A long poem, *Al-Dardara*, was published in book form in 1980.

I REMEMBER HAVING LOVED

To Fatima, 1977

When your spirit shall transcend your time,
your eager spirit,
sorrowful then you shall remain
on a cold shore, with your people,
not knowing them.
                    (Holderlin)

He longs
He strokes with words the place of longing
keeps long vigils on the peaks of days that collapse in cold sand
Saida over Saida
and sea that tumbles into sea
I remember having loved. . . . . .

I loved until I became love
And who saw my soul over the trees of the place

And who saw my voice across the silence opposite the city?
     In silence everything happens
         the rose of the volcano
         the wind's glory
         the talk of the ocean
         the neighing of the ages
         songs
         moans . . .

They do not hear
because
they do not listen
And you are an erect silence
I am thunder advancing
We meet
only for the trees of madness to sprout between us.

—What is the most beautiful of sounds?
—Fatima talking to herself under the stars
—And the most beautiful of rivers?
—Fatima's loving
There . . . in the house, on the sidewalk
                in the book
                or the bottle
I used to lie back and dream of our being two in one name so the gardens
would ignite in bitter sugar, and the bird of the distant sea would fall into
the sea
I would remain standing
and Fatima would still hesitate between entering and not entering a new
    role.
And we say
Fatima is the oceanic distance of the heart minced in the trap
of rigid boundaries
and we say
Fatima is the solar compass of the face walled in by gloom and chains
And we say
Fatima is the rosy distance of the eye that resides in a springtime that
    does not return . . .
That I may see you . . . I remember the last colors:
                    the color of the sea

the color of your two hands
the noontime color of the last Satur-
day
and the last of the words
the lemons leaping from behind the wall
the girls in love with legends
their prince does not come
because they have no windows
pale beneath the weight of dreams and longings.
That I may see you . . . I draw a white step in the morning
near the lemon lake
in one suburb of our blue oceanic
spirit: Saida . . .

Do not hear these words because you are
the distant one
the numerous one
Each time I tried to come near and say what I desire
I fell into endless poetry
you are the sky:
blue
high
and you are the sea:
open upon its eternal pulsing
You are your own opposite
insomnia across the day's roof
and a starry pleasure in the night
ambient ecstatic
Your place: a wave in the sea
Your time: a blue rose . . . that does not come to be
And I: I do not see you . . .
I see only my continuous collapse in the face of
your forbidden embrace
Will you turn into a god that I may organize in you my
bewilderment, invent rites, suitable pleas, a genuine objection
like a sword with which I would strike the sea's head
then
revolve around the wind . . .
I know that you are the arboreal

and the oceanic
and the cosmic
all time
You do not hesitate and you do not fear monotony
And I am the dust of the daily event:
my extremities bloodied
my chest could be crushed any minute
Do you hear within you the echo of my leaving you?
Do you hear the echo of my flames as I am writing?
Do not hear these words because this is the impossible language
for the saying of the unsayable

I make you a gift of my low window
I so that you may see how afraid I am to that extent—I am the deep failure
in the face of this sea—
Where will your face be in the evening, so that I may think in your
direction
Stagnant my age is
and free as the fire my spirit
empty the space of school mornings.
Cruelly . . . the lemon does not flower around me
We do not talk together in silence between one poem and another
Terror gives tongue where there is neither Saida
nor any meeting with you
Once again I declare your great necessity
my dusty solitude
Where will your face be in the evening
so that I may go with it to a moon that has entangled itself
in the sky's adventure?
I give you my window and the map of space
so that you may follow
and you may become weary
my journey to you
Where are you?
Had you forgotten while my heart was suspended in fear?
The soldiers invade my days without let-up, I saw dead doves on their
rifles, I saw like pines my blood yearning for a clear place:
a town or a woman
a snail

or a pavement floating
in light

O our doleful blood . . .
and our crippled stones
How is it that my martyred body did not sprout a garden higher than the
bullets and ignominious helmets? How did this friendly fire pass without
devouring, consuming, destroying the reasons for my death?
Where are you?
Where is your strength that . . . your eyes
                              your voice
I do not call you because you are my second name
        and my first is the shores . . .

And I say Fatima is the departure toward the poem when my hand
fell among the chains
my spirit into the dust
my songs into moans.
And I say Fatima is the light spreading in the days . . . the
prisoner's window
And I say Fatima is the branches
                    while around us there is the desert . . .
She comes I say
She will wear Saida and come
to pick me up from among the shreds of poems, cigarette butts,
                              old and new rubbish . . .
Fatima who is a neighbor to the destruction of the spirit
                        always comes
            to scatter a song over the silence of the place.

Translated by Lena Jayyusi and Christopher Middleton

——Saida: the ancient city of Sidon in the South of Lebanon.

Muhammad 'Abd al-Hayy (b. 1944)

Sudanese poet and critic. Educated first in Khartoum, he went to Oxford University to pursue his higher studies, obtaining a D.Phil. in comparative literature in 1973. Since then he has been Professor of English literature at the University of Khartoum. Aside from his works on literary criticism he translated and wrote studies on contemporary African poetry and published several volumes of his own, including his two long poems, *Return to Sinnar* (1973) and *Ode of Signs* (1977), a poem of deep religious concerns. His collection, *The Last Rose Garden*, is his latest. 'Abd al-Hayy's poetry represents a departure from the direct political involvements that have dominated contemporary Arabic, including much Sudanese, poetry, but in its terseness of style and power of expression it proves to be firmly rooted in the strong poetic tradition of the Sudan.

ODE OF SIGNS

I. The Adam Sign

> With Names we summon Cosmos out of Chaos
> Waves   Dunes
> Stone   Wind   Water
> Forest   Fire   Female
> The Darkness   The Lights
>
> And God arrives
> Wearing His holy Names
> Inside the Names
>
> Tonight is the birth of His vision

II. The Noah Sign

> Into the face of the Lord I almost scream:
> "How could You rest after releasing this
> Terrible flood onto the fields we formed

By the sweat of our brow these many arid years,
This crescent of green we pulled out of the jaws
          of the lion of drought?
          Why must the wilderness
          Begin again?"
Instead I shout
As the universe slides into sunset:
"O Lightning! Flash in the darkness of His wrath
And fill my psalm with light:
My ark of weakness and desire
That teems with new birth for our ancient land."

III. The Abraham Sign

    Will he come?
    Will he come across the night of words?
    Across the silence of speech?
    Across the starry rose at the center of night?
    Bright as the blade of words across the flesh of darkness?

    Will he come, your other angel, tonight? Listen!
    The cry of a hawk   The warnings of nature
    The frothy blood of a slaughtered lamb in the track of heaven
    Horse-bodies shining in the clouds
    Above the trees and in the wind
    The language of green, blazing,
    The night-bird in flight
    Turns to ashes inside the mirrors of fire.

IV. The Moses Sign

    Ashes in virgin morning they collect and rise
    As green trees in clear light
    As red fruit on the fresh branch
    A white bird   A generous well

    Everything
    Is a dream that speaks of the promised land.

V. The Jesus Sign

    This is the ringing of dawn's foot
    On hills and in the trees

Telling how wind boomed through the grand guitar
How Virgin and angel embraced
In canopies of fire
In street-noise and in dust
How they took leave:
He to his heaven
She to her conquered body
And the song of blood began
That comes to light in the throat of sparrows.

VI. The Muhammad Sign

The garden surprised us
The garden startled us and
At its heart like a rose of fire
The lights converged like silver stallions
In this kingdom without clouds the peacocks
Spread their embroidery
Everything held among the branches of truth
Myrtle of fire   A wave in deep seas
Of Flame   of Beauty   of Fortune
Where the bird falls before it meets the shore
And greets, delighted, its own conflagration.

The garden surprised us
The garden of blossoms bewildered us
At the center shines the green-domed shrine
Good news resounds, loud and sublime
Joy for the birth of the Chosen One
The garden arrayed in the new sunlight
Ecstatic
And the names sang.

VII. A Sign

A sun of grass and two doves   singing
Before the beginning   and after the end
Of Time
They burn in the branches
Of the transparent willow

Translated by Matthew Sorenson and Alistair Elliot

Salah 'Abd al-Sabur (1931–1981)

Egyptian poet and dramatist. Educated at the University of Cairo, he served as editor of the influential monthly, *Al-Katib;* as Undersecretary of State for Culture; and then as head of the Egyptian Book Institute until his death. His first collection of poetry, *The People of my Country* (1957), was an immediate success. He received the State Prize for Literature for his free verse play, *The Tragedy of al-Hallaj* (translated into English as *Murder in Baghdad*), and has published several other verse plays since, as well as several other collections of poetry of major significance. 'Abd al-Sabur is one of the most "modern" of contemporary Arab poets, writing in a language nearest to contemporary written Arabic and expressing the predicament of modern man in the Arab world.

EXPECTATION: NIGHT AND DAY

In this way the day slipped
off the slope of the sun
and evening fell
    like a collapsed wall.
Sky and earth: one embrace.
    Windows of the sick,
        lights on bridges, eyes of gendarmes,
and minarets blink now.
    In the market place walls of darkness
are piled up at the doors
    and the dark walls, stacked together,
collapse like tombstones from a fallen mountain.

The night ends with a delicate cloud
    tinged pink, like a petal
lost in the darkness as day rushes forth.
    (O twilight red, color of
my life, that was a real goodbye we said.
    Night has lost you. Day has lost you.
    Memory alone brings you back.)

In this way night dies
with the sun springing to mount the sky
and the streets inhaling
      the sounds of din,
         braziers of light spilling
         illumination to make shadows
         piercing the stones.
      O noon, you fill my heart
      with fear and grief, showing
      me more than I want to see.
      Blessings on you, noontime blaze,
      your light stings the eyes and
      dims sight, changes houses
      and people into solid cubes
      of pastel stone.

And this is how the delicate color gray is born:
      Weariness creeps into the veins
      of the sun at day's end,
      street noises dissipate
      and are absorbed into the
      soft contours of gray,
      (the color of my days
      not days lived in life,
      but in contemplation).

Now dusk. Now a parting glance
from the sun leaning fatigued
      against the hills.
Now, blackness.

And my life passes while I
      live in expectation,
      waiting for one
      radiant moment in
      the darkness of night
or one quiet moment in
the clamor of day.

Translated by Diana Der Hovanessian
and by Lena Jayyusi (first translator)

THE GIST OF THE STORY

She called me the man of sands
I called her the lady of green
We met in my twilight days
Called to each other like happy children
Shyly we got acquainted
Each of us feeling, with wonder,
The color of the other
And exchanged our names.

Then we parted
Don't ask me what happens to things when they break
Or to echoes when they fall
in a silent vacuum!

But I recall that once upon an evening
We dodged the scythe of Death's reaper
Cheated Time's cock-crow
And etched on the wall of the night
An image of our two shadows, blended our colors
On the border of a rumpled pillow
Then subsided
Into an armchair.

And here you see me contemplating this image,
drinking to it in my solitude
So pour a glass of wine to this image, please.

This is the gist of the story.

Translated by Lena Jayyusi and John Heath-Stubbs

THE PEOPLE OF MY COUNTRY

The people of my country wound like falcons
Their songs are like the chill of winter in the rain's locks
Their laughter hisses like flame through firewood
Their footsteps dent the firm earth
They kill, steal, drink, belch,
But they have their human worth and are good
When they have a handful of money
They hold fast to their belief in fate.

As one entered my village there sat my Uncle Mustafa
Who loved the Prophet
Who spent the hour
Between dusk and nightfall surrounded
By musing men
To whom he told a tale
Rooted in experience
A tale that stirred
Within their souls
The pain of man's mortality.
And it made them weep and bow their heads
Staring into silence
Into the gulf of deep terror and silence.
"What is the purpose of man's striving, what is the purpose of life?
Oh God!
The Sun declares Thy glory, the crescent moon is Thy brow
And these unshakable mountains are Thy steadfast throne
Thou art He whose will is accomplished, Oh God!
A certain man rose to eminence, erected castles
with forty rooms filled with glittering gold
And on one faint twilight evening
Azrael came to him
his fingers grasping a small book
And Azrael stretched out his staff
with the secret of life and death
and that man's soul was pitched into Hell!
(Oh God! . . .
How cruel and full of menace thou art,
Oh God!)"

Yesterday I visited my village
Uncle Mustafa had died
They laid him to rest in the earth
He built no castles (his hut was of mud)
And behind his ancient coffin
Walked those who, like him, owned only an old cotton gown
They said no word of God or Azrael
For it was a year of famine
And at the door of the tomb stood my friend Khaleel

Uncle Mustafa's grandson
And when he stretched up his brawny arms toward the sky
A look of contempt flickered across his eyes
For it was a year of famine.

Translated by Lena Jayyusi and John Heath-Stubbs

WINTER SONG

The winter tells me I shall die alone
One winter just like this, one winter
The evening tells me I shall die alone
One evening just like this, one evening
That my past years were all in vain
That I live in a naked world.
The winter tells me that my soul
Shivers with the cold
That my heart died last autumn
Faded with the first fading leaves
And dropped with the first drops of rain
That each chilly night
Thrusts it deeper
Into the stone's core
That if summer's warmth comes
To wake it, it will not
Stretch with the roses
Its arms up through the snow.

The winter tells me that my body is sick
And my breathing is briar
Each step a hazard
That I may die between one footfall and the next
In the torrential rush of the city
Die, none knowing me
Die, none weeping for me
Perhaps it will be said among my friends
When they gather:
Here he used to sit but he is gone

As others have gone
God rest his soul!

The winter tells me that what I thought
Was my cure, was really my bane
That this art when it set me trembling
Brought about my downfall
How many years since I got this wound?
But still my head is bloody!
Poetry my ruin, for this
Everything's run to waste
For this, I became a drop-out
For this, I'm crucified
I hung there, cold, darkness, thunder
Shook me with terror
When I called, there was no answer,
I knew that all was lost!

The winter tells me that
To live in winter
We must hoard warmth and memories from summer's heat
But like a wastrel I scattered
At autumn's onset
My harvest, my wheat, all my grain,
This, then is my punishment:
The winter tells me
That one winter just like this
I will die alone
Die alone
One winter.

Translated by Lena Jayyusi and John Heath-Stubbs

THE SUN AND THE WOMAN

Restless she stirs as she reclines,
A setting sun,
Bleeding with a hidden light
Torn in fragments in the crook of the shadow.

Restless she stirs as she reclines,
Covers up her wrinkled legs
        stretches out all blue
Her eyes now kindle, now go out,
Her lashes droop and tremble
As she recollects a golden age
In company with a man so crazy
He could not keep from laying her down on the grass
And devouring her breasts
        till she wept with exhaustion.

She arises from her bed when night falls
Laves her old age in water of the sea
        and sleeps, to be born a virgin in the approaching morning.

She shakes her pendulous breasts
Searches between them for the key to the room
Looks about her feeling her way through the sands,
And gets up, worn and gray.

From the nearest shop she buys
Bread for her needs, and cigarettes and wine,
Goes back again and drowses in her past
Making it anew.

The morning pulls the tresses of the virgin sun
And spreads them upon the earth.

She smiles in death
Her hands upon her breasts
Water dribbles at her mouth.

Translated by Lena Jayyusi and John Heath-Stubbs

——Azrael: English word for the Arabic ʿUzraʾil, the angel of death.

'Abd al-Razzaq 'Abd al-Wahid (b. 1932)

Iraqi poet. Born in Baghdad, he studied Arabic literature at the University of Baghdad and worked as a teacher for some time before taking up a position as Assistant to the Dean of the Academy of Arts in the capital. In 1970, he was transferred to the Ministry of Information and Culture, holding several responsible positions before becoming a Counsellor at the Ministry of Information and Director of the National Library in Baghdad. His first collection of poetry appeared in 1956, and he has published several more collections, including *Leaves on the Sidewalk of Memory* (1969), *A Tent at the Threshold of Forty* (1970), and *Where Is Your Calmness Now?* (1983). He has also written several verse plays. An exceptional power to use words aptly, and a deep insight into the human condition, its courage, fears, and existential anxiety have given his poetry universal dimensions.

DREADED ROAD

So this is the way it happens
       like a stalk of wheat being snapped off
       like a straw nest abandoned by birds
       you are stripped bare?

So this is how poverty comes
       suddenly you crouch alone
       in utter silence
       not a laugh sounds
       not a quarrel
    between one cigarette and the next
    you are folded down like the match stick,
    bent and old

And this is how all roads fall to ruin
       on the way between you and love
       between you and fear
       on the road. . .
                 that you had dreaded all along

Translated by Diana Der Hovanessian
and by Lena Jayyusi (first translator)

REACHING FORTY

All is passed—all that loomed ahead as evil,
all that loomed ahead as good.
what remains is hidden in time's fold.
Now you pull up the pegs of the tent
of forty years and gather fewer provisions
for the road, fewer hopes, less need
for sleep. But in your wakened heart
one fluttering wing resists chains while
you stifle a long protracted scream.
Whatever is done is over; whatever comes
now will light the lamp of old age.
Whatever is coming blunts the sharpness
of sight, slows the fall of the step,
clouds the eye, but all the while
you resist its arrival.
After this forty year peak, the road slopes
downward steeply. Toward more pain?
The pain to feel nostalgia
even for past misery? And you, the most
anxious of tired men, who seem so
debonair, even haughty, are you laughing
now at things that should bring tears?
Or seem untroubled, in spite of annoyances?
What do we see, meeting you, except the cheerful countenance?
But the greatest tragedy is having to please
when no one pleases you,
when no one praises your virtues or
forgives your faults.

What is past is past. You grappled
life's challenges avoiding caution.
In spite of that war which life wages
against you, it was you who always
welcomed the uninvited.
Did you ever want anything except
the unacceptable? Now you stand perplexed
in the wake of events wondering
what to take, what to leave.
But even if you shielded yourself

from all arrows how could you
have escaped your own? O anguish,
that has no end, O anxiety that cannot
be calmed, the seeds are planted
and it is time to reap.

Translated by Diana Der Hovanessian
and by Lena Jayyusi (first translator)

YOU RISE AMONG TRUTHS

So tired, your footsteps drag
toward death,
so anxious, but you pretend calm,
you feign strength, Husain Ben Mardan.

But the refuge you sought,
the shelters are closed. All help fled.
Who would share death with the dying,
Ben Mardan?

Stripped and alone,
your huge frame, that bulk, squeezed
through death's door, you feign strength.

But every pool of water where you bend
to quench your fear
sprouts a skin of leaping flames.

And you surrender, foresaking
the numbers, the conquered sums,
to drop them one by one.

The road to zero is a miracle,
Ben Mardan, and you own the road.
You alone own regret.
You can meet, head-on,
that dread you have always feared.

The moment of revelation has arrived
and only you have the power
to hear, touch, feel it.
Only you can see it.

Now only you know if footsteps are possible
without feet
and without ground.

The secret of death is yours alone
to possess.

And as the unknown creeps toward you
you rise among truths
stripped of pretense.

The road to zero is a miracle.
And what of fear now?

You who never acknowledged fear,
now you are surrounded by something
beyond measure which
erases all paths where you moved
except the road back to your youth.
And there you are on it, barefoot,
the collar of your shirt gaping.

Walking past
the faces,
the years,
the women,
until you arrive, Husain Mardan
with hair grown to your shoulders,
beating the road with a stout cane,
the road between Dayala and Baghdad,
to climb a ladder
which like all our ladders,
is placed vertically.
(And was this how we planned to welcome death?)

One day we tied the bells of our names
on the tree of death and waited for the wind.
And the wind came.

Do we exaggerate our vigor in those times?
Or were they truly the years of heroes?
When did the ladders fall,
break, while we crawled toward fear?

Remember the welcome we planned for death?
Every time the wind whistled
    whoever heard his name ringing would go.

Those were years of happiness, Ben Mardan.
Man and tide fastened those bells for the winds.
We hid the smallest bell, the death bell
in thick branches.

You spent your life perfecting that bell
and its hanging, its size, its sway.
Then widening your eyes, you waited
in alarm for its ring.

Meanwhile what did you reap, Ben Mardan?

You played with the toy of your life like a child;
like a child you were bored and broke the toy
dreaming of the time
you would be the working
government official
buying the new suit,
finally, not owing,
but being owed!

But before the sleeves of that dream suit
could be soiled, Ben Mardan, the knock came.

Before it was time to be paid what was owed you,
the knock.

The gong of your death was rung,
O Emperor,
O two-month employee.

Translated by Diana Der Hovanessian
and by Lena Jayyusi (first translator)

Shauqi Abi Shaqra (b. 1935)

Lebanese poet. After working as a teacher for three years, he chose a jour-
nalistic career and is now the cultural editor of *Al-Nahār*, a prestigious Leb-
anese daily. In the fifties and sixties he was actively involved with *Shiʿr*
magazine, a quarterly devoted to poetry. As a member of its editorial board,
he devoted much energy to the promotion of the modern poetry movement.
He writes an experimental poetry which reflects a modern vision without
losing touch with his country background, whose attributes of warmth and
simplicity are still alive in Lebanese consciousness. Six *diwans* to date have
been published, including *The King's Footsteps* (1960); *Water to the Family
Horse* (1962); and *Running, He Follows the Magician and Breaks the Wheatstalks*
(1979).

WATER FOR THE FAMILY HORSE

My grandmother kneels to thresh the grain. The grain remains while
chaff flies away like children running to another house. She chases it with
her broom like a witch, and makes it a pillow for my father. He will catch
cold without this pillow to lay his cheek on.

My father was a policeman who neglected his precinct. He wore an over-
coat whose buttons shone like stray coins at the beach, where he used to
fire at submarines. Our generals and the allies were delighted. They invited
him to tea and promoted him to sergeant.

He was blond as baked figs, so women, both white and black, committed
suicide for so much beauty. He got married and wrapped my mother under
his warm overcoat so he could create me and beat me when I broke the
mirror. The mirror is a white street where we twirl our moustaches.

He was the horse of the family and during the war he didn't run away
to the hills of Houran. He remained brave as an oak tree; his blood was hot
and he drank no water.

. . . .

The fox ate our red cockerel and immediately worry ran all over my
grandmother's dress. She uttered a great gasp which hung upon her breast
like an icon to the day she died.

When the pain comes on, she hangs a ring of keys in her braids, pushing the hurt downward till it falls from her, like a cup.

· · · ·

She loved me, and I kissed her hands. When she had her pains I massaged her back by walking barefoot on her. She always brought me to the place when it was time for the eggs to hatch. She passed the mother hen under my knee because I am the firstborn male of our house.

The weather in our village changes with the song of the foxes. We keep watch on the roof by the light of our lantern, and the moon does her best to help it. The cost of our lantern? Five liras—and its number is 3. Bought by my grandfather from a pedlar who rolled from village to village like a wheel.

There is a cloud of water and bananas glittering inside my grandmother. Her chest is a shop where she has hidden the Ottoman golden coins— probably between her breasts which have suckled the mouths of the family. She doesn't brush her teeth and she never goes to the movies. She can spot the eye of a needle inside a tunnel or a ruined palace.

· · · ·

She was always sad and covered with grass. To cure her arthritis, which weighed on her as heavily as a turtle, she oiled her legs with spirit of alcohol. When my father fell in the valley, and scattered among the trees like banknotes, she went on a fast. Then she used the wall as a crutch and supported her stumbling by leaning on a breeze.

· · · ·

My grandfather Mikhail up and left us for America. His ship tracked the waves like a nightingale. He became sick on the voyage, so he lifted his moustache and spat in the sea when the captain wasn't looking. He thought of his wife in the attic and wrote her a letter which would make you weep.

· · · ·

Her skirt was as famous as the hero Abu Zayd al-Hilali. It made the rounds of the province. When the sun was wilting behind the hills, the peasants paid homage to the skirt and rang the village bells.

· · · ·

She died at four o'clock. Her children left their money on the table and got into cars to carry her corpse to the village graveyard. The students and the local poets recited their elegies, and the priest sprinkled her with incense.

Death followed after her with the rapidity of water. It began to chop off

all the old women and dragged them off to its den. As for us—we kept
eating bread brought in from the capital, stained with dyes and asphalt,
and we longed for logs of wood and thoughts of birds and rain. We kissed
the unpaved roads like men returned from exile.

Translated by Sargon Boulus and Peter Porter

THE STUDENT

My sister comes from
the mountain of dwarfs.
A tired shepherdess
leaning on her staff,
she has walked on foot
to expel the devil
from the kingdom of her breast,
and to learn geography.
So she entered the capital of candles,
the capital of mirrors
like a bee—
she got lost on her way home
like a drop of oil
spilled on the sea.

Translated by Sargon Boulus and Peter Porter

FUGUE

October in my country
at the café of bitter drinks and jazz—
I lost consciousness
and slept right across the month
as my center-of-gravity desired.

I dreamt my language was
a sheep
a sparrow
or a man kneeling

by the foot of the Caucasus
plucking berries for the guests
from the mythic tree.

Translated by Sargon Boulus and Peter Porter

——*Houran:* the mountainous area in Western Syria where there is a large Druz community, along with people from other denominations.

——*Abu Zayd al-Hilali:* legendary hero of the famous Banu Hilal folktale, in which he is represented as black-skinned. The folktale revolves around his great feats of courage and horsemanship as the leader of the Banu Hilal tribe, which emigrated from Arabia to North Africa. His tale, which acquired many versions over the centuries, was fascinating to the many Arab nations under imperialist regimes, who found in Abu Zayd's heroism a great consolation and hope.

Adunis (ʿAli Ahmad Saʿid) (b. 1929)

Syrian poet. Born in the Alawite mountains of Northern Syria, he studied first at Tartus, then at the Syrian University, and later earned a doctorate for *The Static and Dynamic in Arabic Culture* from St. Joseph's University in Beirut. From 1956 to 1986 he lived in Beirut, and then moved to Paris. In 1968 he founded the avant-garde magazine, *Mawaqif* (Situations), dedicated to culture and literature. One of the greatest poets in Arabic literature, he is also something of an iconoclast. His prose writings have aroused much controversy in the Arab world, particularly his views on the Arab heritage and other subjects treated in the above-mentioned work (published in 1974) and other writings. There can be no doubt as to the influence of his ideas about innovation and modernity on a whole generation of poets. Equally important is the leading role he played in revolutionizing poetic language, imagery, and approach. Seven collections of his poetry have appeared, of which *Songs of Mihyar the Damascene* (1960) may be regarded as a turning point in his work. It has been translated into French, and there have been several English translations of selections of his poetry, including *The Blood of Adonis* and *Transformation of the Lover*, both translated by Samuel Hazo.

A MIRROR TO KHALIDA

I. The Wave

Khalida
Sadness around which
the branches burgeon
Khalida
Voyage that drowns the day
in the water of the eyes
Wave that taught me that the light
of the stars,
the face of the clouds,
the moaning of dust
are but one blossom.

II. Under the Water

We slept in a garment woven
from the red berries of night—
the night dissolved, the blood
of our innermost being was singing
with the rhythm of cymbals,
the glitter of suns under water . . .
The night was pregnant.

III. Lost

. . . Once
I was lost in your hands, my lips
were a fortress yearning
                for a strange conquest
                and enamored of embraces.
You advanced
Your waist was a king,
your hands the herald of the army,
your eyes a friend and a hiding place.
We fused, were lost in each other and entered
the forest of fire—I taking the first step
                you paving the way.

IV. Weariness

The old weariness, my love,
is blooming around the house.
It has now pitchers of water
and a balcony
in whose nooks it sleeps and disappears
And how we worried
about it in its journeys! We ran
circling around the house
asked every grass stalk about it, prayed,
we glimpsed it and shouted:
                "How, what and where?
Every wind has come
and every branch
                has come
but you did not . . ."

V. Death

After those moments the same time comes
and the repeated footsteps, the repeated roads,
after them the houses grow old,
after them the bed
puts out the fire of its days and dies
and the pillows die too.

Translated by Lena Jayyusi and John Heath-Stubbs

BEGINNING SPEECH

That child I was
came to me once
an unfamiliar face

He said nothing—we walked
each glancing in silence at the other
One step
an alien river
                    flowing.

Our common origins
                    brought us together
and we separated
a forest written by the earth
and told by the seasons

Child that I once was, advance,
What now brings us together?
And what have we to say to each other?

Translated by Lena Jayyusi and John Heath-Stubbs

A SONG

O close of night, I would have you linger
                    Fall into ecstasy
                    Turn into a magician on my bed

I ask you to tell me:
>   What does love say to the lover
>   at the end of the seasons?

Translated by Lena Jayyusi and John Heath-Stubbs

WHO ARE YOU?

My eyes are on a butterfly
terror lashes my songs

—Who are you?
—A spear at a venture
>   a god that lives without prayer.

MIHYAR, A KING!

A king, this is Mihyar,
A king, his dream is a palace
>   and gardens of fire.

Today a voice that has died
Told of him to the words.

A king, this is Mihyar,
He dwells in the kingdom of the winds
and reigns in the land of secrets.

Translated by Lena Jayyusi and John Heath-Stubbs

A GRAVE FOR NEW YORK

I.

Until now the earth has been drawn in the shape of a pear
>   or rather a breast
But between a breast and a tombstone there is only a difference
>   of geometry:
>   *New York,*

A civilization with four legs; in each direction murder and
                    a road leading to murder
        and in each distance the moaning of the drowned.
NEW YORK,

A woman—the statue of a woman
    lifting in one hand a rag called liberty by
    a document called history, and with the other
    hand suffocating a child called Earth
NEW YORK,

A body the color of asphalt. Round her waist a damp belt, her face a locked
window . . . I said: Walt Whitman will open it—"I speak the first pass-
word"—but no one heard it except an overthrown god. Prisoners, slaves,
thieves, the desperate and the sick pour out of his throat and there is no
way out for them, no path. And I said *Brooklyn Bridge!* But that is the
bridge which connects *Whitman* with *Wall Street*, which connects the green
leaves with the greenbacks . . .

NEW YORK—HARLEM,
Who is it who comes on a silk guillotine, who is it departing in a grave as
long as the *Hudson?* Explode, O climate of tears, and all you exhausted
things forge together into one. A blue, a yellow, roses, jasmines, the light
sharpens its needles, and in their pricking the sun is born. Have you ig-
nited, O wound concealed between the thighs? Has the bird of death vis-
ited you and have you heard the final death rattle? A rope, and the neck is
weaving the gloom, and in the blood runs the bleakness of the Hour . . .

NEW YORK—MADISON—PARK AVENUE—HARLEM
An idleness which resembles work, work with a resemblance to idleness.
Hearts stuffed with sponge and hands puffed like reeds. And from the piles
of rubbish and the masks of the Empire State history rises up in odors that
hang down in sheet after sheet:
    It is not eyesight that is blind but the brain,
    It is not speech that is barren but the tongue.

NEW YORK—WALL STREET—125TH STREET—FIFTH
    AVENUE
A Medusa phantom climbs up between one shoulder and another. A market
for all kinds of slaves. Human beings who live like plants in glass houses.

The wretched, the ones nobody ever sees, filter like particles of dust into the network of space—victims spinning in endless circles,

    The sun is a funeral   ;

    Day is a black drum

II.

Here

On the mossy underside of the rock that is the world, no one sees me except a "negro" about to be killed or a bird about to die, I thought:

A plant growing in a red clay pot was metamorphosing as I drew back from the threshold, and I read:

About rats in Beirut and elsewhere that parade themselves lavishly in *White House* silk, that arm themselves with paper and gnaw at human beings, About the remnants of pigs that trample on poetry in the kindergarten of the alphabet,

    • • • •

I saw

the Arab map a stallion dragging its steps while time droops like a saddle toward the grave or toward the darker shadow, toward a fire dying or already dead; discovering the chemistry of the other dimension in Karkuk al-Dhahran and what has remained of such citadels in Arab *Afro-Asia*. And here is the world ripening in our hands. Hah! We prepare for the Third World War, and set up secret bureaux, a first and a second and a third, to establish·

    2—In this house someone who owns nothing but ink,

    3—In this tree a bird singing,

Let us proclaim

    1—That space is measured with a cage or with a wall,

    2—That time is measured with a rope or a whip,

    3—That the system by which the world is built begins with one
        brother murdering another,

    4—That the moon and the sun are two coins gleaming under the sul-
        tan's throne,

And I saw

Arab names as vast as the earth, tender with affection, shining only as an uprooted star shines "with no ancestors, and its roots are only in its steps . . ."

Here,

On the mossy underside of the rock of the world, I know, I confess: that I
remember a green shoot which I call life, or my country; death, or my
country—a wind that freezes like an icy mantle, a face that destroys
joy, an eye that expels the light; and I create in the teeth of you, my
country,

> I go down into your hell and I scream:
> *I am distilling a poisonous elixir for*
> *you—and I greet you!*

And I confess: *New York*, in my country you own the corridor and the
bed, the chair and the head. And everything is for sale: night and day,
the stone of Mecca and the waters of the Tigris. And I proclaim: and
yet you strive and you compete in *Palestine*, in *Hanoi*, in the North and
in the South, in the East and in the West, against those who have no
history except fire,

And I say: Since John the Baptist each one of us carries his severed head
on a plate and waits for the second coming.

III.

Disintegrate, you statues of liberty, you nails driven deep into the breast
with a wisdom which imitates the wisdom of the rose. The wind sud-
denly blows again from the East, uprooting the tents and skyscrapers.
Two wings write:

> A second alphabet rises among the contours of the West,
> The sun is the child of a tree in the gardens of Jerusalem.

This is how I kindle my flames. I start all over again, I shape,
>   and specify:

NEW YORK

A woman of straw and the bed sways between one empty space and an-
other, and lo! the ceiling rots away: Every word is a sign of a fall,
every movement is a spade or an axe. And on the left and the right
there are bodies that like to change love, eyesight, hearing, smell, touch,
and change change itself—they open time like a gate, break it, and
invent the remaining hours

Sex, poetry, morals, thirst, speech, silence, bodies that want to banish locks.

And I tempt Beirut and its sister capitals,

> She jumps from her bed and closes the gates of memory behind her.
> She comes close, clings on to my poems, and hangs down. The axe

for the door and the flowers for the window; and burn, O you history of locks!

I said, I tempt Beirut,

"Search for action. Words are dead," others say. The word is dead because your tongues have given up the habit of speech in favor of the habit of blather. The word? You want to discover the fire of the word? Write then, I say write and I do not say blather; I do not say copy, I say write.

From the ocean to the gulf I hear no speech, I read no words. I hear squeeking, and therefore I see no one lighting any fire.

The word is the lightest of things and it carries everything.

The act is one direction, a moment of time, the word is all directions for all time. The word—the hand. The hand—the dream;

I discover you O fire, my capital,

I discover you, poetry

And I tempt Beirut. I wear her and she wears me. We wander like rays of sunlight and we ask: Who reads? Who sees? *The phantom is for Dayan and the oil* flows to its destination. God is truth and Mao was not wrong: 'Weapons are a very important factor in war, but they are not decisive. Man, and not arms, is the decisive factor.' There is no final victory, and no final defeat.

I repeated these proverbs and aphorisms, as Arabs do, in Wall Street, where rivers of gold of all colors pour in, flowing from their sources. And among them I saw the Arab rivers carrying millions of torn limbs of victims, and offerings to the *master idol*. And between one victim and another the boatmen laugh out loud, as they tumble down from the *Chrysler Building* and return to the source.

. . . .

IV.

NEW YORK, woman sitting in the arc of the wind,

Shape more distant than the atom

A point that scurries in the

wilderness of numbers

One thigh in the heavens and one

in the water,

Say, where is your star? The battle between the grass and the electronic brain is about to begin. The whole epoch is hanging on a wall, and here is the hemorrhage. At the top, a point that unites North Pole and

South Pole, in the center *Asia*, and at the bottom two feet for an invisible body. I know you, corpse floating on the musk of poppies; I know you, game of breast with breast. I look at you and I dream of ice, I look at you and I wait for autumn.

Your snow carries the night, your night carries people like dead bats.

Every wall in you is a cemetery. Each day is a black gravedigger carrying
a black loaf and a black plate and planning with them the history of the
White House.

A (Alef)—

There are dogs that link together like a chain. There are cats that give birth to helmets and chains. And in alleys that creep along on the backs of rats, white guards are breeding like fungus.

B (Ba)—

A woman comes towards us led by her dog which is saddled like a horse. The dog's footsteps are the footsteps of a king, and around him crawls the city like an army of tears. And where children and old men with black skins have accumulated, there the innocence of bullets grows as plants grow, and terror strikes the heart of the city.

C (Geem)—

Harlem—Bedford Stuyvesant: People like sandgrains, thickening into tower after tower. Faces that weave the ages. Trash makes a feast of the children, the children make a feast for the rats . . . In the long banquet of another trinity—the tax-collector, the policeman and the judge—stands the authority of slaughter, the sword of extermination.

D (Dal)—

Harlem (the black hates the Jew)
Harlem (the black does not like the Arab when he remembers the slave trade)

Harlem-Broadway (human beings permeate like laxatives into flasks of drugs and liquor)
Broadway-Harlem, a festival of chains and batons, the police are the bacteria of the age. One shot, and ten doves fall to the ground. The eyes are caskets bulging with red ice, and time is a walking stick with a limp. Old black man, young black child. Go on until you are infinitely weary. Go on, infinitely weary, forever and forever.

V.

HARLEM

I do not come from the outside. I know your rancor, I know it's good bread. There is no cure for famines except sudden thunder, and there is no end for prisons except the thunderbolt of violence. I see your fire advancing under the asphalt in hoses and masks, in piles of garbage carried on the throne of the freezing air, in outcast footsteps wearing the history of the wind like a shoe.

HARLEM,

Time is dying and you are the Hour:

    I hear tears roaring like volcanoes

    I see jaws munching human beings like bread

    You are the eraser that will wipe out the face

                 of New York,

    You are the storm that will seize it like a leaf and

New York = *Subway* + *IBM* coming from mud and crime

                          going back to mud and crime

New York = a hole in the earth's crust out of which madness

                       gushes in torrent upon torrent

Harlem, New York is in its death throes and you are the Hour.

VI.

Between *Harlem and Lincoln Center,*

    I, a vagrant number, advance in a desert covered by the teeth of a black dawn. No snow, no wind. I was like someone following a phantom (the face is not a face but a wound, or tears, the body merely a pressed rose), a phantom (would you say a woman? Or a man? Or a woman-man?) carrying bows and arrows in its breast and ready to pounce on an empty space.

    A gazelle passed by and he called it earth, a bird appeared and he called it the moon. And I knew that he was hurrying to see the rebirth of the *Red Indian* . . . in Palestine and her sisters,

             Space is a ribbon of bullets,

             The earth is a screen of corpses

I felt that I was an atom undulating in a mass, undulating toward the horizon the horizon the horizon. I came down into parallel valleys that stretch away into infinite distance, and I even began to doubt that the earth was round.

. . . .

I put New York in brackets and walked in a parallel city. My feet had their fill of streets and the sky was a lake in which swam fishes of the eye and the mind, and animals of the clouds. The *Hudson* was fluttering like a crow dressed in the body of a nightingale. The dawn came toward me like a child sighing and pointing to its wounds. I called the night but it gave no answer. It carried its bed and surrendered to the sidewalk. Then I saw it covering itself with the most tender wind—a wind so tender, nothing surpassed its tenderness except the walls and columns . . . A cry, two, three . . . and *New York* flinched like a half-frozen frog jumping into a waterless pond.

LINCOLN,

This is *New York:* leaning on the cane of old age and strolling in the gardens of memory, preferring artificial flowers. And while I look at you among the marble stones of Washington, and discover your likeness in Harlem, I think: When will your next revolution come? And my voice rises: Set *Lincoln* free from the whiteness of marble, from *Nixon,* from the guard dogs and the hunting dogs. Let him read with new eyes what Ali ibn Muhammad, the Black leader, read, what Marx and Lenin and Mao Tse Tung read, and what al-Niffari read, that heavenly madman, who reinvented the earth, allowed it to live between the word and the sign. Let him read what Ho Chi Minh would have liked to read: the poetry of Urwa ibn al-Ward: "I distribute my body among many bodies . . ." Urwa never knew Baghdad, and he probably refused to visit Damascus. He remained where the desert was another shoulder that shared with him the burden of death. He left to those who love the future a portion of the sun soaked in the blood of a gazelle he called 'my beloved!' And agreed with the horizon that it should be his last home.

LINCOLN,

That is *New York:* a mirror in which Washington is the only reflection. And this is Washington: a mirror that reflects two faces, Nixon and the tears of the world. I join in the dance of tears, I rise up. There is still a place to go, there is still a part to play. And I love this dance of tears, which changes into a dove, which changes into a flood. 'How the earth needs a flood!'

VIII.

. . . .

I woke up in the morning screaming
before the hour of departure: *New York!*

> You mix children with snow and produce the cake of the age.
> Your voice is an oxide, a poison beyond the grasp of chemistry, your
> name is insomnia and suffocation. *Central Park* flings a banquet for its
> victims, and under its trees you see ghosts of the dead, and bloody
> daggers. There is nothing for the wind except naked branches, nothing
> for the traveler except a blocked road.

I rose in the morning crying: *Nixon*, how many children did you kill
today?

> —"This matter has no importance!" (Calley)
> —"True that this is a problem. But is it not true that this decreases
> the enemy's numbers?" (An American General)

How can I give the heart of *New York* a different size?

> Does the heart also widen its boundaries?

New York—where *General Motors* and death are one and the same "We will
replace men with fire!" *(Macnamara)*—they dry up the sea in which the
revolutionaries swim. "They make a desert of the land and they call it
peace!" *(Tacitus)*

I got up before dawn and woke Whitman up.

IX.

WALT WHITMAN,

I see letters to you flying in the air above the streets of *Manhattan*. Each
letter is a carriage full of cats and dogs. The age of cats and dogs is the
twenty-first century, and human beings will suffer extermination: This
is the American Age!

WHITMAN

I did not see you in *Manhattan*, and I saw everything. The moon is a husk
thrown out of windows and the sun is an electric orange. When a black
road, round as a moon leaning on its eyelashes, leapt out of Harlem,
there was a light behind it that scattered along the length of the asphalt
highway, then wilted away like a plant when it reached *Greenwich Vil-
lage*, that other Latin Quarter. ∴ .

. . . .

WHITMAN,

'The clock announces the time.' (*New York*—*Woman* is refuse, and refuse is
time moving toward ashes.)

'The clock announces the time.' (*New York*—the system—*Pavlov*, and peo-
ple are dogs used in experiments . . . where war is war is war!)

'The clock announces the time.' (A letter has come from the East. A child
has written it in his own blood. I read it: the doll is no longer a dove.
The doll is a cannon, a machine gun, a rifle . . . Corpses in streets of
sunlight link *Hanoi* with *Jerusalem*, *Jerusalem* with the *Nile*.)

WHITMAN,

'The clock announces the time' and I

'See what you have not seen and know what you have not known.' I
move over a vast area of boxes set down side by side like yellow
crabs in an ocean of millions of persons, lonely as islands; each
one is a column with two hands, two feet and a shattered head.
And you

'O you emigrant, exile, criminal'

You are no more than a hat worn by birds unknown in the skies of
America!

WHITMAN, Let it be our turn now. I make a ladder our of my glances. I
weave my footsteps into a pillow, and we shall wait. Man dies, and
yet he outlasts the grave. Let it be our turn, *now*. I wait for the *Volga*
to flow between *Manhattan* and *Queens*. I wait for the *Hwang-Ho* to pour
down where the *Hudson flows*. Are you surprised? Did not Al-ʿAasi flow
into the Tiber once? Let it be our turn now. I hear the tremor, the shells
falling. *Wall Street* and *Harlem* meet—paper and thunder meet, dust
and storm meet. Let it be our turn now. Oysters make their nests in
the waves of history. The tree knows its own name. There are holes
in the skin of the world, a sun that changes the mask and the ending,
and weeps in a dark eye. Let it be our turn, *now*. We can revolve faster
than the wheel, we can smash the atom and float in an electronic brain
whether faded or bright, empty or full, and we can make the bird our
homeland. Let it be our turn, now. A little red book is rising. Not the
wooden plank that once rotted under the weight of words, but this
plank that expands and grows, the plank of wisdom in madness, and
rain which wakes up to inherit the sun. Let it be our turn, now. *New
York* is a rock rolling across the forehead of the world. Its voice is in
your clothes and in mine, its coals color your limbs and mine . . . I
can foretell the end, but how can I persuade time to keep me alive so
that I can see it with my own eyes! Let it be our turn, let us lift the
axe, *now*. And let time swim in the waters of this equation:

New York + New York = The Grave and anything that comes from the Grave
New York − New York = The Sun.

X.

. . . .

And so,

 I carry Cuba on my shoulders and ask in New York: When will Cas-
  tro arrive?
Between Cairo and Damascus I wait on the road leading . . . . . .
 Guevara met Freedom, entered into the bed of Time with her, and
 they slept. When he woke up, he did not find her. He left sleep and
 entered the dream
In Berkeley, in Beirut and the rest of the cells, where everything prepares
 to become everything.

. . . .

But,
Peace be to the rose of darkness and sands,
Peace be to Beirut.

Translated by Lena Jayyusi and Alan Brownjohn

——Mihyar: the name was adopted by Adunis in reference to the poet, Mihyar al-Dailami (d. 1037). Al-Dailami was of Persian origin and was born in Dailam, Persia. He probably came to Baghdad as an official translator of Persian and stayed there until his death. He was origi- nally a Magian (i.e., of the ancient Persian religion whose followers worshipped fire) but was converted to Islam and became a fanatical Shi'ite, attacking in his poetry even the followers of the Prophet. This caused some people to regard him as a blasphemer and to reject him. In his poetry, he also boasted of his Persian origin. "Mihyar" was adopted by Adunis perhaps to represent his own situation as a man attacked in some quarters because of his own beliefs and unorthodox ideas. Himself an Alawite, which is an extremist Shi'ite sect, he might have found some affinity with Mihyar's own unorthodox ideas about what he regarded as orthodox rigidity in traditional religious (particularly Sunni) circles.

——Harlem: a section of upper Manhattan, New York City, which was a black ghetto and where one of the largest black communities in the United States still lives.

——Karkuk: an oil town in Iraq

——Al-Dhahran: an oil town in Saudi Arabia

——Alef, Ba, Geem, Dal: the first four letters of the ancient semitic alphabet originally used by the Arabs but changed into the present order of the Arabic alphabet around the middle of the eighth century. It is used sometimes now to number prefaces and introductions just as the roman letters are used in English for the same purpose.

——Ali ibn Muhammad: Al-Zandji (the Black man), known as the leader of the Zandj, or blacks. These were black rebel slaves who for fifteen years terrorized southern Iraq and the adjoining territories (868–883 B.C.). He tried to establish himself first in Bahrain and then in the Basra region in southern Iraq, where he sought support among the black slaves working in gangs on the salt-flats east of the town. He professed the egalitarian creed of the Kharidjites and had a long period of military successes, capturing several towns in the region. However, his army was finally defeated by the Abbasids, and he was killed and his head carried on a pole to Baghdad.

——al-Niffari: Muhammad ibn Abd al-Jabbar (d. 965), a famous mystic who flourished in the fourth century of Islam. His main writings are his two books, *al-Mawaqif* and *al-Mukhatabat*, which constituted brief apothegms on the main aspects of Sufi (mystical) teachings. Influenced perhaps by his great predecessor, al-Hallaj, he was a fearless and original thinker, and had a thorough conviction of his own mission.

——Urwa ibn al-Ward (d. 616): pre-Islamic outlaw poet whose philosophy in life was to take from the rich in order to give to the poor. He distinguished himself as a valiant horseman and was famous for his great generosity and his firm ideas on social justice. He always gave to other outlaws, to the sick and needy, and to any quest.

——Calley: see *My Lai*, in the notes to Samih al-Qasim.

——Macnamara: Robert Macnamara, hawkish secretary of defence during the Vietnam War whose policies led to the escalation of the war.

——Tacitus: Cornelius Tacitus (c. 55–120), Roman historian who lived through the reigns of nine emperors, including Nero and Domitian, whose last three years of rule are known as "the reign of terror." This period had impressed itself on the historian's soul, and when he wrote his *History* he could see little but the darkest side of imperialism.

——Pavlov: Ivan Pavlov (1849–1936), Russian physiologist, 1904 Nobel Prize winner, world famous for his systematic experiments on the conditioning of dogs and other animals, which profoundly influenced the psychology of learning. His discovery of techniques for creating "experimental neuroses" in dogs did much to pioneer the scientific approach to the study of human mental disorders.

——Hwang Ho: a river in mainland China

——Al-ʿAasi: Nahr al-ʿAasi (the Orontes river), an unnavigable river 246 miles long, rising near Baalbek in central Lebanon and flowing north through western Syria. It follows a tortuous course to Homs, north of the Beqaa' valley.

'Ali Ja'far al-'Allaq (b. 1945)

Iraqi poet. Born in a village of Southern Iraq, he was educated in Baghdad
and England, and obtained a Ph.D. in Arabic literature from the University
of Exeter. He is at present editor-in-chief of the prestigious literary maga-
zine, *Al-Aqlam* (Quills). He has published three collections of poetry, *Noth-
ing Happens, Nobody Comes* (1973), *A Homeland for Water Birds* (1975), and
Family Tree (1979); and a book of criticism, *Gypsy Kingdom* (1981).

POET

Who among you has begun his days
seeking out the color of the dew and stones,
searching and searching
for themes that have neither been profaned
nor sung to satiety?

Whenever he felt
that the stallions he pursued were too elusive,
that the songs he tried to work were too abstruse,
he would cast his vexed eyes
over the flock of his days,
as one filed by behind the other,
every one the same.

This is the dusty song of papers.
Can you smell its blossoms
as it draws him to his room,
to the loved ones he has been neglecting,
and lists for him the number
of his dreams, his deserts, and his books?
He surveys his days
and his preoccupations,
gazes on his loved ones,
sincere and cast aside.
He counts his books: one, two, four.

Then he slips away,
restless and morose.
Of him they say he is, as usual, dazed,
as one well might be
who contemplates a stream to touch the taste of dew.
They say he is impervious
to offenses,
they say he is too quick to find offense.
They say he is dismal

                  elated

                          absent-minded

as one well might be
who is given to the contemplation of streams and crows.

He remembers his friends
and forgives them their taunts.
He laughs
and releases all his birds into the fog.

Translated by Sharif Elmusa and Thomas G. Ezzy

LADY OF CHAOS

Where has she come from, this lady
who churns up our calm fountains?
Has no one warned her to be wary
of our own cold winds?

Never have we seen a passion
such as hers. It is said
that she was abandoned by some tribe,
marooned by some fugitive ship,
and dropped here by a light, rising cloud.

It is said,
it has been said . . .
but still she spreads confusion as she likes,
bends the winds to blow the way she likes.
She has aroused all our instincts
and holds us all enthralled.

Translated by Sharif Elmusa and Thomas G. Ezzy

Muhammad al-As'ad (b. 1944)

Palestinian poet. Born in the village of Um al-Zeinat near Haifa, Palestine, his family became refugees in 1948 and eventually settled in Basra, Iraq, where the poet received his early education. Despite great financial difficulties, al-As'ad was able to complete his studies and move in 1968 to Kuwait, where he still lives and works as a journalist. Al-As'ad's poetry is rich in sensuous imagery and emotion and reflects the poet's involvement in the themes of personal love and the collective suffering of Palestinians living in the diaspora. He has published three collections of poetry, the last of which is *To Your Shores Come the Birds Today* (1980). He has also published a book of criticism titled *Poetic Diction*.

GARDENS FOR THE FIRE AND THE RAIN

Blue, dew-drenched
these birds come
carried to you from my body by the wind
they come   disappear   dwell
Open up sister, the dew has soaked me
in its age-long night
the ringing sound of water
      the silence of the sea
            warmth of blue coastlines
and the rustle of birds
      stealing across my body
have all left me
Will you live in my life like a red lily
      that recites one page for the sea
      and another for the fire?
You burn

      Here is my body
It groans   it comes   it begins
possessing gardens for the fire and the rain

a sorrow of leaves around you
a blue color of water
for the beautiful night sojourn
a ringing of bells
for the taste of wild mint
the long night's sojourn.

      Open up
child of pleasure and dew
night has encircled me
and fed me to distant voices
myrtle around your face has given leaf to desire
sadness that gives us tears to drink
a distance to the sea
closed gardens dwell in us
where birds return
        and dream
where fountains meet within your eyes.

Are you absent?
Around you the echo overwhelms me
Or are you present
and around you a lover unraveling in the eternity of absence
these birds disappear
      departing from my body
disappear
      disappear
        fires engulf them
Open up sister,
      the dew has awakened me
    night has besieged me
      and left me to the distant voices.

Translated by Lena Jayyusi and Charles Doria

THE PRINCESS

We stood at the edge of the crowded bar drinking
amidst the noise of all the trains, all those
who come and go nowhere

She cast shadows within me like coastal trees
illuminated like the transcendental
while present in time.

She asked me who I was
    one day she found me a child
    and the next a wise man
                Who might I be?
At the edge of the bar I was performing an ancient rite
creating two people who depart
                      while we stayed
two who burn
                      while we stayed
two that smile
                      while we wept
She embraced me like tears
she knew that my explosion was near
that the limits of myth were smaller than the bar
that the trains were here
that we were destined to absence
and I knew
that the princess happened only once in life.

Translated by Lena Jayyusi and Charles Doria

ʿAbd-Allah al-Baraduni (b. 1929)

Yemeni poet and literary historian from Baradun in North Yemen. At the age of six he contracted smallpox and subsequently became blind. He studied language and religion in the town of Dhamar at the Shamsia Mosque school. After that he moved to Sanʿaa, where in 1952 he obtained a degree in Arabic language and Shariʿa and taught for a while. He currently works in the cultural section of the Broadcasting Service in Sanʿaa. He has published eight collections of poetry and several books of criticism. Much of his poetry involves Yemeni (and Arab) social and political situations. He is one of the best explorers of the ironic mode in modern Arabic poetry. His verse exhibits a vigor, originality, and potent spirit that have won him pan-Arab recognition. His *diwans* include *City of Tomorrow* (1968); *From the Land of Belkis, Journey to the Green Days*, and *A Time Without Quality* (all 1979).

FROM EXILE TO EXILE

My country is handed over from one tyrant
to the next, a worse tyrant;
from one prison to another,
from one exile to another.
It is colonized by the observed
invader and the hidden one;
handed over by one beast to two
like an emaciated camel.

In the caverns of its death
my country neither dies
nor recovers. It digs
in the muted graves looking
for its pure origins
for its springtime promise
that slept behind its eyes
for the dream that will come

for the phantom that hid.
It moves from one overwhelming
night to a darker night.

My country grieves
in its own boundaries
and in other people's land
and even on its own soil
suffers the alienation
of exile.

Translated by Diana Der Hovanessian with Sharif Elmusa

FROM "A ROSE FROM AL-MUTANABBI'S BLOOD"

His fame stole his real name.
Alone, he rose from himself to himself
creating his own roots. The past is dust.
He carried his life in his hands like a spear.
He carved a route, his way, on hearts,
abandoned himself to the desert winds,
putting fate and kings to shame.
The volcanoes gave him birth and he in turn
fathered hurricanes and volcanoes, showing
the world what the power of will can do.
He was the "No" man, the lover of danger,
the most dangerous of outlaws.
When his era indicted him he became judge
of his age, a judge of his judges.
"They killed him" it was said, and it was said
"He died in agony," and "Death was a stallion
which he rode like lightning, which he
spurred on like an arrow."

Ink grew leaf in his hand
and every leaf gave birth to a star.
The grapes sang his praises to the cup.
The dew offered his name to the sun.
The road grew old under his feet.
Yet old age seemed merely another
youth overtaking the past.

But whenever he felled a killer
a worse one took his place.
Do tyrants die bragging
as they live bragging? Where is
the predictability of Time?
Does Time see a change of heart
as inevitable? No. True spirit
resists, refuses to inhabit false clay.
Now earth is beyond his feet.
All destinations now beyond
the reach of his lightning
And what of the enemies? Should
he befriend them now? Friendship
has many faces, and although grim,
the foe, only one.
And when did he meet affection
except in the form of a serpent?
When was he greeted by anything
but a twisted smile?
Every lightning bolt, every blaze
is his kin. Every desert is the face
of his beloved.
All distance is wiped away. His size,
his measure erased, but only to increase.

Recognition illuminates him,
even by overlooking him.
Denial meets only with defeat.
All of "them" eat of him while
he hungers. All drink of him
while he thirsts.
All, all deny seeing him although
he is a flame under their
eyelids, hotter than any ember.
Those who try to constrain him tie
chains on their own hearts.
One day Death tried to sweep
away his name but until now it is
Death itself who died in his place.

Translated by Diana Der Hovanessian with Sharif Elmusa

——*Al-Mutanabbi* (915–964): one of the greatest Arab poets of classical times. Having declared his courage and horsemanship in his poetry, he doggedly refused to back down from an uneven fight where he was completely outnumbered and killed, in accord with his own profession of valor in his poetry.

Saleem Barakat (b. 1951)

Syrian poet of Kurdish origin. He lived in Beirut for many years working in journalism and is now associate editor of the prestigious quarterly, *Al-Karmel*, the literary review of the Palestinian Union of Writers. One of the most original poets writing in Arabic today, he has enriched modern Arabic verse with his portrayal of complex human situations, as in his long poem "Diram and Dilana," a story of love between a youth and a mature woman. He has also written about animals, a theme which once flourished in classical Arabic poetry but is now almost extinct, as contemporary Arabic poetry has come to concentrate more on the great upheavals of the human situation in the Arab world today. Barakat has shown courage in using words and expressions which are rare and unfamiliar but semantically apt and esthetically exciting. He has had several collections of poetry published as well as a novel, entitled *The Sages of Darkness* (1985). In 1981 he published a collection of all his previously published *diwans*, under the title *The Five Collections*. Barakat now lives in Nicosia, Cyprus, where *Al-Karmel* is published.

DILANA AND DIRAM / PART ONE

A wild goat on the hill
and silence that lifts its horns high as the mountain goat.
Do not come closer then, you who guide,
and do not retreat:
yours is the place from which roots detect roots
and the earth views its heritage.

A wild goat on the hill,
and a solid silence that lifts its horns, high as the mountain goat.

I
Look at her, Diram, she is the harvest of golden baskets in the gleam of your blood. Watch how she sleeps clinging to your side, her breath cascading flame by flame into the vast terrain of your manhood. Do you remem-

ber, Diram, the moment you came to her, meek and gentle, wrapped by fields, your steps singing of the day and the quiet frenzy of corn stalks? Do you remember the evening that shimmered in your eyes, that first evening you took hold, with kisses, of creation's treasures and uncovered a strange stream-bed beneath the rock of the soul? Take your time, Diram, take your time as you magically stroke the nests of her heart—Dilana's heart suspended like a wound full of life.

6

Look at him, Dilana, see how he clasps his hands 'round thunder bolts and scatters winds across your bed. Look how he dangles from your rapid breath like fruit; he traps waterborne plants as though boasting about you to the lances of water. Look how he encircles the waters like land, enclosing your pulse that rises up with boats and foam . . . but when he lays open his nets, at day's end, and cranes and planets scatter forth, leave him sleeping in his prophecies. Leave him, Dilana, for all that he holds of the earth is a fistful of baked brick, and all he can see are the wings of your breasts spreading across the earth, the shadow of evening and manhood.

8

Then wake him, Dilana, wake him from his sleep gilded with the sweetness of a thousand drunken hearts, awaken the morning with him, so they may rise to you together, dusted with desire and joy, for he is the last one whom you will see so delirious, blowing into giddy trumpets, or, like a cup-bearer, filling the cups of the drowned with heroism, standing in the same ancient path swept by roots and the joy of wild things in each other. He is the last whom you will see approaching like a storm-signal before the wind dons its violent helmet and rips at the tablecloth, scattering vessels across the marble of souls. Wake him, wake him up, Dilana.

9

Wake her up, Diram, awaken the butterfly of mystery and its golden drone . . . Wake Dilana up, and the house with her, stone by stone, then awaken the yard that encloses the house, and awaken the hedge. When you have finished with all that, awaken the morning that sleeps by the hedge, and say, Come Dilana, let us witness the bewildered radiance of the earth as she sheds power and splendor over our human shield, and after that let us reveal our breasts so we may reach the fields, trembling from the sweetness of the blade sinking to where sesame and saffron flow, as though we were trying, together, to be wounds beyond which there are no wounds . . .

Come, Diram, wake her up.

17

Wake her up, Diram, wake up Dilana, the fulness of foam, and spread your sails when she stirs from the caresses of your morning-fresh energy, for you approach her dressed only in mist. Wake her up, wake her up, Diram.

Wake him up . . . Wake her up . . .
I did not wish to wake up the earth that morning.
I did not wish the earth to wake me up.

Everything passes when the signs are complete, and whoever clings onto a sigh is carried off by it: that is how they went, Dilana and Diram, so I did not wish, that morning, to awaken the earth, and she did not wish to awaken me.

I was in full view of them, a youth and a woman, and I was their silent guide, opening before them pathways of dew. When they wandered amidst cymbals of blossom, I transformed the vivid blossoms into the celebration of wanderer with wanderer.

· · · ·

But, as a guide who led a pair of lovers only to a bitter brevity, I said, let me tell what happened. I said I would begin with the sorrowful, that I might tunnel forward to the sweet. As I speak, various others recount with me: the roots of bulbs and jute and golden blood that braided together in celebrant winds.

I thought I would start from where dust encircled the baskets of Dilana and Diram, they were returning from the truffle harvest, a dusting of grain pollen on their heads, as if they had bathed in blossoms and the blossoms had coated them with their sensual play. As though they had left behind some kisses in the grass, so the grass bounded forth to them with what they had forgotten.

They were returning, and the earth was returning from its daily harvest with a thousand stalks of corn and a thousand flames, a thousand raids in which the brave open their fates to invisible waves, a thousand cracked shields, a thousand thunderbolts drenched with kisses and twenty men who aimed arrows of ash at Dilana and Diram, so they bowed down to the silence that scatters fountains in its wake, and ravages carnations.

· · · ·

Ah, Diram, you were a youth fleeing the plains wrapped up with the
   thunderbolts of the fields.
Ah, Dilana, you were a woman fleeing her spouse, racing toward a choice
   and a choiceless youth.

A youth and a woman bonded together in purpose, who kindled the delir-
ium of ignorance around them.

. . . .

Each of them a child. A youth and a woman: two children. And I, the
mute guide, leading them amidst peach trees, and the beaks of
drunken clouds.

. . . .

I was not an ordinary guide. I went wandering between their eyelashes,
seeing what they saw, praising as they praised, the splendor of kings
who spun cities into an uproar like packs of greyhounds, and emerged
looking for their people.

. . . .

Allow me, Diram, I shall clothe you in a prince's mantle.
Allow me, Dilana, I shall clothe you in the cape of a princess.
And I will kneel, exposing my whole breast to the blows of the priestly
river.
Ah, anger, did I have to lead a fleeing youth and a fleeing woman?

. . . .

(With the fortitude of moles and the earned wages of a youth, Diram began.
He would lift books from their secret places into the memory of the dead,
and bundle up sands and arguments for word-peddlers, then return at the
end of the day, to sit on the roof of his building, sipping his evening tea
and the fragrance of a woman who had not yet emerged from her clay. But
he met Dilana, after two hundred suns followed one another in an empti-
ness punctuated by iron and noise. And he cried.)

. . . .

(Dilana was waiting too, after forty cycles of corn. And she was hoping to
make of her two daughters a reason for blood's submission to blood.)

. . . .

FIRST PRELUDE

They would run together around the mast of the city, muffling themselves
with winter's messages, joyous as seagulls, panting like ravens. Dilana would
try to catch hold of his youthful lightning and he reached out for her tender
mist. When they tired, they would sit together near the city's flagpole, she
receding a little, like a wave, and he receding, wavelike also, leaving their
surf-spun shirts strung across ropes of rain, with the dangling sash of an
unfinished kingdom.

. . . .

THIRD PRELUDE

. . . .

(I remember how helmets surprised one another after two celebrative pages
of Diram and Dilana's joy had been turned. I remember the pages ended,
and the city began. I remember that twenty stabs were thrust and two
lovers were dispersed from the banks of fountains. Diram was not killed,
nor was Dilana; instead they returned, each to their evenings. I remember:
Diram smashed the vessels of a woman who let down her heart after the
siege. I remember: Dilana shut her vision on the image of the youth, and
bowed to the carriers of middle-age after the siege. So I drank the last
lightning down myself, and awaited more ruin.)

. . . .

No lover remains. All of them have departed. All of them rolled the great
    pearl of the soul to the slopes and departed.
Each of them awoke, one morning, found his heart still sleeping, bowed,
    and departed.
Sighs! They create their own waves and break the masts.
So sleep then, heart, sleep a little. All you are is a wine jug where wan-
    derers take turns drinking, where invaders flirt with conquests, then
    forget them.
Sleep then, sleep.
(Dilana has not fallen asleep yet.
Her husband has gone to sleep and she has not.
Half of her is for Diram, and half for her two daughters.
Half of her is for a home, and half for the open wild.

It is the uncertainty of all ages and places.
It is the uncertainty of the silent song the body sings between the lover
    and the husband.
It is the uncertainty of the entire choice, the uncertainty of the blow that
    explodes what is to come, or erases what has passed.
    Ah, . . . half of her lies awake there, and half of her lies awake
    here.)

Sleep then,
sleep, delirious heart.

(Diram has not gone to sleep yet.
His new woman is sleeping, and he has not yet slept.
The city and ruins have gone to sleep, and he has not slept yet.

The bridges have gone to sleep and he has not slept yet.
The waters and clouds and spirits have gone to sleep
but he has not slept yet . . .
All of him is for Dilana,
all of him for a bewilderment that joins no one to anyone.
Ah, he was given no choice in the matter:
the sedate middle-aged men came and decreed that Dilana should remain
    for her spouse.)

Sleep then,
sleep, delirious one,
for your heart is simply a heart, and you were only the guide
for two lovers who did not complete the plundering of their souls.

DILANA AND DIRAM / PART TWO

DIRAM

He is what I have described, what I have told the earth and the air: a youth, delicate as an evening which women set aside for their own celebrations. A shy youth, streams washing the silt of his depths down to the sea, where the outcroppings of rock set traps for him. He was alarmed, at first, by the city of tumultuous stone, the rooms of stone with brazenly decorated windows, like the priestess of war. But he adopted the guile of the ruler, copied the temper of bridges, and blessed the unsmiling crowds. That truce gave him no real peace, for the fields which haunted him with their fern thickets continued to whistle in his ears, and northern mornings continued to whet, near the city, his scythes of longing. Ah, Diram, you used to say:
"The comedy begins with a kiss,
With a kiss the entire war begins,
With a light kiss which intensifies little by little growing huge.
With a gentle kiss filled with the tumult of man and woman,
the tumult of two bodies hollowing out of the muscle's wave
to hide their limbs each in the other's living cemetery.

This is how the dialogue of a man and a woman is completed,
the dialogue of their guts;
When the heir to the light kiss awakens, to inherit all the anger, and all
    the comedy."

You used to say that, Diram, and blow the sweet trumpet of the fields, delicate as the evening which women reserve for their celebrations. But you succumbed to desolation at last, to hear the farthest trumpet blowing, the trumpet that only awakens the ruins.

DILANA

Each day she opens the same door to her two daughters.
Each day she lays the same table for her two daughters.
Every day she watches the same spouse.
For twenty years
she has observed the same spouse.
Her future is what has passed: her future repeats the same movements,
    the same distractedness.
She is what I have told you. She is what I told the earth and the air, and
    she has fallen into loneliness again, hearing the most distant trumpet,
    the trumpet of her years that stand, like a lynx, on a hill with noth-
    ing left to be hunted.

Translated by Lena Jayyusi and Naomi Shihab Nye

THE WILD GOAT

Sage of the tribe, nay, most resplendent of sages, raises the animal's sign and its vows to the king of the wild, ascending and descending that rocky slope overlooking the canopies of sunset, where thunderbolts retire to bed, leaving their fires outside to flash in the shadows, the fitful shadows, and in the air their royal recklessness.
The silent sage of the tribe raises his horns, high, above mountain mist, as one who guides the wandering stone.

THE COWS OF HEAVEN

Luminous cows, mysterious cows, with inscrutable hides, enter the celestial passage, one after the other, graceful, jingling into the vast stretching emptiness. From comet to comet, planet to planet, space to space, their tails move like hands shooing the bees of falsehood from the honey of the gods.

Cows enter the heavenly passageway,
and from beyond their horns the evening assumes the rites
of thunder and virility.

THE GREYHOUND

They gamble on you,
and it is not your fate, graceful one, to rest calmly at all.
You will run long, very long.
You will run from thicket to thicket,
lake to lake,
carrying slain game in your mouth, across the water,
rousing the ducks and hens of the field within range
of the hunters' arrows.
Pampered, favored with choicest food . . .
But one day, in pity, they will take aim at you—that day when your
    lungs, which once sniffed out the hiding places of trembling game, or
    your slender legs, will let you down.
For a long time after you, flocks of birds shall live on in fields untread by
    masters following their dogs.

THE HOOPOE BIRD

It is as if the birds have segregated you,
as though you woke one morning, felt estranged from the kingdom,
and retired from it, fleeing from spring to spring,
a coxcomb your only mark of royalty,
and a middle-aged temperament.
Still, you are a living observatory;
the hard land beneath your wings hears the drums of water.

THE FLAMINGO

The enclosed, self-possessed one spreads his wings across the lake, beak
    pointing downwards, eyes searching out the bright movement of
    water serpents and green flies.
How he wishes for his victims to be sad when he pounces on them from
    above, but they are mute and merry,
merry in the mirthful water:
This is what makes him sad,
what saddens the mute flamingo, as he continues to pounce,
generation after generation, upon the mute gaiety of the water.

THE SQUIRREL

The first hazelnut trundles down from above.
The second hazelnut, the third, the fourth, the fifth, and
the sixth, trundle down from above.
The hazelnuts trundle down, nut by nut, to the ground beneath
the dumb tree, the tree whose memory the squirrel collects
nut by nut, rolling it into his den.
Each year a memory of hazelnuts rolls, nut by nut, into
the den of the prince with the merry tail,
and the tree forgets.

Translated by Lena Jayyusi and Naomi Shihab Nye

——Dilana and Diram: the true story of the love of a young country youth for an older woman of the city, commemorated by the poet in a very long poem *(The Crane)* from which these excerpts were selected.

——The Cows of Heaven: imaginary objects which, according to the poet, he created and wrote about.

ʿAbd al-Wahhab al-Bayyati (b. 1926)

Iraqi poet. He studied at the Teachers Training College in Baghdad and taught Arabic language and literature. He published his first collection in 1950, and in 1954 he published *Broken Pitchers*, the collection which made him famous all over the Arab world. Involved in radical politics from early youth, he lost his job more than once and suffered exile, living in Syria, Lebanon, Egypt, and the Soviet Union. Despite this he continued to write and is one of the most prolific Arab poets alive. He returned to Baghdad in 1972, was honored by the present government, and was eventually appointed as cultural attaché to the Iraqi mission in Madrid, where he still lives. His committed left-wing poetry has been the subject of many studies and has been translated into many languages. It is one of the most important avant-garde experiments to dominate the literary scene during the last thirty years.

THE IMPOSSIBLE

With dawn it comes or does not come,
My love that took to stony silence,
Round the walls it goes, begging,
Torn by talons of death whenever
Out of the depths and gnawed by despair
It shouts: O you creature you!
The Ship of Fate moved on,
Sinbad of the Wind never came,
How was it you came when our wells
Are poisoned, where can you have come from?
Did we meet before I came to be?
But love is blind and now I write
On water what you said, our Spring
Completes its journey through disgust
And sorrow from the wilderness,
Light fills the swimming butterflies,
Sister, fling the portals open wide!

Your eyes, beloved, before you were born
I loved them so:
                    Whoever might you be?

Translated by Salma Khadra Jayyusi and Christopher Middleton

LUZUMIYYA

Sorrow, mute, a guitar
Too soon by misery sharpened,

Its chords burn in my hands, I seek
shelter in it, seek shelter from it.

"Ah, tomorrow, sweat
tickles, the soul, ardent,

Craves flight. My clothes carry
the stain, I wish my soul as pure."

You who drill with your pain the well-hole,
Leaving your mercy in the water,

Making of my words a mouth
To shout in a night without friends,

Drill deeper, your black pain
Will end tomorrow.

Your bread poisoned, eat what your soul
Desires, and may your life be long.

Translated by Salma Khadra Jayyusi and Christopher Middleton

THE BIRTH OF AISHA AND HER DEATH

I
Assurbanipal loved me
He built for my love
A walled city

Thither he drove
The sun in chains
Fire, captives and slaves
And the Euphrates
River of paradise.
Half his heart was imprisoned
In the world-enchanted well
The other half devoured
By Assyrian eagles: thus
He loved me.
He was a storm
In destiny's hand he was
The axe that fell
On the skulls of kings
On cities and fortresses
Because I never could
Reciprocate his love
Trees withered and died
The Euphrates ran dry
The city disappeared
With its fires and ceremonies.
A stony rooster crowed
In place of it
Whenever the iron man
Returned from death kingdom
On his horse of rain and wind.
Through magic cities
Where high priests cast their spells
In their twilit temples
He looks for my face.
At the bottom of the world's
Enchanted well
He awaits my birth:
A gazelle that runs
Behind the chariots of banishment
In Assyria

2
Sold by the slave trader
Sick with love I dream

Of red carnations grown
In the Euphrates gardens
They cover my flesh that is haunted
By life and death
A bird of prey
Cawing its lonely cry
Dies in my depths
Its beak deep
In the bodies of things

3
The magician, poet
And warrior loved me
Offered his sacrifice
Built his obelisk
Where he recorded
His spells and the wafting
Scent of the motion
Of wind and stars.
Names he inscribed
Of flowers in my far country
He wept at my grave
Sprinkled the blood
Of a slaughtered child
And he kissed me:
I cried out naked
Held in his arms.
Submerging my tomb
The red Assyrian moonlight
Stained my hands and face
Turned my cheeks to rose
With black magic.
Blood began to flow
Into my veins
And back to life
Came nature once
Dead at the root
With thunder and lightning
Flowers from the sky
Of the world's night rained.

A hungry bird
Circled my nipple
The hand of the wind
Spread my hair. Keen
On my starting body it sought
In the garden of vision
A sapphire spring
A grove of fiery specters.
As I brushed from my braids
The birds he said:
"Ishtar, cypress
O Mother of gods
Of clear weather and rain
You who were born
In the bloodstream of earth
In the weeping of Tammuz
On the Euphrates
Tonight let us run
Away you and I
Over the mountains
Disguised as shepherds."
No more he could say
Soldiers trampled him to the ground
And plucked out his eyes
And waiting for them
In the hall of mirrors
Combing his beard
And drowned in light
Was Assurbanipal.

4
They sell me into slavery
While I wait for my labor pains
In the cities of the East
Ravaged by whirlwinds

5
For the chariots of banishment
In Assyria
For the king of the world

For the green wheat ears for the sun
For the sacred bird
In the underworld prison
Beneath this enchanted mountain
For the ritual fire
For the body of earth raised up again
By summer's kiss
For the Euphrates
I carry these marks
The signs of my slavery.
In the kingdom of God
I wander
And in the kingdom of Man
Searching for Tammuz
Weaving a wreath
Of red carnation
For his head that was severed.
Sleep in a seashell
With pebbles and light
Silver fish and polyps
In the bed of a river
A deserted planet.
On tablets I carve
Prophetic deciphering
My prophecy tells
Of mysterious essences
Defeating death
And primordial matter.
Carving a prophecy
I embrace beauty and terror
See the eagle upon the shore
Straddle a doe
Assurbanipal stab with a spear
The sun that is setting
Captives hang from the gallows
Dim in the twilight
To the Lord of Hosts
A high priest praying:
"And Jeremiah said—

Princes and kings
Thus shall I let them
Be drunk and sleep forever."
What then did I tell
To my death in slavery?
And fate: Whatever
Is hiding there tonight
Under the paw of the beast
Crouched at the gate of the unknown?

Translated by Sargon Boulus and Christopher Middleton

ELEGY FOR AISHA

Like Galen even him
The shepherd waiting dies
Orpheus swallows the sun disk
Ishtar shedding tears
Looks for a lost ring
O boats of smoke
On the Euphrates
Whose water sings
A dirge for Tammuz
Aisha she-who-lives
With winter has returned
Returned to the orchard
A stripped willow
Leaf on leaf it weeps
Into the Euphrates
By the keeper of the dead
Its tears are woven
Into a chaplet
For dead love a chaplet
In the world of inbetween
Where Aisha sleeps
Her head cut off
On a cushion
And in the dark of her braids
The rats play and scuttle
Worms devour her eyes

My queen I saw a vision
When thunder clapped
The earth replied
With a cloud of fire
A clawless eagle
Took my breath away
Stripped me naked
Clad my hand
In shell and feathers
A bird's wing an oar
And the eagle guided me
To the keeper of the dead
There discarded crowns
Lay in heaps the doors
Would not close or open
The Lion of the Dust
Had dirt for daily bread
And the sacristan
Of this underworld
Honing his blade shouted
Who has brought to me
This wretched man?

Aisha has returned
To her distant country
A poem on a gravestone
Sayings old and wise
A rhyme of the rarest
A leafless willow
Weeping on the Euphrates
In a cloud of smoke
Day departed
And three or four
After this vision sick I die
My queen like you
Bedded on stone and flame
In blood I write on leaves
Of floating willow
What the fortune teller
Spoke to the wind

To the bird and the ashes
O thin sustenance
Each night to die
Sober and drunk I go
Through houses of the dead
In Babylon through ruins
Along the river shore
Alone
Speak to clouds
Wallow in dust
Shout in despair
From the grave I wait in
Tell the willow
What the fortune teller foresaw
Aisha has returned
To her distant country
Let the poem
Let wind and ash and dove
Let the cloud and stars
Let the temple sacristan
Let the Euphrates mourn for her
I wept until the walls
Melted in Babylon
Ishtar on your mattress
I laid you down to die

What did I ever come by
Oh Phoenix
While you returned only
As virgin field a hearth
That dies again in the cold
A door not holding
Against the wind
Again you were
A worn book read by lovers
A book sold by the scribes
A tattered bone
A hope envenomed
When Aisha had returned

To her distant country
Let the Euphrates mourn for her
Let all the poems mourn

Translated by Sargon Boulus and Christopher Middleton

——*Luzumiyya:* a poem in which the monorhyme has the last three letters of the rhyme-word similar. Abu al-ʿAla' al-Maʿarri, the famous Abbasid blind poet, wrote much poetry using this kind of rhyme. Bayyati's above poem invokes al-Maʿarri's spirit.

——Assurbanipal or Ashurbanipal: Last of the great kings of Assyria, who reigned from 669 to 630 B.C. Aside from his many wars to secure the settlement of Egypt, which had been conquered by his father, and wars with Tyre, Lydia, and other neighbouring states, he was a great patron of culture, showing a sustained interest in literature. He collected a great library of cuneiform texts at Nineveh, which still forms the basis of Assyriology and is of great and unique value for the light it sheds on ancient life and thought.

——Ishtar: Chief mother-goddess of Babylonia and Assyria, the counterpart of the Phoenician Astarte. Her chief trait was her life-giving power, and it was under this symbol that she was used in contemporary Arabic poetry.

——Tammuz: Summerian, Babylonian, and Assyrian god who died and rose annually with dying and reviving vegetation. He was loved by his sister, goddess of earth and heaven, Innini or Ishtar, who descended annually into Aralu or the underworld at the time of Tammuz's death and brought him back to earth in her bosom. Tammuz represents the mystery of life and death, as seen in the withering vegetation of the hot Mesopotamian summer, and the rapid renewal of its life at the season of the spring rains. Tammuz is therefore the patron of flocks, irrigation, and vegetation. Many Arabic poems in the fifties and early sixties revolved around the content of this myth, emphasizing the lamentable withering of Tammuz and his glorious return.

——Galen (c. 130-200): renowned Greek physician, founder of experimental physiology and, after Hippocrates, the most distinguished physician of antiquity. In search of knowledge, he roamed through Greece, Cicilia, Phoenicia, Palestine, Crete, Cyprus, and Alexandria, and eventually settled in Rome in 164.

——Orpheus: son of Apollo and the Muse Calliope and a musician so marvelous that the wild beasts, and even trees and rivers, came to listen to him. His wife Eurodice, whom he loved dearly, was bitten by a serpent and died. Orpheus, inconsolable at her death, went down to Hades (the underworld) to get her back. The infernal deities, softened by his music, allowed her return, on condition that she should walk behind Orpheus and he should not look back. However, he failed and she became a ghost once more.

——Phoenix: a fabulous bird of gorgeous plumage, always male and the only one of its kind. It lives a long life and, at the expiration of its time, it makes itself a nest of twigs of spice trees, which it sets on fire, burning itself with it. From the ashes another phoenix is born. It has been used in contemporary Arabic poetry as a symbol of resurrection after death. Among the Arabs the story of the phoenix was confused with that of the salamander or *samandal*, or of al-ʿAnqa', which is a bird like the *roc* or *rokh*. According to Qazwini, al-ʿAnqa' lived 1,700 years, only to die and be resurrected.

Mohammad Bennis (b.1948)

Moroccan poet. Educated in Morocco, he is the editor of the avant-garde magazine *Al-Thaqafa Al-Jadida* (New Culture). He is interested in poetics, translation, and Moroccan graphic arts. He has published four collections as well as a critical study of contemporary Moroccan poetry, and his poetry has been translated into French, Spanish, and Swedish. His collections include: *Before Speech* (1969), *Something about Joy and Oppression* (1972), and *A Face Shining Across the Stretch of Time* (1974).

THE SECOND COMING

Forward! Announce the dust cloud's coming
Revolution in you I see my feet
in you outlaws
I know you are me   Forward!
naked radiant angry resentful full of fire
                            Forward!
in you I see our hunger in you I see
                our blood in you
                    I see our death
                        Forward! destroy
the authority of lies, those "mind-forged manacles"
                        Forward!
                                    in you I see
                                    kings' tombs
in the fury and the dust, in you I see
                        brazen cities driven by sand
turning red, seething in the air, I see a gaping chasm
a bird singing of blood and fire
Forward!   in you I see children growing with anger
            Forward!
                        before the world has time to turn
        they'll free the bird of those killed
        again and again on the streets,

buried headless again, and again
who've brought our language back to us
taught rebellion to turn tragic
and become a demon redoubled
                    Forward!
a prophecy shakes us out of our graves
away from bullets
away from old loyalties

                    Forward forward!
In you I see
those authority has slain
put on leaf and flower, and fly
to create out of those killed senselessly
the banners of the end
                    and the beginning.

Translated by Sharif Elmusa and Charles Doria

BELONGING TO A NEW FAMILY

My father recommended safety
fearing to contradict law and order
he memorized the legal code, advised me:
if you're wise, stay out of politics

But how crowded courts and prisons have become
how gallows have swung, bullets whined
how much blood shed, enveloped castles of anger and mutiny
down through the ages!

How this question turns colorless, emptied of meaning
                    whether I dream or wake?
How the silence that reigns behind numb curtains
slips away in the absence, pierces walls
and becomes tablets of wrath? How such curtains reveal
voices spreading on flame to bring us to the massacres of history?

How can we sit on chairs, strapped down by advice
recommending safe submission?
How return?

Without taking action
words lie dead on library shelves
canned in manuscripts, newspapers, books

Translated by Sharif Elmusa and Charles Doria

Sargon Boulus (b. 1944)

Iraqi poet and short story writer. Born in Habaniyya, Iraq, he left in 1967 for Beirut, where he worked as a journalist and translator. He later emigrated to the United States, and since 1968 has lived in San Francisco. He studied comparative literature at the University of California at Berkeley, and sculpture at Skyline College, San Mateo. An avant-garde and thoroughly modern writer, he has published his poetry and fiction in major Arab magazines and has translated Merwin, Ginsberg, Snyder, McLure, and others. A selection of his poems, *Arrival in Where-City*, was published in Washington, D.C., in 1982. He has also given readings in Berkeley, Los Angeles, New York, and Washington.

LIGHTER

I try the dead lighter.
It is the dark.
And all I want from the world
now is a match
just one
not two!
But the flame
as it quickly expires
like history succeeds only
in scorching the edges
with its final breath.
This is really what happens.
Who knows in what ways
God is liable
to think?
So then:
I want to spend tomorrow morning
as though it were a new *dinar*
that lures me into dubious places

where I steal off from instant
to instant, like a wave
of conspiring figures
lashing the walls of secret
passages with the tongues
of their lanterns, till I find
you somewhere there
a creature of music who invites
me to play
all night long

Translated by Sargon Boulus and Alistair Elliot

POEM

I want to know today
who planted these blind statues in my way?
Miracles are cheap.
With a cigarette you can buy
a magician. And money
is the MC
it is history that arranges
a meeting between life and death
so that
whenever war flares up in the East
the price of gold is bound to rise in the West

But that addicted gambler the world
reshuffles the deck of cards this time
to put the villains off the track
to uncover the sand shifting
under the podium
every sign reverses its course
as if nature had forgotten something
important, and turned back suddenly
It is time for these multitudes of the forgotten
to toss their torches onto the pyramid
of forged documents
—If you are the fire

I am the burning
if you are the big tree
I'm just a humble axe
but with my blows I'll cut you down

There are rivers with courses
still to be chosen
that will betray your maps
this time

Every killer shall kneel
before an ant!

And if you happen one day
to enter the cave of mythical monsters
where history used to hide
you will only find
the rusted helmet of the hero
and excrement of gods that grow extinct
with every blow
on the wall

Translated by Sargon Boulus and Alistair Elliot

MY FATHER'S DREAM

One night
my father saw a saint in his dream
He saw a tall saint
who spoke to him
with eyes burning like two embers
in a voice full of authority
very sure of being obeyed

In the morning
my father went out
to knock on village doors
one after another
to tell his dream
while he rolled a cigarette

of cheap tobacco
with the face of somebody
returned from war
or a soldier staring in amazement
at the stump of his amputated thigh

He had forgotten to shave for many days
and was jobless for as long as history
In his hands that knew
only how the hammer weeps
as it drives his days with cuneiform
tears into the heart of wood,
in his hands of skin and bone
he stubbornly clutched the rosary
of the future with orphan beads
and saw winter
after winter
send the carriage of hope
rolling off into a snowstorm
to disappear, trailed by a star
and a pack of emaciated wolves

He kept knocking on the doors
one after another
the sack of burlap on his back
filling up as evening advanced
with loaves of bread, the village's
black rice, tea, and salt
whenever he told his dream
which he did more than fifty times
till I knew it by heart

He had taken me along
to carry the sack when he got tired.

Translated by Sargon Boulus and Alistair Elliot

SIEGE

I found myself in this house
kept by a woman who disappears

throughout the week to roam
along rivers. When she returns,
she moors her boat to my thigh
while I sleep
and drags her mauled body
in heavy silence to my bed.
Animals recently set free
have been growing more ferocious daily
pouncing on children and the sick
in alleys.
There are rumors, other news: they say
a great famine, plague, massacres . . .

When the dawn arrives
with its carts piled with ammunition
my neighbors bang their heads
against doors,
a sign of complete servility
or unbearable pain.

Translated by Sargon Boulus and Alistair Elliot

———*Dinar:* the highest monetary unit in such countries as Iraq, Jordan, and Tunisia.

Mahmoud al-Buraikan (b. 1934)

Iraqi poet. Born in al-Zubair near Basra, he studied law in Baghdad and teaches at the Teachers Training Institute in Basra. A poet of great originality and a universal outlook, he rarely publishes his work and has no known collection in print, thus depriving the literary world of his versatile themes and distinctly different tone, outlook, and approach, which could be of great benefit to the rising generation of poets in the Arab world.

TALE OF THE ASSYRIAN STATUE

In a glass room
In a museum that squats
in a lost city that crouches
in a deserted land
on a vast continent
I live, elevated, confronting the eyes of men,
and paralyzing them.
At silence's end, I shake off
the events of time, and the
terror of the ninth century.

Idol of Nineveh
Its Master.
In an inscrutable moment
My being emerged
to the echo of a chisel
in the hands of a sculptor
in the hall of stones and clay.

In terror, tribes of the dead
make me blood offerings.
              How many voices
tremble with the nightmare in the cadence
of the chant
I was called many names

Scented with perfumes and essences,
Hung with rings
My eyes, two diamonds that pierce
the night,
come from mines whose secrets
no man has discovered.

Does Time admit to this memory?
I have seen the gentle moon
at night's beginning, heard the tumult
of the earthquake before the hour of ten.
I have seen the horses
invade women's cloisters
I saw the lances rise high
with skulls of men
I saw the heads twitch
after the sword's descent
I saw how the bride dances in the ceremony
of death,
and how suns extinguish
the storms of capitals.

Does Time admit to this memory?
The fall of castles and walls
drought and rains
wheat and iron
and the power of the sword, at which men stare
with awe, as it lies
in its leather scabbard?

Does Time admit
to that allusion?
The secret date
for the death of a legend
and the beginning of an impossible undertaking,
the plagues of history,
cycles of unknown duration,
the blaze of fires coloring
faces, coloring the gardens and sky,
the will to power
the lust to destroy.

I have lost my jewels
been stripped of my rings,
my locks sheared
I've been rolled off my original base
moved from place to place
The owls and eagles spoke to me,
little boys climbed my ribs
A hammer was once tested on my body
I was tied with ropes,
dragged along, stretched out on my face,
behind a pair of mules.
Once I guarded a wall
Another time I stood at the gate of a palace
Marched in file in one of the armies,
Was abandoned in the desert,
spread out, to be washed by the gales,
for the hot sandstorms to dry out
my deepest chambers,
casting an eternal gaze,
my white sockets open
to the world of stars.

The sea recedes, only the shells remain
                                    at the bottom of the earth
wind after wind
redistributes the red sands.
                        The ravens
have landed here, and meshed into the cycle of the horizon
Eagles' wings have fluttered
on my neck, then burned on the summits
of sand dunes.
Old wolves made a pillow of my body
as they passed by, fleeing to somewhere.
Caravans of thieves
took shade at my sides, where precious stones
left their mark, where ants built
the earthen kingdom of blind balance.

In the glass room
I stand erect, women stare

at my uncomplicated body,
(stare precisely at the center of the crotch)
children take delight
because my ear has fallen off, and my eyebrow is broken,
because in my chest
there is a gaping hole (so frightening in the light).
In the glass room
sound does not enter
the surface of death is not touched
Some men appear, and continue whispering,
perhaps about my left nail.
In the glass room
the worn-out fingers do not fall off
the sun does not penetrate, but the microscope does.
In the glass room alone
the solitary corpse stands erect.

Translated by Lena Jayyusi and Naomi Shihab Nye

MAN OF THE STONE CITY

From the world submerged beneath the ground, in a maze
carved out from iron, cement and stone
where the spider of fear and boredom
spins out its threads along silent paths, and there is no escape
In death's labyrinth, where humans perish
longing for life
where sound disappears spinning as though the ages gasped
through you
You are here . . . What is it you sing to the graves?
What is it you say to the harsh darkness and the icy cold?
And what is it you confide to solitude?
You turn! In your eyes there is
something about the spring
about a skyline untouched by dreadful nothingness
about a gentle laughing place
washed by the dawn, watered by light alone
You are here in your stone prison, on trails

that twist, converge, and twist again
whose prisoner never returns,
dreaming of the world, of escape
from the brutal silence, from tired imagination
from a hoarse voice, from the grey footsteps
visions that wither and desiccate
like flowers, like a bunch of grapes after the harvest
dreaming of the world, of the sun that lights up
colors the earth, of the flower's innocent dance
Dreaming: expanses, horizons and songs
Laughing eyes that speak marvelous languages
Outstretched endless shores
Islands laden with perfumes and dew
Strange cities, undulating with life,
Capitals of an awesome roar and echo
Features that trace strange encounters in the mind
Tears, sorrows, loud bursts of laughter,
Dreaming of the land where roots sink firm
and winds frolic
where night is a glad dream emboldened
by the rise of morning!

How many hours did you stand on a sad evening
Looking at the limitless sea?
What is it you say to waves which return
after colliding with green rocks
(the everlasting rocks . . . the meaningless rocks)
What is it you say to the birds that hover
over the water's flame? To the straw
that floats through it (perhaps it came from some deep
sprouting place,
and will end at some ancient hidden shore)
What is it you say to the white waving sail?
And to the wind that wanders with abandon
like children's joy?
What is it you say in your painful calm
to the sealed circular horizon, the beams of light?
Were you not once free of heart and vision?
Were you not once a child with a beautiful secret,

a child who did not judge others?
Did you not once hasten toward the sun and long for the moon?
Where did this devastation in your heart come from?
How did time fade leaving a colorless image
and where, human, do you hope to encounter
what you lost of your love?

Translated by Lena Jayyusi and Naomi Shihab Nye

Ahmad Dahbur (b. 1946)

Palestinian poet. He was born in Haifa, but his family had to flee to Lebanon when the city fell to the Zionist forces in 1948. Because of the great poverty of the family, Dahbur had no formal education, but he avidly read all the books and magazines he could lay his hands on. His highly sensitive poetry is dedicated to the Palestinian situation, mixing themes of heroism with a deep recognition of the dangers and tribulations of the contemporary Palestinian experience. He has eight collections of poetry to date, among which are *The Story of the Palestinian Boy* (1979), *Mixing Night and Day* (1979), and *Twenty-One Seas* (1980).

IN MEMORY OF ꜥIZZIDDIN AL-QALAQ

His blood is on us
I do not exonerate the vipers of the oil wells
or pass light sentence on their petrodollars
for I pursue a black rose growing in my heart
while the evidence overwhelms me.

ꜥIzziddin came laughing toward me
whipping out that old notebook of his
and proceeded to list his would-be killers.
He did not speak about his strange uncertain nights:
"Each day under a different roof!
Behind you creep plagues, fools and the cops!"
He laughs, "It's Paris, you know."
Whispers, "This is half the price we pay."
He never complained but suspicious
of men in strange suits on the streets
he'd suddenly quicken his steps
then just as suddenly slow down.

His blood is on us
His blood is on us

Here in the street where he drew his last breath
I saw (and do not exaggerate)
a gang of killers opposite a martyr's poster
their boss shows up, gun on his hip
his mind on that gun
and 'Izziddin smiling his distant smile,
leaving it behind with me
on the street where they murdered him
I see him still
whipping out that notebook
writing down new names.
Am I watching mountains fall
or writing a poem?
He said goodbye and made a joke
"You probably won't see me again."

His blood is on our hands
his blood is on our hands

He is our wretched land
If danger misses,
why, gravity pulls it back again to strike
He unmasked the tyrants with their lies
capitals deserted him
while he toted up their rulers:
"They kill you in defeat
they kill you in hollow victory
mornings and evenings they kill you
and buying and selling they kill you
do the wells bubble over? They kill you
They praise you? They kill you
but each morning tells again
the story of your resurrection
and the killers shiver
murmuring, "Why don't the refugees just die?"
Say, "They will not die!"
Tents and . . . sunny nights
an axe . . . and heads that will not bow
prisons . . . they fight back.
Say, "The refugees will never die!"

You hear the news about the Palestinian?
Wherever he is they knife him
famine strikes him and flees
rumor hacks off an arm here, a leg there,
the media joyfully spread the news
the Palestinian rejects
he accepts his days as a sword
a hand that scatters the illusions of others
I testify "Endurance is his strength."

He said, "Till final victory
I shall wear the sash of patience
till either we are disposed of, corraled and die
according to our guardians' whim,
or until we win!
This is the special realm
where our madness dwells."

His blood is on our hands
his blood is on our hands

I saw a bomb walking on hindlegs
in the capitals of the ebbing Arab tide
Palestinian blood shall reverse that tide
I know the secrets of the proud capitals.

One judgment day we shall appear
arrayed in our Arab poverty
I will step forth to give witness
accusing the enemies within:
"You kill me nights
while days you toast my health
tell me how is one bullet different from another?
Both shatter my head"

I see him standing there
whipping out that notebook
adding new names

His blood is on us
his blood is on us

Will he be a memory?
No, for the embers of thought sputter and die in our hands
while the snow falls
A fragrance?
No, the oil smells stronger than perfume
a vision?
No, night's ink blots out what we have seen
. . . Yet 'Izziddin remains 'Izziddin
forever
if we can't reach him
he'll find a way to find us
this recording spirit
whose blood unites, inflames us
but if we do not rise up
to meet him worthily
then his blood is on us
his blood on us.

Translated by Lena Jayyusi and Charles Doria

THE DEATH OF THE SHOEMAKER

Poet's Note: This poem was inspired by the death of the poet's friend and comrade Muhammad Najeeb Abu Rayya, who died in an explosion which destroyed a nine-story building in the Fakhani district of Beirut. Abu Rayya was killed along with his wife and eight children. He used to make shoes, and gave many of them away as gifts to the fighters and the poor. Behind his sarcastic smile he carried the memory of seven years he spent as a young man in jail because of his political struggle.

His eight children and their mother
blew up together,
he flew up with them to the second frontier, the sky.
The stunned trees considered it the work of an unknown
while the stooges' laughter echoed throughout the city.

There is a locust in the field
who will warn the fields?
Who can speak with a locust in his throat?
Together let us lift up the slain
gather their shredded limbs.

But who can follow the track of barefoot nights
from Abu Rayya's prison cell
to his house scattered in space?

There is a butterfly in the field
who will tell them the good news?
He was here
I can still picture him listening to the newscast,
apricot sheets, a glass of tea nearby;
he said, "Glory to the fighters!"
He also said, "We shall renew the land with hammer and sickle."

His news travels on the winds,
who will reassure the winds?
He used to drive nails into leather,
bandage wounds with roses,
"Our flesh is on our enemies' whips
we walk along the people's path
we will not deviate. . . ."

He was ever present, his rough voice sarcastic
he did not like patience:
"The grave strides toward us on a thousand feet . . ."
He was quickwitted (too late I realized
I was just listing his personal traits),
he said, "The grave strides toward us on a thousand feet
and I shall not give the grave one pair of shoes."

He used to give away shoes
to the poor and the fighters
when they asked how much
he'd make it a joke,
"So much you'll curse the deal."

The instant the bomb went off
I imagine him shaking twice with anger:
once at the noise and again
because the explosion gave him no time for sarcasm
He was not dreaming when he flew
how can a busy man dream?

That evening I was not dreaming either
I was not accusing the unknown.

I ask him now to rise up
prove the innocence of the unknown,
expose the guilt of the known,
but as usual he mocks,
whispers, "Will you vouch for my safety?
If today I reveal my killer's face
won't they say I'm the one to blame?"

His eight children and their mother blew up together
he flew up with them to the second frontier, the sky.
The stunned trees considered it the work of an unknown
while the stooges' laughter echoed throughout the city.

Translated by Lena Jayyusi and Charles Doria

——ʿIzziddin al-Qalaq: PLO representative to Paris assassinated there in 1978.

——Fakhani: district in West Beirut inhabited mainly by Palestinians. It was the object of numerous Israeli air raids, the worst of which, before the Israeli invasion of 1982, was a raid in July 1981.

Mahmoud Darwish (b. 1942)

Palestinian poet. Born in the village of Berweh, east of Acre, which was razed by the Israelis after the war of 1948, he lived as a refugee in his own country and entered the political struggle early in his life, joining the Israeli Communist Party, Rakah. As a result, he experienced constant harrassment and repression at the hands of the Israeli authorities, including imprisonment and house arrest. While in Palestine, he lived in Galilee and for some time edited Rakah's newspaper, *Al-Ittihad* (Unity). He left Israel in 1971 and went to live in Beirut, where his reputation as the foremost poet of the resistance continued. Several of his poems have been put to music as emblems of the Palestinian struggle. His poetry developed great sophistication with the years, and is widely acclaimed today. He has produced more than ten collections. He now lives in Paris and is editor-in-chief of the Palestinian literary review, *Al-Karmel*. PROTA is preparing a collection of his poetry in English.

DIARY OF A PALESTINIAN WOUND

Quatrains for Fadwa Tuqan

1

We do not need to be reminded:
Mount Carmel is in us
and on our eyelashes the grass of Galilee.
Do not say: If we could run to her like a river.
Do not say it:
We and our country are one flesh and bone.

2

Before June we were not fledgeling doves
so our love did not wither in bondage.
Sister, these twenty years
our work was not to write poems
but to be fighting.

3
The shadow that descends over your eyes
—demon of a God
who came out of the month of June
to wrap around our heads the sun—
his color is martyrdom
the taste of prayer.
How well he kills, how well he resurrects!

4
The night that began in your eyes—
in my soul it was a long night's end:
Here and now we keep company
on the road of our return
from the age of drought.

7
And we came to know what makes the voice of the nightingale
a dagger shining in the face of the invaders.
We came to know what makes the silence of the graveyard
a festival . . . orchards of life.

8
You sang your poems, I saw the balconies
desert their walls
the city square extending to the midriff of the mountain:
It was not music we heard.
It was not the color of words we saw:
A million heroes were in the room.

11
This land absorbs the skins of martyrs.
This land promises wheat and stars.
Worship it!
We are its salt and its water.
We are its wound, but a wound that fights.

12
Sister, there are tears in my throat
and there is fire in my eyes:
I am free.

No more shall I protest at the Sultan's Gate.
All who have died, all who shall die at the Gate of Day
have embraced me, have made of me a weapon.

14
Ah my intractable wound!
My country is not a suitcase
I am not a traveler
I am the lover and the land is the beloved.

22
The archaeologist is busy analyzing stones.
In the rubble of legends he searches for his own eyes
to show
that I am a sightless vagrant on the road
with not one letter in civilization's alphabet.
Meanwhile in my own time I plant my trees.
I sing of my love.

24
It is time for me to exchange the word for the deed
Time to prove my love for the land and for the nightingale:
For in this age the weapon devours the guitar
And in the mirror I have been fading more and more
Since at my back a tree began to grow.

Translated by Lena Jayyusi and Christopher Middleton

BREAD

(Written for Ibrahim Marzouk, a painter, killed on the morning of Wednesday, October 8, 1975, as he was buying bread at a Beirut bakery, one of many victims of the Lebanese civil war.)

From early dusk the day was inscrutable
The sun shows up, lazy as usual
A mineral ash, eastward, blocks the horizon . . .
In the veins of clouds
In household pipes
The water was hard . . .
A desperate autumn in the life of Beirut

Death spread from the palace
   to the radio to the salesman of sex
To the vegetable market

What is it wakes you now?
Exactly five o'clock
And thirty people killed
Go back to sleep
It is a time of death and a time of fire

Ibrahim was a painter
He painted water
He was a deck for lilies to grow on
And terrible if woken up at dawn

But his children were spun of lilac and sunlight
They wanted milk and a loaf of bread
           . . . .

Inscrutable day. My face
A telegram made of wheat in a field of bullets
What is it wakes you now
Exactly five o'clock
And thirty people killed
           . . . .

Bread never had this taste before
This blood this whispering texture this grand apprehension
   complete essence this voice this time this colour this
   art this human energy this secret this magic this
   unique movement from the cavern of origin to
   the gang war to the tragedy of Beirut

At exactly five o'clock
Who was dying?

Into his hands Ibrahim took the last color
Color of the secrets in the elements
A painter and a rebel he painted
A land teeming with people, oak trees, and war
Ocean waves, working people, street vendors, countryside

And he paints
In the miracle of bread

A body teeming with a country pulverized
And he paints
The festival of land and man: a warm loaf of morning

The earth was a loaf
The sun a loaf
In a loaf of bread Ibrahim was a whole people

Hide from him
The autumn, hide from him his blood,
Hide from him the finger accusing, the hard water
Let him complete the victorious painting
Let him complete the heroic epic

Now he is finished
Exactly six o'clock
His blood in his loaf
His loaf in his blood
Now

Exactly six.

Translated by Lena Jayyusi and Christopher Middleton

FROM: BEIRUT

An apple for the sea, marble narcissus flower
Stone butterfly, Beirut
Shape of the soul in a mirror
Description of the first woman, smell of early mist
Beirut is built of gold and fatigue
Of Andalusia and Damascus
Silver, seafoam, bequests of earth in the plumage of doves
Death of a cornstalk
Vagrancy of a fugitive star between my love and me
Beirut—I did not hear my blood before I uttered
The name of a mistress
Who sleeps across my blood, who sleeps
•   •   •
Captives we are in this flabby age
Invaders have delivered us up to our kin

No sooner had we gripped the earth than our protector
Pounced on our weddings and memory
So we distributed our songs among the sentries. . . .
We found nothing to indicate our identity
Except our blood that climbs the walls and in secret
We sing:

>Beirut our tent
>Beirut our star

. . . Beirut, shape of shade. . . .
She tempts us with a thousand overtures
And with new alphabets

>Beirut our only tent
>Beirut our only star

. . . .

A grey horizon scatters in the distance
Circle paths of mother-of-pearl, not roads
And from Hell to the Atlantic
From the Gulf to Hell right left and center
I saw nothing but a scaffold
With one single rope for two million necks
I see armed cities of paper that bristle
With kings and khaki

. . . .

I see cities crowning their conquerors
And the East sometimes is the opposite of the West
Sometimes the East of the West
Its image and commodity
I see cities crowning their conquerors
Exporting martyrs in order to import whiskey
And the latest thing in sex and torture

. . . .

I see cities that hang their lovers over branches of iron
And drive away the names at dawn

At dawn the guardian of the only idol comes
With a million keys and one scaffold
What are we leaving if not a prison
What have the prisoners got to lose?
We walk toward a distant song
A first freedom

We sense the world's enchantment for the first time
This dawn is blue
And the air can be seen and eaten like figs
    . . . .

Is Beirut a mirror that we can break
To enter into the fragments
Or are we mirrors for the drizzle to shatter?
    . . . .

Beirut, markets hung over the sea
An economy that destroys production
To build hotels and restaurants
A government in a street or an apartment
A coffee bar that turns like the sunflower to the sun
Description of departure and free beauty
Paradise of documents
A seat in the plumage of a bird
Mountains that bow to the sea
A sea that ascends to the mountains
A deer slain by the wings of a sparrow
And a people that do not like the shade
    . . . .

We burned our boats and hung our stars over the outer walls
We did not search for our ancestors in the family trees
We did not travel further than pure bread and our clothes of mud
To the mother-of-pearl of ancient lakes we sent no pictures of our fathers
We were not born asking. . . .
We were born every which way
Spread like ants over a mat of straw
Then we became horses that pull carriages

We who stand in the line of fire
We have burned our boats and embraced our rifles
We shall awaken this land that rested on our blood
And extract our fallen victims from its cells
We shall wash their hair clean with our white tears
Pour over their hands the milk of the soul
    . . . .

We who stand in the line of fire declare:
    Until the night shall pass

We are in the trenches
    Beirut eternal we gaze upon the sands
In the beginning we were not created
In the beginning was the word
And now in the trenches
A birth is being prepared
                . . . .

A moon shattered over the bench of darkness
Beirut is a lily of rubble
A first kiss
Eulogy of the *Zanzalakht* tree
Cloaks for the sea and the slain
Roofs for the stars and the tents
Stone poem
Collision between two nightingales hidden in the heart
A bereft sky
Thinking on a stone
A rose that can be heard, Beirut
A voice that separates the victim from the sword
A little boy who flung away the regulations and commands
And the mirrors—
Then fell asleep

Translated by Lena Jayyusi and Christopher Middleton

POEMS AFTER BEIRUT

I. EARTH SCRAPES US

Earth scrapes us, pressing us into the last narrow passage, we have to dis-
    member ourselves to pass,
Earth squeezes us. Wish we were its wheat, to die and live again. Wish it
    were our mother,
Our mother would be merciful to us. Wish we were images of stones that
    our dreams carry
Like mirrors. We have seen the faces of those who will be killed defending
    the soul to the last one of us.
We wept for the birthday of their children. We have seen the faces of
    those who will throw

Our children from the windows of this last space of ours. Mirrors that our
    star will paste together.
Where shall we go, after the last frontier? Where will birds be flying, after
    the last sky?
Where will plants find a place to rest, after the last expanse of air?
We will write our names in crimson vapor.
We will cut off the hand of song, so that our flesh can complete the song.
Here we will die. Here in the last narrow passage. Or here our blood will
    plant—its olive trees.

II. WE MOVE ON TO A COUNTRY

We move on to a country not of our flesh. Its chestnut trees are not part
    of our bone marrow.
Its stones are not goats in the song of mountains, its pebble eyes are not
    lilies of the valley.
We move on to a country that suspends no singular sun over us.
For us the women of legend clap their hands: a sea for us and a sea
    against us.
If wheat and water are cut off from you, then eat our love and drink our
    tears.
Black handkerchieves for the poets. A line of marble statues will raise our
    voices up
And a stone mortar to guard our souls from Time's dust. Roses against us
    and roses for us.
You have your glory and we have ours. Ah, how we are troubled by a
    country of which we see only what is invisible: our secret.
Ours is the glory: a throne carried on feet torn by roads that have led us
    to every home but ours.
It is for the spirit to find spirit in itself, or to die here.

III. WE TRAVEL LIKE OTHER PEOPLE

We travel like other people but return to nothing. Traveling was the
    clouds' way.
We buried our loved ones in the clouds' darkness, among the trunks of
    trees;
We said to our wives: Bear children from us for hundreds of years, so that
    we may complete this departure
Toward a single hour of homeland, one span of the impossible.

We travel in psalm wagons, rest in the tent of prophets, we emerge from
    gypsies' words.
We measure space by the hoopoe's beak, or sing to repel from us the dis-
    tances, wash out the moon's light.
Your road is long: dream of seven women, so that you can carry this long
    road across your shoulders.
Shake the palm trees, to know their names, to know which mother will
    give birth to the child of Galilee.
We have a country full of words. Speak, speak so that I can rest my road
    against a rock.
We have a country full of words. Speak, speak so that we may know what
    is the limit of this traveling.

Translated by Lena Jayyusi and Christopher Middleton

——June: a reference to June 1967, when the Six Day War took place between Syria, Egypt, and Jordan on one side, and Israel on the other, ending in a disaster for the Arabs which inflamed poets all over the Arab world.

——Andalusia: the region of southern Spain where the Arab Islamic kingdom prevailed from the eighth century up to 1492, the date of the fall of Granada, the capital of the last Muslim kingdom in Spain.

——Zanzalakht: known also as *zalzalakht* or *izdarakht*, the china tree or the Indian lilac, a handsome tall tree with lilac-colored flowers and rich shade. Some references state that it is the "shade tree" of America. The name is probably derived from the latin term, *melia azedar-ach*. It is one of the large trees that abound in Galilee.

Zuhur Dixon (b. 1933)

Iraqui poet. Born in Abu al-Khasib, south of Basra, she later came with her husband to Baghdad, where they have been living for many years. Largely self-taught, she draws on the strong poetic tradition that has remained alive in Iraq. Her poetry reflects a suppressed emotionalism related to her position as a woman in a highly traditional society, but conveys at the same time a deep message of freedom and individuality. Her style is well-knit and her imagery both original and evocative. She has published several collections of poetry, including *Cities Have Another Awakening* (1976), and *A Homeland for Everything* (1979).

OVERTURE

Who can open the door
of the green river,
of the golden clouds,
of my heart?

Translated by Patricia Alanah Byrne with the help of the editor

DIALOGUE OF THE NIGHT OF THE ROSES

You were forgiven
when you burdened
me with the unbearable.

Do grant me, love, what I can never bear;
perhaps I can embrace again
through separation
my lost space
suffer and perhaps
wake up!

The most painful part of silence
is the echo of an echo.
The most distant thing in the distance
is the constant taking of the
same road.
    Night of the Roses
    sends forth its dew,
    evoking my homeland.
    Night of the Roses
    bestows its fragrance,
    the lilies of sleeplessness
    pour forth.
Oh, my homeland
this limitless land
that has no frontiers
is called longing.

Translated by Patricia Alanah Byrne with the help of the editor

SEASON OF BEGINNING AND END

Behind the gate of light
the lady of the languishing moon,
of the echoes,
of vanishing dew,
rests.

Shall we begin at zero point?
What harm in that?
The season of creation begins in the
season of nothingness:
    the arduous climb
    is the beginning of the end.

Behind the gate of light the lady
of the quiescent moon
of the vanishing sunset watches
the snows about to melt while
moonrays drown in the mirror.

Show me a place where I could
lie quietly among corners
a jungle where I can take shade,
a flower whose dew and fragrance I can breathe.
Grass loves all depths and distances,
but is also found in the surface
of the road that contains it.

The desert sun flirted with the clouds
in the hall of silence, or of those thirsty sands;
nothingness delivered the blow of death.
What harm to repeat the story?

What harm to us?
The season of creation begins in
the season of nothingness
if it is tended carefully.

But
by climbing,
one reaches the top of the slope.
Shall we begin?
Or is this
the beginning of the end?

Translated by Patricia Alanah Byrne with the help of the editor

TWO HANDS ON THE WATER

A face reigned on the water
      but did not sleep
It was the face of pain.

two hands that grew green with prayer
      were
         the hands of the poor.

A face floated on the water
      but did not sleep
It was the face of God.

The guardian of the morning wanders
       between the Khalili Bazaar
   and the Mosque of Husain
He stretches two hands:
   one bargaining with the Khalili Bazaar
   playing with the Khalili Bazaar
   stringing bracelets on the wrists
      of the Khalili Bazaar
and the other
   picking autumn flies
   off the children's faces
      in the Grand Mosque of Husain

Translated by Patricia Alanah Byrne with the help of the editor

Amal Dunqul (1940–1982)

Egyptian poet. Although he did not complete his formal education, he was able to carry on the tradition of modern poetry in Egypt with vigor, winning immediate recognition with the publication of his first collection in 1969. He later drew greater attention when he took a strong stand in his poetry against the disruption of ties with other Arab countries in favor of appeasement during the rule of Sadat. Before his death in 1982, he had published six collections of poetry, gaining great recognition with his collection, *The Coming Testament* (1975).

THE SCAFFOLD

You shout and hurry through
the rows of soldiers.
We kiss. At last, the moment:
at the last step
of the scaffold's ladder
I feel your face.
You are beyond me now.
Are you my child
or my widowed mother?
I feel your face . . .
(I am blind.
They have bound my eyes
and hand with the folder
of my confessions.
The authorities will go through it,
authenticate my statements and my
signature . . .
Perhaps it was the interrogator
who added the sentence
that sends me to my death.
And yet they promised they would give me back

my eyes and hands
after a fair trial . . .)

The era of death is not yet over,
my grieving child.
I am not the first one to predict
the age of earthquakes,
nor am I the first
to have said out in the marketplace
that in its nest the dove is perched upon a bomb.

I will pass my secrets to your lips.
I will pass my only desire on
to you, to the sheaf of wheat,
to next year's flower.

Kiss me, and do not cry.
Do not let the cloud of fear
block me from your eyes
in this heavy moment.
Already between us there are
too many iron mantles.
Do not add a new one . . .

Translated by Sharif Elmusa and Thomas G. Ezzy

CORNER

He sits in the corner,
writes, as the naked woman
mingles with the nightclub's patrons,
auctions off her beauty.
She asks him how the war is going,
and he answers:
"You needn't worry about the treasures of your body,
our country's enemy
is just like us,
he circumcises males and loves foreign
imports, just like us, he hates pork
and pays for guns and hookers."
She cries.

He sits in the corner
as the naked woman passes.
He invites her to his table.
She can't stay for long, she says:
since morning she's been combing army
hospitals, searching for her brother,
whose unit was encircled
across the Suez (The land
returns, her brother doesn't . . .)
She tells him she has had to earn
the bread in her brother's absence,
how she will wear again her modest clothes
when he gets back.
She shows his picture with his children
on a holiday.
She cries.

Translated by Sharif Elmusa and Thomas G. Ezzy

TOMORROW

When you get there, do not greet them.
Now they are carving up your children
on their platters;
they have charred your nest,
set fire to the straw
and sheaves of wheat . . .
Tomorrow it is you they will slay
and dig for treasures
in your craw
Tomorrow, our ancient cities
will turn into cities of tents
pitched along a stairway
to the scaffold.

Translated by Sharif Elmusa and Thomas G. Ezzy

TRAINS

Trains travel on a two-railed course
of what has been and what shall be.

The sky is the ash
that Death has brewed his coffee from
and scatters now to make the living breathe it.
It seeps inside their hearts and veins.
Through the glass, everything eludes us:
flecks of dust in a beam of light,
songs of wind, the barrage on the river,
flocks of birds,
the poles that hold the power lines . . .
Everything eludes us. Water
cannot be held in the hand,
nor do dreams linger
on the balconies of eyes.

Trains depart, and passengers
arrive,
and do not arrive.

Translated by Sharif Elmusa and Thomas G. Ezzy

THE CITY A WRECKED SHIP

I feel I am alone tonight;
and the city, with its ghosts and tall
buildings, is a wrecked ship
that pirates looted long ago
and sent to the ocean's bottom.
At that time the captain leaned his head
against the railing. Beneath his feet
lay a broken wine bottle, shards
of a precious metal. And the sailors
clung to the silent masts,
and through their ragged clothes
swam sad fish of memory.
Silent daggers, growing moss, baskets
of dead cats . . . Nothing pulses
in this acquiescent world.

Translated by Sharif Elmusa and Thomas G. Ezzy

Salah Fa'iq (b. 1945)

Iraqi poet. He was born in Karkuk, Iraq, and is largely self-taught, having left school at fifteen. He has worked in journalism and is at present the literary editor of the weekly, *Al-Dustur*, issued in London. He writes his poetry in prose and inclines toward a surrealistic style as well as a philosophical outlook on life and experience. He has published two collections of prose poetry, *Hostages* (1975) and *That Country* (1978).

POEMS

1.   If I speak always of the dead
            it is because I'm their friend.
    I row with them in empty boats
    and we shout if the shape of the peaks
    is changed and if we see someone wipe out
    the footsteps of the beasts in the snow.
    This is what makes me plunge deeper to touch
    the waves that flow
    and this is what makes me see
    God's creatures circling distances
    trying to understand if the din of the jungles
    is merely a joke, or
    a sign of anguish.

2. As I traveled from the city
    toward the country
    old age fell off my shoulders.

3. Nothing is more cruel than to see
    workers
    in the early morning
    stooping to build a jail.

4. I know
   how fascinated we are with clarity
   the clarity of a country dawn
   the clarity of the pangs of death.
   But what I care about is what the trees think,
   and what makes a madman laugh.

5. When the dream departs leaving
   the memory of a real world, I stay
   in front of the hearth watching
   my fear raising its arms
   toward gypsies dancing
   in a picture hanging on the wall.

Translated by Patricia Alanah Byrne with the help of the editor

Muhammad al-Faituri (b. 1930)

Libyan poet. Born in Alexandria to a Sudanese father with Libyan family ties and an Egyptian mother, he studied in Alexandria before moving to Cairo. Later he became a Libyan citizen and has been in the employ of the Libyan government ever since. The main theme of his early poetry was the problem of color and racism, and he felt one with the black people of Africa, writing about human dignity and freedom for all blacks. It was primarily in this vein that he wrote the poetry in his *diwans: Songs of Africa*, *Sorrows of Africa* and *A Lover from Africa* (all published in or before 1964). However, his poetry later took on wider horizons as he came to address the large Arab audience, and wrote about political freedom and other pertinent Arab problems. His slim volume, *The Fall of Dabshalim* (1968), heralded this new direction.

THE STORY

And Bidpai said:
the thieves have stormed
across the harbor mole,
they've broken the ship's mast
and plundered its precious cargo,
the captain is still
searching through the alleys
for his old telescope.
It is this story, Dabshalim
I see unfolding, chapter by chapter.

INCIDENT

And Bidpai said:
while the clowns laugh
the corpse is dangling

like a windless flag
from the gallows,
the sun is white-haired in the sky.
It could well be, Dabshalim
that what we see with open eyes
comes sated with the blindness of the core.

THE QUESTION AND THE ANSWER

—With what sword shall I
strike down tyranny?
—With the sword of the weak of the earth,
Bidpai answered.
—What fire will burn
the winding sheets of death?
—The fire of humiliation
Bidpai said.
—And how might I make man anew?
And Bidpai answered:
—You will make him if you fall
while standing up for him.

THE DERVISH

And the Dervish spat
in his cloak and said:
When at last
we screwed the coffin lid down on him,
he was saying, GOD IS MY LORD,
DEATHLESS, ETERNAL.
He loved God and stood in fear of Him,
he held Him in reverence
in himself and in others.
But, Sire, should you happen to catch
a glimpse of God
it would make the mountains
and the sea get up and follow you.

THE CLOSED DOOR

The tavern is closed for the night,
the tapster bent double with age,
the old drinking crony is dead.
Chew over your sorrow, Dabshalim
yesterday our black cat aborted her kittens
and the wise man's dog spent a sleepless night
barking at something it could not see in the stars.

A SCREAM

I understand Death's contract
and the finite ends of life:
however long a man lives
he lives only to die.
At the end, every scream
pours like a river into silence,
but the most dazzling star
is that which shows the caravan its way
when moss has covered our memories
and grief runs wild through the house.

THE VISION

Suddenly horizons clouded
and the day grew dim,
trees shed their leaves
and the skeletons of fish
danced in the seas,
every face confronted another,
each destiny found its mate
and the father repudiated his son
walking away from him.
Then I woke up, and Bidpai
said to Dabshalim:
Man is whatever choice he makes.

Translated by Sargon Boulus and Peter Porter

——Bidpai and Dabshalim: Dabshalim was the Indian king who figures in *Kalila Wa Dimna*, a book of beast-fables written first in Sanskrit and then translated into Persian and then into Arabic in the eighth century A.D. The poem refers to the relationship of Dabshalim and Bidpai, his counselor. The king was directed by a dream to a cave in which an old man would give him treasures. Of these treasures, he keeps fourteen pieces of advice for rulers, and takes them to Ceylon, where the Brahman Bidpai explains each of the precepts by stories which form the separate chapters of the book.

Muhammad al-Ghuzzi (b. 1949)

Tunisian poet. Born in the ancient city of Qairwan, he studied literature at the Tunisian University and worked as a schoolteacher in his birthplace. As with his friend, al-Munsif al-Wahaybi, his upbringing in this center of Islamic learning has had a major influence on his poetry. His book, *The Book of Water . . . The Book of Embers* (1982), demonstrates a refreshing new direction away from the often militant verse and loud tones of poetry east of the Mediterranean, and is characterized by a compact mystical language and a philosophical outlook. Ghuzzi has translated, with al-Wahaybi and Sigrid Kahle, a collection of poetry by the Swedish poet Östen Sjöstrand.

FEMALE

Do you not see that we pitched our tent on the banks of night
And called out to you to enter in safety
So that we could wash your face at night with sea water,
Your face where ancient terror dwells?
Did you not crave sanctuary of the wind, and we gave you shelter?
Did you not tremble and we called to you
To drink our wine from earthen vessels,
That wine whose praises you have sung?
Did we not call upon you to seal in the blue of night
A covenant with the land you seek?
This is your drawn countenance
The water birds enter it in flocks
And this is your house, open,
                                        pledged to the flood-tide of the sea.
The Female called out your name saying:
"Do not betray me, Master,
Descend into my body, cleanse
With night rituals its estrangement;
Of antique cedar wood is our bed,
And full of gladness is the night; be with me."

Why did you lose her, Master? They say she cast
Her girdle and earrings to the waters of the sea,
They say we saw her before people crying out:
"Who of you can restore to me my Master whom I love,
A young man like the cyprus tree, all the birds of evening
Are reflected in the depth of his eyes;
I invited him into my mother's house,
I said do not saddle your horses for the valley of God
That path has no guide and winter is on the roads,
What should you seek?—God is here in my body."

Why did you lose her, Master?
They say we saw her, face to the sea, arms open, calling:
"Come to me now, my body celebrates you."
Why did you lose her, Master? Here you return
Dust on your shoulders, heavily burdened,
In your open face the osprey finds a home.
Descend in safety, let's wash
Your face at night with sea water,
Your face where ancient terror dwells.
Did you not crave sanctuary of the wind, and we gave you shelter?
Did you not tremble and we called to you
To drink our wine from earthen vessels,
That wine whose praises you have sung?
Did we not call upon you to seal in the blue of night
A covenant with the land you seek?
This is your drawn countenance
The water birds enter it in flocks
And this is your house, open,
                    pledged to the flood-tide of the sea.

Translated by May Jayyusi and John Heath-Stubbs

QUATRAINS FOR JOY

When joy surprises me, I ripen
Before the gathering of figs and grapes,
And call to my master who is one with my soul:
"Pour out your wine for all, my body is the cup."

When joy surprises me, the sea
Floods in upon the thresholds of the night
Carrying in a basket all the fruits of the season
And I make myself a necklace of the sea's treasures.

When joy surprises me, I cry out:
"Master alight at my side,
I will hide you tonight in the cloak of my love,
Here's my body flowering for your wayward stallions."

When joy surprises me, I come forth
With my loosened hair, following my lovers,
I open my breast to the bird flocks, "who," I say,
"Will repair to the regions of the Female if lovers go?"

When joy surprises me, I come forth
From my hidden cities and kindle my incense-burners,
And bless the tree of my body; then all I've hidden
shows on my face and my secret is out.

When joy surprises me, I inhabit
The incadescent kingdom of lightning
Sleep with the sap in the heart of the leaf,
Return when the palm branch is heavy with dates.

When joy surprises me, I cry out,
"Priest of the Nile Valley, here are my fish
Dead, and my horse is slain before me.
With what chant then shall I open this requiem?"

When joy surprises me, I go
To the soothsayer bearing my broken pitcher
And he lays his hands on my chilled body and declares,
"For seven nights shall this glad face be grieved."

When joy surprises me, I behold
A hawk perched on the castles of the winds
I loosen my locks over my face and cry,
"From what frontiers does this portent come?"

When joy surprises me, and its white gulls
Alight on my body, I see my shroud

Through my ecstasy, and so I strew
All I possess on the waves and I depart

Translated by May Jayyusi and John Heath-Stubbs

YOUR EYES

Your eyes will not mark the advent of the season
    Nor the joy of grasses thronging from the earth
Nor will they notice the burgeoning of the trees
    In the stillness of the night
    Nor the glow of sap in the heart of the leaf
They will not remark, your eyes, the silence of the seed
    As it goes back to its closed-in kingdoms
They will not perceive, your eyes, this death as it returns
    Hiding all the freed birds in its basket.
Conceal yourself, then, behind the herbage of words,
    Know for a truth that the world
    Is wider than is your anxious glance.

Translated by May Jayyusi and John Heath-Stubbs

A DREAM

When he surrendered his eyes to the dream, this lad,
The evening star entered his house, trembling,
The wood of his bed turned into a ship for him,
The cosmos turned to an oyster in his hands.

THE PEN

Take a pen in your uncertain fingers,
Trust, and be assured
That the whole world is a sky-blue butterfly,
and that words are the nets to capture it.

MY SISTER

Do not ask how, before cock-crow, my sister had departed
Making her way through arcane cities
Deep within us she lives
As the tree hides in the kernel.

TAGHORE

What does the old man hope from those books like graves
When the whole earth is his carpet,
And the stars are a rosary within his hands?

THE BEGGAR

Noiselessly,
       in the blue of night this heart of mine
       Comes full of joy to you
       But
       When it perceives your silver door closed fast
       It gathers its tattered robes about it
       And lies on the threshold
               like a beggar.

Translated by May Jayyusi and John Heath-Stubbs

Ghazi al-Gosaibi (b. 1940)

Saudi Arabian poet. Born in al-Ihsa' in Eastern Saudi Arabia into a well-to-do and influential family, he had his early education in Bahrain, then obtained a B.A. in law from the University of Cairo in 1961. In 1964, he obtained an M.A. in international relations from the University of Southern California, and in 1970 obtained a Ph.D. in political science from the University of London. He had held important positions in his country's government, becoming the Minister of Industry and Electricity (1976–1983), then Minister of Health (1983–1985). At present, he is Saudi Arabian ambassador to Bahrain. Dr. Gosaibi is widely read in literature, religious studies, and history and has been very active as poet, anthologist, and writer. He has at least twelve books in print, including *Verses of Love* (1975), *You Are My Riyadh* (1976), *Fever* (1980), and his lovely collection, *Chosen Poems* (1980). Despite his formal status, Gosaibi's poetry, written with clear language and an eloquent style, reveals a deep involvement in Arab life and political experience, and reflects great love for simple beauty, innocence, and uncomplicated human relations in contrast to the pomp and flourish of the high life around him.

OCTOPUS

One arm circles my neck
another my limbs
another and then another

I feel these black arms
sucking at my veins
draining the life from my body
Where's my hand?
The knife I held?
Once I had thousands of hands
thousands of knives!

With my own hands
I can cut off my arms
here I am armless
wrapped in black arms

I feel those black arms choking me
the beast's hideous eye staring at me
in his greed seeing my death
        when he draws me toward his jaws
and rends me

Suddenly a knife sprouted from my forehead
a knife from my ribs
the wound blossoming with fresh blood
every drop growing a hand.
Cursing me,
the hideous eyes died.

Translated by Sharif Elmusa and Charles Doria

WHEN I AM WITH YOU

I set sail
(although there's nothing more beautiful
than your eyes' sea where stars meet
where they shine with love
and their lighthouse beacon smiles
beaming home the voyager
ports have denied entry
because he tried to land passportless)

I set sail
searching for beautiful women
wearing perfume, kohl, and smiles
women who've never known joy
But like a child's
your face, loveliest of faces
has never been defaced with makeup
it still shows sorrow, hunger, fear
smiling one moment, frowning another

I spread my sails and wandered
grappling with life's mysteries
I crossed the sea of riddles and enigmas
however you in your mind
never wrestled with philosophy
or searched beyond nature's bounds
asking questions
never pretending to knowledge
yet knowing right from wrong
penetrating through the fog
of hypocrisy

I set sail
changed my clothes and the color of my eyes
honed my tongue so others could understand me
danced to their tunes
donned eloquence, fine manners
shedding my old face
But when I am with you
I'm still the one you always knew
as I know myself
I show the sun my warts
the winds my faults
I accept myself as I am
as your generous love accepts me.

Translated by Sharif Elmusa and Charles Doria

SILENCE

Our words are dead
like the tyrant's conscience
They've never bathed in the fountain of life,
never known birth pangs or wounds,
the miracle of walking on spear points.

We dream of a world free of chains
rising from our paralyzed pens
That a season of roses

will blossom in our dying hearts
We dream of a fresh miracle
born from our pens

When the brave poet is afraid to die
his best poem is silence!

Translated by Sharif Elmusa and Charles Doria

Qasim Haddad (b. 1948)

Bahraini poet. Born in Bahrain, he did not finish his secondary education and is largely self-educated. He rose to fame both as a poet and as a revolutionary, writing much verse on political subjects dealing with freedom and progress. At present, he is Director of Culture and Art at the Ministry of Information and the head of the Union of Bahraini writers. The most famous poet of Bahrain, he has published seven collections of poetry, including *The Good Omen* (1970) and *Doomsday* (1980), which contain some of his most popular poetry.

THE CHILDREN

Those many children running in your space,
Have you named them
or shall the gardens do it?
those green children
    climb from the pit
    or do they descend
    from the mountain top?

These very tiny children
    I see now like fish
    of many colors
    in the fishbowl of space.

You are their water.

Translated by Sharif Elmusa and Charles Doria

ALL OF THEM

Everybody said it was useless
Everybody said, "you're trying to lean on sun dust"
    that the beloved before whose tree I stand
        can't be reached

Everybody said, "you're crazy to throw yourself
    headlong into a volcano and sing"
Everybody said that salty mountain
    won't yield even one glass of wine
Everybody said, "You can't dance on one foot"
Everybody said there won't be any lights at the party
That's what they all said
but everybody came to the party anyway

Translated by Sharif Elmusa and Charles Doria

LIKE THE WHITE

From blue sky birds come
bearing bright kerchiefs in their beaks

From lilac sky moon yawns
        weary from not sleeping
        washing her face
        in the water of wakefulness
        then sets to work

From azure sky the dreams of strong nations stir
harnessing alert steeds to assert themselves

From the rose unfold the desires
        that fold the banners of modesty
        unfurling the red flag
        that breaks all established rule

From the joy I see in your eyes
        I begin like a myth
        Looking behind me
        I find only swords
        that wave like thickets
        of branches in the storm

When your cry assaults me
        the current sweeps me away
        where neither ship nor shore
        can gather me in

I desire you
as the white does all colors.

Translated by Sharif Elmusa and Charles Doria

FROM: STANDING WHILE WE DIE

Book of the defeated man:
In you let me write
one red letter that plants
green sadness leading to crystal joy
so that a song comes dancing forth
dressed in elf's clothing

Book of the fallen man:
You know what it means to a man
to live without song
live his wedding without feeling joy
live without a sky that knows him
his life ignored, address unknown?

Book of the future:
Set down the history
of our love of our land
for the effective word
record a moon, record a child
record a branch that grows
out of a fighter's sacrifice

Book of the resistance fighter:
Flame comes from the beating pulse
rebellion from the vanquished heart
revival from the bleeding wound
and our message is still a river of moons

Translated by Sharif Elmusa and Charles Doria

INTERROGATION

This terror in whose thrall I am
I have inherited

From the knock that comes in the night
And has no appointed time
Being given at all times.

Translated by Lena Jayyusi and Christopher Middleton

Yasin Taha Hafiz (b. 1938)

Iraqi poet. Educated in Baghdad, he is currently editor-in-chief of the pres-
tigious magazine, *Al-Thaqafa al-Ajnabiyya* (Foreign Culture), issued by the
Ministry of Information in Baghdad. His poetry reveals an interest in self-
analysis and in the personal experience of daily life, which he delineates in
graphic detail. He has published several collections of poetry, including *The
Tower* (1976) and *Abdallah and the Dervish* (1980). He has also published
some critical studies and several translations from English.

THE GAZELLE

Incessantly
A wild gazelle
Leaps and flounces,
Runs, madly glances, looks around
                                        Right
And left
In fear of a trap

This wild rebel
Is tethered now in a stone bower
She remembers her quick leapings
How she fell
How they jumped on her . . .
Reprovingly she looks
At her tragic world

In this little coffee house
I am alone
My spirit is tethered to a fence
Powerless to run
To the nearest tree
It contemplates the crowd moving
The flood of the street

And a desire swells deep
Inside it
For the great escape
That can expand the spirit
In this human wilderness.

Translated by Sharif Elmusa and Christopher Middleton

WORDS AND TRUTH

These city streets, the labyrinthine black roads
These tubes, they suck me in
I hear the rustle of dry fronds, owls in the roof
I hear the chink of money on the brain
Those who resent us patting us on the shoulder

No, Sir, I said
Then stopped, remembering the face
Of a country I had for a long time yearned for
I wished I could turn into oil
Into loaves of bread and into fruit
I wished . . . but I had not turned into anything at all
Down the streets of the city now I slipped
I shouted (in my heart): "I'll keep myself clean,
I'll stay . . ." but then I completely lost the thread

In this street of the rushing human wave
There was dancing
Signs with inscriptions. A film, a murder
Down the city streets I slipped as down long tubes
To the square where I had wished
To meet the lady I had been told came every night
To general applause. Joyfully she'd come down
Among the neon lights and microphones.
But this is my fortieth evening here and I see nothing.
Has anyone seen her?
    The lady has the time
    The lady has the joy
    The lady has her homeland

O well I could do worse
Than read the signs, telling myself and her:
    Nothing in it for me
    I know there are things I wish for
    And dream about
    I know I can touch them, even

But

    Hypocritical words
    And only one thing's true:
    Nothing in it for me.

A haberdashery now and a lady
Just like the one that I imagine, in she comes
Ten minutes, takes her fur and turns away
The chauffeur opens the door . . . in she slips
This lady, the dream, the temporary joy . . .
All disappear

    Hypocritical words
    And only one thing's true:
    Nothing in it for me.

Thousands of faces have crowded the neons of Spring
The microphones and the vehicles
Observation machines . . . But now they've gone away
Perhaps somebody glimpsed her crossing the square
Perhaps somebody saw her face clearly
Perhaps some people took away gifts she gave
But I saw nothing!
In my room the books are climbing the walls
My face is alone with the desk
I'm thinking:
She might have been the woman
Who stepped out of the bus when I was getting in?
Or the maid who enchanted her master?
Let her be what she likes

    My words are hypocritical
    And only one thing's true:
    Nothing in it for me

I only have this city with its labyrinthine tubes
My skin is bursting with the din of machines
Smelling of kerosene and gas
My face was white but now it's motley hued
With the minutes quickly passing
You read
Numbers and addresses and you read
What is flung in your face from office and shop and sign
I have no other road to the lady
   I have seen the truth
      I deserve to see her, don't I?
And tripping here I have collapsed over a heap
Of newspapers:

O swoon of love! You were my silken coverlet
And my deep, deep well . . .

Translated by Sharif Elmusa and Christopher Middleton

A WOMAN

In the Kifah Street, near the Fadl Mosque
   One evening I happened to notice
A woman crossing the street
   A stranger she was
Flitting through time
   Swathed in a black cloak
   On her face the stamp of bygone days
   And a shadow of ancient Babylon
She might be a hierodule who'd come out
From the temple darkness to the market place
Perhaps to buy an incense burner, or a candle
To light up the gloom of the cloister.

I followed her, gazing at her,
Approaching her, wanting to say a word,
Then drew back:
      Ah! The awsomeness of bygone times!

Translated by Salma Khadra Jayyusi and John Heath-Stubbs

BREAKING THE PRECEPTS

When we were small, folks taught us these precepts
Concerning trees: he'll go to Paradise
Who smothers the fire of a burning tree,
It is a sin to cut off water from a fruiting tree,
You can eat fruit to your heart's content,
It is hallowed; but God will strike you dead
If you destroy even a single fruit;
And fear God's wrath if you cut back a tree in the evening
Or if you dig around its roots.

The village is gone, and gone are the precepts!

A tree bough was beating against the cable
Making the lamp post sway
I climbed the house fence, I caught hold of the cheeky bole
It was evening! All my old lore
Came back to me, and time's misdeeds:
One mad leap down to the ground
And it lay dislocated
It shattered the lamp
And the cable was dangling
And my forehead was bleeding
But my gaze froze:
How white it was, it put me to shame
The flesh of the tree!

Translated by Salma Khadra Jayyusi and John Heath-Stubbs

Buland al-Haidari (b. 1926)

Iraqi poet. Born into a Kurdish family, he studied in Baghdad and was a political activist from his early youth. He lived in exile in Beirut between 1963 and 1976, then returned to Baghdad. At present he lives in London. From the beginning, he was involved with the movement to develop the techniques of free verse. He has published seven collections of poetry. The first two, *Songs of the Dead City* (1957) and *Footsteps in an Alien Land* (1965), portrayed his deep political and social alienation, which was never to leave him and which has conveyed, with untiring persistance, the somber tones of terror and suffering caused by oppression and the curtailment of freedom.

THE DEAD WITNESS

Who killed the last fighter?
I know who . . .
Your Royal Highness!
I know who put out his eyes and who
cut off his hands and who
mutilated his glorious dream
I know who . . .
I've watched that youngster grow
long before he was born again
in his vision and longing
long before he lay in ambush
at every bend of the road
long before
his dream spanned all this earth
and his love embraced it
long before he became
sometimes a bleeding knife
I know, Your Royal Highness
who killed that last fighter.

I know who . . .
for a thousand, thousand nights
I stood vigilant at his door
stayed awake in the blackness of his eyes
became part of his bitter nights
part of the rays that shone in his exile.
For a thousand, thousand times
I was the mired blood on his skin.

I know who. . . . .
—Who killed the last fighter?
Who killed the . . .
—I know who . .
—Who killed him?
—Speak out, who?
—If I should say who,
My Royal Prince
I would become
the slain witness of the last fighter.

It was you and I,
My Royal Prince,
You and I!

Translated by Patricia Alanah Byrne with the help of the editor

AGE OF THE RUBBER SEALS

Oh Age of ours
(Age of rubber seals,
of whips rasping on our skins,
of chains without crime)
      Return to us our old eyes
our grim, black doors open
to night and gale.
      Return to us our shadows
shaken by trembling candlelight
in the dark night.
      Return to us
our children bare in winter's anger;
their little hands craving to tear down the sky.

O Age of ours
(Age of rubber seals,
of chains without crime,
of rasping whips)
    Return to us our old eyes
so we can see the victory that looms
in defeat.
    Erect for us
from the feet of locusts in our desert
from the dry cactus
from the limbs of our dead sons
scaffolds that charge us
with anger that can carry us
on a great song.

We're bored with your face plunged in rubber
    implanted
    in the earth
      in crime.

Translated by Patricia Alanah Byrne with the help of the editor

GENESIS

His bed is like his death.
The prince lies down and
the princess:
two shadows abandoned on
an island.

In my island the sun does not rise, nor set
shadows do not grow shorter
nor longer
nor change.
People are not born on this island,
the shadow
sees only its dubious reflection
in the mirror,
never its conscience!

Island-world grows bigger
    time grows bigger
the two shadows move.
Under the weight of night and day
of the noonday sun
Death is born to man
and the cursed and angry devil
is born to the island.

Time revolves,
it drowns man and his death
    and the island.
Nothing is left
but the noonday sun.
Without man's shadow.

Translated by Patricia Alanah Byrne with the help of the editor

DIALOGUE

Sad guard
Haven't you slept?
When will you go to sleep?
You've been awake in our lamps
for a thousand years
crucified between your outstretched hands
for a thousand years
Won't you go to sleep?
—For the twentieth time . . . I want to sleep
but I fall into sleep
and do not sleep
for the fiftieth time
I fall into sleep and do not sleep.
Sleep to the sorrowful guard
is like the blade of a knife.
I'm afraid of falling asleep
I'm afraid of waking up in dreams.

—Let them burn Rome, let them burn Berlin
Let them steal the China Wall!
You *must* fall asleep.
It's time for the sad guard
to have a moment of rest, to sleep.

—Sleep? When every moment
Berlin is burned again and again?
When every hour a wall
is stolen from China?
When between one glance and another
a dragon is born?
I'm afraid of sleeping
for slumber to the sad guard
is like the blade of a knife.

Translated by Patricia Alanah Byrne with the help of the editor

Unsi al-Haj (b. 1937)

Lebanese poet. He studied at al-Hikma College in Beirut and chose jour-
nalism as a career, joining the team of the prestigious Lebanese daily, *Al-
Nahar*, and eventually becoming editor of its weekly cultural publication,
Mulhaq al-Nahar, a job which he still holds. The publication of his volume,
Never (1959), written in prose poetry, launched him as an avant-garde poet.
The volume contains an introduction defending the cause of prose poetry
as an important vehicle of expression. He has published several other col-
lections since. His poetry displayed strong surrealistic leanings at the begin-
ning, but has now moved toward greater simplicity without losing depth
and insight. Of his other collections, the one titled *What Have You Made of
the Gold, What Have You Done with the Rose* (1970) became very popular in
avant-garde circles.

HE KNEW JOY ON EARTH

He looked for her and found her
puzzled what he should do
so he let her go and began
to search for her again when she had disappeared
God! he said when he found her
make my sight large enough to encompass her
make from my stone water to quench her thirst
use me like a prison to wall her in
let me be round her like a wall of gratitude
otherwise break me over her my God
like a storm
at sea

He was lost but when he found her
he knew a little joy on earth
and then he flew to heaven

Translated by Sargon Boulus and Alistair Elliot

THE ONE WHO LAUGHS AND LAUGHS AND LAUGHS

You are the echo when my body calls
tree of abandoned houses
the one who picks for me the words I also pick
at the mention of whose name I lose my words
You are my yearning and my finding out
bride of the soul and instincts
and mother of desires
You are my silent screams and my white mare
that tramples down my night of stars
You carry my sword now in domestic fragments
you who are brighter than the fruit-tree blossom
and stronger than wild fruit
blue lily of pain who laughs and laughs and laughs

Translated by Sargon Boulus and Alistair Elliot

THE WOLF

In the grownups' stories for the young
there is always a wolf
behind stones
behind journeys
behind trees
behind flower beds

And the wolf breaks out
in the grownups' stories
to eat the young

The grownups left
the young arrived
the young left too

When there wasn't a wolf
to eat me so I could go to sleep
I wept for twenty years
and died longing for you
dear wolf
longing for you!

Translated by Sargon Boulus and Alistair Elliot

BLUE CREST OF FONDNESS

my shifting ground from season
to season became an excuse
for begging meals, poised
for more migration
and, like the birds in their
wise flight, I kept on
beating from ocean
to ocean
from peaks to branches
from night to night
till I was struck
with the reputation of a gentle madness

after we have seen how
wise birds are
I remind you that
it is in the nature
of beings
to hurt themselves

lying on stones I was
a tortoise
carved into trunks
of trees and armrests
carved inside rings
carved on mountains' ankles
and I saw space
    then I really saw space
when I found it beautiful I fell
in love with a dove
who carried me up high
she came down in the dust
when I admired
the fragrance of the earth
I lifted my spirit off the dove
and it stood erect like a spear
in space

no other fragrance actually
after Danae's

I laid the treasure between her wings
over my knees
she lowered down
ignorance and knowledge
and in my mouth she hid
witnesses of love
together we knew
the unnamable things

like a spear she froze
and lived like lightning
I wallowed in dust like a dervish
a fortune-teller in my tent
an acrobat, a wanderer
my strings droned like a bee
storming inside a bottle

I reminded you before
that beings by impulse
hurt themselves
and that between one being
and another
there is a tortoise and a dove
likewise between a tortoise
and a dove
the kiss of solitude in flight
generous blade of the impossible
and the blue crest of fondness

let my departure
from season to season
become a plea to you all
I am the truest testimony
on this matter sealed like glue
illiterate like the lion
which has a simple name
among the names:
a fable.

Translated by Sargon Boulus and Alistair Elliot

AUTUMN LEAVES ARE VIRGIN MARY

That melancholy that inhabited me once has died.
Master Time, with its winds and rains, has taken its place.

Now, I find poetry strange:
I call children "children,"
I call a woman's knee "a woman's knee,"
and a severed willow branch "a severed willow branch."
But, in the days of that tearful mist,
I never spoke the prevailing, the common names,
not just out of pride
for, in the days of melancholoy I called
autumn leaves, for example, "Virgin Mary"
and how I felt they really were!
As I said,
I never called these things by name
I only saw them,
and Ah! How rich I was!
Everything that touched me, charmed me.
Everything I touched, I charmed.
I was not ignorant,
but I did not know.
I believed that I was immortal,
until, one morning,
        the melancholy evaporated
and I did not know how
it died like musk!

Translated by Patricia Alanah Byrde with the help of the editor

————Danae: daughter of King Acrisius of Argos, who did not want her to marry because he
had been told that he would be killed by his daughter's son. He kept her imprisoned, but
Jupiter came to her in the disguise of a shower of gold. Their meeting resulted in a son,
Perseus (who was later the slayer of the Gorgon Medusa). Danae and her child were set adrift
in a chest but were saved by a fisherman on the island of Seriphos.

Khalil Hawi (1925–1982)

Lebanese poet and scholar. He was educated in Beirut and Cambridge, where he obtained his Ph.D. in Arabic literature. He was professor of Arabic literature at the American University of Beirut and had been working on the production of the *Encyclopedia of Arabic Poetry*, of which four volumes have appeared, before his unexpected death by his own hand in protest at the Israeli invasion of Lebanon in June 1982. He was one of the foremost pioneers of modern Arabic poetry, and his death put an end to a unique poetic experiment which relied on symbolization, a mythical sense of time and experience, and above all a pan-Arab vision of great purity and ardent sincerity. After his first collection, *River of Ashes*, which made an immediate impact in 1958, he published four other collections.

FLUTE AND WIND IN THE HERMIT'S CELL

(At Cambridge University)

1.

Ink bottles and pens
stand between me and the door
muttering complaints
that echo inside my head.
Sheets of paper pile up.
Worries stack up,
to trip my every step
on my way to the door
and the road outside.

2.

These are lies, all lies.
My blood boils, scalds,
then scolds me.
How long will this contamination

continue? How long should
I spit out my brains and cough
out my lungs merely for a chair
and a title? How long shall I sleep
with this preserved mummy?
I am not one of you, not one
of your fellowship of monks and
ascetics with dehydrated flesh
in cold cells.
My blood is too thick
to turn to water.
I am living a lie.
Take me to the city square
and rip the university insignia
from my lapel and strip me naked.

3. THE FLUTE

"God protect my child, my son.
He is his father's treasure,
the staff and bridge of our house,
he who carries its weight and burden . . .
The new year waits outside the door, my daughter,
and tomorrow he will return to you.
Have patience."

But tomorrow she might be dead
She has withered waiting
for me. In fantasy her blood
mingled with mine long before
she could taste the pleasure of flesh.
And she might die
with the flute she loves
dragging its sadness through
the evening hours. She might die
with the drooping white roses, she,
whose wedding gown was woven
by winter snow.
All day long her funeral
cortege winds through my nerves.

All day long the flute
she loves shrills its sad refrain.
She dies before she can celebrate
or know the comfort of a home,
the luxury and strength of a hand
that can provide shade.

4. THE WIND

All day long,
O Lord, to break away
from my mother and father, to escape
from my books, my cell,
from her who lives and dies waiting,
to step over hearts
including my own,
to drink from bitterness
without turning bitter
so that words will bloom again
on my lips, and my road
lead to the dark Bedouin girl
in the oasis of her untouched flesh,
in the valley of the noonday sun,
in the bitter sandstorm.
That wayward Bedouin girl
cannot be tamed except
by him who wears the patience
of a camel. And him in
whose heart a child builds a paradise.
Except by him who lives on
strange fruits
some grown with difficulty
some picked with ease.

She rises shaking off desert tales
from her braids, chanting,
whirling wherever I point
but eluding me
like a joyous storm.
The wind has its season
of rage.

Alone with the dark Bedouin girl,
alone with the words,
I drink from the bitter cup
without feeling the bitterness.

The wind blows wherever my fingers point
and the virgin soil aches
at the sound of night thunder,
drinks in the dream of rain,
and turns it into vine,
and roots of the pine.
What else but to join
the white domes into a single dome,
reflecting in its glow
the forests of young cities
that welcome all.

Can the waters of
a single sea be separated?

Now I see the peacock
sailing in a fan of its feathers
swaying
in the shade of fences
thinking that
elegant poems and roses
can cover up the shame
of his comic existence.
He has two breasts
greater than any nursing mother's.
Harvests gold and ivory.
If he were worthy,
I would have led him to Golgotha,
to the Cross. But he is not.
And I leave him to the winds
of sand,
mud and dung
to cover the honey and treasure
of his breasts
The season of the raging wind
will wipe off the antique
and rusted fences of the mind.

5. THE HERMIT

The hermit questions me in my imaginings
"You have neglected your studies?
Were you following the jinni?
Or were you tempted by Satan?"

"I was alone with the dark Bedouin girl
drinking from the bitter cup
without turning bitter."

"Mad riddles!" the hermit
returns to his old goods.

6.

All day long blurred
images visit my mind
like waves
My mother and father and she
who lives and dies in waiting.
The defeated hermit in my head
gathers up his strength and
begins to scold again
while I wake and see
a desert of paper, old paper,
piled between me and the door.
And beyond, a valley of more paper
and beyond them both
a lifetime of old paper.

Translated by Diana Der Hovanessian with Sharif Elmusa

THE BRIDGE

It is.enough for me to
have the children of my comrades.
Their love is bread and wine.
From the harvest
I have provisions equal to the day
and can anticipate

the feast of harvest whenever
a new light shines
in my village.

I have never been in love
with the dead.
Neither with perfumery, gold,
wine and treasures.
A wizened bat is born
out of such love.
Where is He who destroys,
and gives life?
Where is He who restores
His creation cleansing him
with oil and sulphur
from the stench of pus?
Where is He who destroys,
gives life, and restores
by bringing forth young eagles
again from the progeny
of slaves?
Now the child, bearing no
resemblance to father and mother,
disowns both.

How can our house be cleft
in two with the sea flowing
between old and new?
With a scream, a ripping
of the womb, tearing of veins?
Why are we, who are under
one roof, divided by
seas, walls, deserts
of cold ash and ice?

How lightly they cross the bridge
in the morning.
My ribs, a bridge, stretch out for them,
reaching from the caves, from the swamps
of the East to the new East.

My ribs—a steady bridge for them.
"They'll pass and you will stay alone,
a relic left by priests
to the winds that lash you."

Silence, owl, beating inside by breast!
What does this owl of history
demand of me?
In my coffers are countless
treasures:
joy in the gift of hands,
joy in the essence of life,
joy in memory and faith.
Embers and wine.

I have the children of my comrades.
And their love is bread and wine.

From the harvest I have provisions
equal to the day
And it is enough for me
to anticipate the feast of the harvest.

I do not fear your coming,
season of snow,
for I have stores enough
of embers and wine.

Translated by Diana Der Hovanessian
and by Lena Jayyusi (first translator)

THE MAGI IN EUROPE

"And it came to pass that the Magi, led by the Star of
the East, found the Child, and fell on their knees before Him."

O Magi of the East, did you continue?
Did you follow the ocean flood and
civilization to the new lands?
Did you find what god reveals himself now
again in the cave? Come. The road starts here.
The star shines here. And here again
provisions for your travel.

Let the star of the adventurous lead
you to Paris where you can try the doors
of the laboratories of thought and where
you can discard thinking for celebrations
with buffoons. And in Rome you may watch
the star shroud itself and be
extinguished by the glow of censers
swung by eager priests.
Then in London it can disappear
and lose you in a fog of coal dust and in
ciphers of commerce. And now
it is Christmas night and you have
no star, and no hope left for
finding child or cave. It is midnight
and there is no child in sight. But
what is this tightness in the chest?
A street empties below you. And you follow
the sound of sad laughter past
corridors. Your eyes move from
door to door as you ask for the cave.
And you are told how to reach a door
with a sign, "Earthly Paradise." "A place
with no tempting serpent. And
no divine judge to cast stones.
Here roses have no thorns.
And nakedness is called purity."
You hear, "Now take off those
borrowed faces, those horrible masks
you formed out of chameleon skins."

"But these are our true faces.
They are not masks to put on and
peel off. We are from Beirut.
Don't you know? We are born with
borrowed faces. We are born with
borrowed minds. We are a tragedy.
Thinking is born a whore in our markets
and spends its life inventing
virginity."

"Come on. Take off those borrowed
faces."

And you enter as those who enter
a graveyard night. A fire is lit.
And you see bodies undulating
in a dance to the tune of some
sorcerer. Suddenly the dark ceiling
becomes blue crystal hung with
chandeliers. And the decaying putrid
walls have spigots of pure wine.
And the mud of the street is gold.
The writhing bodies are purified
and no longer clay but merged
into each other as nerve, blood,
heart.

"This is earthly paradise. Now pray.
Heaven is on earth here."
You kneel to worship chemistry
and the magician who fashioned
paradise from burial and grave.
Yes, worship him,
the god who reveals himself in the cave.
Hailing him:
"God of the weary and lost,
god fleeing from the sun's madness
and the terror of certainty, who
conceals himself in the underground
cavern in the land of civilization."

Translated by Diana Der Hovanessian
and by Lena Jayyusi (first translator)

Ahmad ʿAbd al-Muʿti Hijazi (b. 1935)

Egyptian poet. He studied first in Egypt, then worked in journalism before going to France to continue his graduate studies. At present he holds a position in the Department of Arabic Studies at the University of Paris. He has published five collections of poetry, the first of which, *City Without Heart* (1959), made an immediate impact. He treats various subjects in his verse, particularly the problem of alienation and powerlessness in the face of modern city life. His work has a confessional, self-denuding tone that is rather different from much of contemporary Arabic poetry.

RENDEZVOUS IN THE CAVE

Don't ask me for a date,
tomorrow we shall meet regardless,
just as we did today.

Night has driven me here.
Wandering aimlessly I looked for friends
and found only this cave.
I have imposed myself on you
feeling I am still pursued,
I am that ancient shepherd.
And who remembers me?
After I lost my faith,
after I became a heretic,
who remembers me?
Only the beast that tears
soundlessly at my breast.

Your eyes are my last refuge
where I hide my face in your gaze,
waiting for my end
where light is most intense.
Your eyes are grass and dew

where for a moment I spread my shadow
then continue on my way.

Don't ask me to tell you tomorrow
what I have told you today
because I am trying to forget—
O my short-lived love,
I am trying to forget
so that the light of day
will not see me, know me,
and tear the mask from my face.

Once I used to be brave
but I tasted my enemy's food
and was crippled.
I was a wise poet once
but when I managed to make
two different words mean the same
I lost my wisdom, poetry eluded me.
I was a faithful lover once
but now I am robbed of my soul
by day and turn
into a shivering ghost
in the small hours of the night.

When I wake up alone
lying limp on top of my shadow
crushed against the wall
on the floor of our cave,
I ask myself, has our time run out?
I thought it had just begun.

Your eyes are two words never uttered.
Having failed to be spoken
they remain themselves,
two nuns in black habit
waiting despairingly for their wedding night.

Wait for me here every night.
I might show up,
or never come.

Our kiss is long,
the night of our misery warm.

Translated by Sargon Boulus and Peter Porter

THE LONELY WOMAN'S ROOM

She shuts out the city now
by closing the door and lowering the drapes—
she puts on the light by daytime

Those are her things,
the animals of her solitude
reaching up to her from the corners,
and in the wall
a built-in gas stove,
a sink,
and shelves for groceries.
A small exile
with a bed in its recesses,
and a table,
with stories to induce sleep,
and ashtray
and small candles

Everything has its predestined place,
a presence that nourishes itself
on bread and water
from the steps of time,
a mantle and a slumbering
in its shifting shadow

Everything has its lust, its weeping,
the flavor of the body
grown used to solitude,
meditating on itself.
Everything is a mirror
possessing her face,
the same intimacy and brokenness
of her limbs

Perhaps she came in childhood
upon such a place as this,
and a light,
a vase which casts
a shadow on a spotless sheet

Perhaps by way of necklaces
and candelabra, she summons up
a spirit who will take her back
to gardens long since left,
springs where faces spread across
clear water,
smiling in the depth.

It wasn't me
she was talking to,
but somebody else
whose borrowed face
she stared in.

Translated by Sargon Boulus and Peter Porter

SECRETS

(To the handicapped Arab veterans I met in the streets of Paris.)

There . . . you are revealing your secret to me alone.

When you move through foreign cities
you hide your secrets in your grim-colored clothes,
behind black spectacles;
But *here* you reveal your secret to me alone.

Perhaps you saw my blood
sniff at you for a trace of its youth,
or maybe you glimpsed your houses under my skin
and so showed me what you hide.

A strange, beautiful flock
evasive to every call
hiding behind its sagging color
those frozen, inveterate tears.

Your blood surged forth unaware
on roads you had grown attuned to
blood you tried to bar from a wilted hand,
eyes brimming with beads of tears—
And where did you give away your eyes?
Beneath the stars which once shone on my cheek.

Who did you offer your leg to?
I gave it to those who will be born after me.

Look!
You who come
with half your bodies
from villages that lack their share
of the flesh of sons—

Look!
How attractive these foreign cities are,
how much a stranger needs his arm or leg there.
But you pass the city's beauty
like gracious heavenly birds,
and I keep tracking you
lost in its streets,
groping in my own rotting flesh
and entering my grave at night.

Translated by Sargon Boulus and Peter Porter

ELEGIES, OR THE STATIONS OF THE OTHER TIME

That time stands up vertically
in the rushed span of horizontal days,
separates itself from the pouring strands
of lit-up streets.

How can departure from the sun,
from warm moments, be measured?
There was a time like winter,
when childhood chickens pricked me teasingly,
in a courtyard spread with remnants
of withered fruits.

A time like sundown
  at the height of noon,
  with the sun in the zenith
I was watching a bird
crucify itself in the nets of light
wondering when it would wake up
to resume its roving in the heart of this
frightening whiteness
till it disappeared
and the thread was completed
from the point of beginning
to arrival.

A time like sin—
though still a child
I'm middle-aged, befuddled by wine.
Failings nip at the flesh of my soul.
Not to mention my wicked falls.

A time both present and impossible—
I lured the guest, encouraged him to drink profusely,
thinking he might spill out his secrets,
but he stayed composed until my drinks were finished
while I crumbled on my side of the table,
vomiting up all that I've lived
for many loathsome years.

   Mornings, the grounds of the city open their mouths
to the little women
who rush out with sleepy faces.
 You have a small nest on the surface of Paris,
 little lady, like the nest of a bird
 perched on a sill.
 What do you see before you
 but your city's sloping black tiles?
 You have a little rope to hang your bras,
 a flower vase,
 a bed.
Mornings the women rush out. Like birds

with tinted feathers, on escalators,
aging rapidly, staying awake
with perfumes and tobacco
emitting a fragrance their bodies mull over,
these bodies now fitted onto a frightening machine.

Every day he has this experience!

A SONG:

> You are exquisite
> and I am middle-aged
> contemplating my face on the surface of the Seine,
> smiling in tears.

> You are exquisite
> looking for love, but I follow
> lost traces.
> We should have met when I was young—
> then I would have loved you to madness and
> we could have departed together.

The human body descends alone to the pit,
searches for itself in stations,
sliding down dark alleyways
that transpose it to a faraway time.

Sad human body penetrates deeper,
hops like a monkey from one darkness in the road
to another,
following the traces of a woman who faced him
but she turned his eyes away.
He watched her in the glass of shop windows
till he disappeared. He is dazed,
late for his appointment,
enters apologizing,
taking off his clothes,
beating himself with his own hands.
Regretfully he offers up his limbs
to the throbbing machines.
Then he looks around,

finds himself thrown back
to the beginning of the same road.

Every day he has this experience.

Translated by May Jayyusi and Naomi Shihab Nye

Rashid Husain (1936–1977)

Palestinian poet from a village near Haifa. He first worked as a school-teacher, but was dismissed by the Israelis for his political beliefs. An organizer of the Al-Ard party in Israel, which was founded in 1958 and later banned, he spent many years in Israeli prisons. He became an editor of the Arab journal *Al-Fajr* (The Dawn), which was banned in 1962. He translated selections from Hayyim Bialik's poetry from Hebrew into Arabic and translated Palestinian folk songs into Hebrew. After the June 1967 war, he chose exile and lived in poverty in New York City, dying in a fire at his apartment. Husain has three collections, the last of which, *I Am the Land, Don't Deprive Me of the Rain*, is his best. His poetry is mainly concerned with the predicament of the Palestinians under siege both in Israel and in the diaspora.

LESSONS IN PARSING

THE FIRST LESSON

He was sixty years old . . .
And still teaching.
One day he came into class and said:
"Parse this sentence: The teacher came."
We thought he was joking,
So we laughed and answered:
    "*Came*, an active verb,
    The teacher . . . !!?"
Suddenly we understood . . . in a second
So we were silent . . .
We heard him muttering:
    "*Came*, an active verb,
    The teacher . . . !"
The teacher did not come!
The police brought him
And he will teach.

THE SECOND LESSON

Our classes grew up together until
Our teacher neared seventy but was still teaching.
For instance, the teacher said:
My teacher dreams of the revolution, but does not fight—
A sentence complete a thousand times over,
And he who parses it becomes a fighter.
So we were silent,
We said nothing
But our silence was the struggle,
Our silence was . . .
But there was a boy in class who had fed the earth with his hands,
Its olives nourished his lips.
"Adnan" was his name . . . a peasant without land.
He fought not with silence,
He fought with everything within him.
That day I watched the teacher juggle the rules of grammar;
He taught:
"*My teacher* is not a subject
Dreams is not an active verb
Of is governed by a preposition
The Revolution does not take a preposition
But
Does not fight is the truth"

THE LESSON BEFORE THE LAST

The next day the teacher entered the classroom
He was happy and mysterious like the scent of oranges.
A child at seventy, he greeted us and said:
They put Adnan in prison.
"Parse it, you young girls,
Parse it, you young men!"
We were happy . . . we wept and exclaimed:
"*Adnan* is a subject
Prison is an object" . . .
And we burned the rules of syntax,
We burned the chains of grammar
And converted to the struggle.

Translated by Lena Jayyusi and Peter Porter

JERUSALEM . . . AND THE HOUR

In Jerusalem the hour was: someone killed
                             someone wounded
                             and a minute gained

The hour was: a child's legs
Stolen from him by napalm
      and when he went on walking
They even stole his road.
The hour was an Arab O
The hour was the birth of truth.

The hour struck . . . it struck
But the people's protector was in a bar,
Suppliant to a mistress
Making her a gift of the people's blood,
roses watered with humiliation
never fed by garden soil.
The hour was a gigantic O
The hour was the birth of truth.

The hour was
that nails should sprout on trees,
on stone, on flowers, on water,
that a million men might conceive—
So a great idea might be born,
So a revolution might be born.
But the hour was
it was
The hour was sterile
Then the hour in Jerusalem became
virgins who got pregnant in seconds
gave birth in seconds
and in seconds
the hour in Jerusalem turned into struggle
                             and a minute gained
The hour strikes . . . it strikes
The hour cries with love, with torture, with desire
The legless child walks on his hands and eyes
To carry dreams, bread and greetings to a fighter.
He whispers the simplest prayer a child ever said:

"They've killed my legs, they've stolen my road,
And so I must stay here
Changed into a grave and fight."

The hour struck its final chimes
then died.
Jerusalem had no more need of clocks,
A little girl destroyed their clocks.
Her age—a hundred million victims,
A nation which despite
Sedation and stupor
Will one day rise in wrath.

Whenever a child passes those
Who occupy and rule Jerusalem,
A child, a little girl,
Their eyes and their devices
Search in her breast, her womb, her mind
for weapons, for a bomb.
And when they discover nothing (O)
they insist: "This little girl was born here,
All those born in Jerusalem
Shall be made into bombs."
And they are right.
All born in the shadow of bombs
Shall become bombs.

Translated by Lena Jayyusi and Peter Porter

Hasab al-Shaikh Ja'far (b.1942)

Iraqi poet. Born in Maisan, Iraq, he studied literature in Moscow and now works as Director of the Language Section at the television and radio station in Baghdad. In his poetry, there is a mythic sense of history, envisaging human experience in terms of ever-recurring cultural patterns, but also acknowledging present-day dilemmas and today's special kinds of repression. He has published four collections, of which *Visit to the Sumerian Lady* (1974) and *In the Mirror Across the Wall* (1977) are the most famous. He has also translated selected poems from Pushkin, Mayakovsky, and Alexander Bloch.

SIGNATURE

Every day I see her in front of clinics, surgeries, huddled and clasping her little girl, staring at the passing elegant women. Her own dilapidated house glows in its village of smoke and straw. She prepares tea for us. Her husband arrives with the political mail from the dark palm grove. At the end of the night we leave some of our secrets behind in his house, where we discuss countryside problems. Trembling with cold over a dim lantern. Suspicious foreign birds scream. The surgeries close up. And the glittering cabarets open to reveal soiled nakedness. On which bank did he stumble to fall bleeding, stopped by the bullet in his shoulder?

> He said nothing
> but bled in the stone police station
> until the night ended
> and they wrapped him up
> in the bloody mat.

The political mail waits in the dark roots of the palm grove. The door of the crumbling house bursts open. A bloody dust falls. And the net of the law falls over her. Water, let me go to the bank of the river to carve his face on its stones. Let me hang, like posters, his papers on the palm trees. Let our dim lantern be lit with an eternal flame. Let the surgery doors spring open and al-Rumaila fling its arms around the palms where we first felt the pulse of politics. Waters, take me to that bank where I can spread the waves of his shirt where the bullet pierced. Let me catch a boat to cross. And write on the cheerful face of the water.

> Let me write a name
> which the files have folded away
> in the stone police station
> to be wrapped in a bloody mat.

Her name fades on petitions. Every day in front of government offices I see her clasping her little girl under her cape and staring at the elegant women passing. The agricultural superintendent scolds her through the steam of coffee and smoke of his cigarette. Waters, take me to that bank where I can dig in the dark palm grove, and take out sheets of growing grass to hang like flags over the collapsing house in al-Rumaila. On the horizon, the stone police station. Water, take me to the bank where I can carve a face on the rocks. I see him every day in front of the surgeries, humiliated. Elegant women pass by. I am carving something about palm trees where we began to feel the pulse of politics.

Translated by Diana Der Hovanessian with Salma Khadra Jayyusi

DESCENT OF ABU NUWAS

(Shortened version)

Jinan means eternal waiting.
Jinan means defeat.
Jinan means death by your own hand.

Be what you choose, Ibn Hani. Be a stone. Be the drinking companion whose black laugh coughs up his old defeats. Be the road to the tavern where the parrot is everyone's favorite friend.

Your banner remains the muddy coat you dragged, tossed
in the tavern and forgot there.

At end of night

You bend under pearl clouds to hold up the walls and pull out the illusory thread from wine bottles as you sit among drunken friends until the dawn brightens your face.

The wine skin is empty and your coat is in tatters. Between the star of
Babylon and its light there is a door and a door keeper. A virgin with small
round breasts since Noah's times.

We follow the starlight
and descend damp stairs.
The sound of our steps fades
on worn-out stone.

Oh space, receding space, you can repeat anything except the echo.

Jinan is in every land,
in every spark and fire
Be what you will, Ibn Hani,
be rock, or echo,
space or dew
waiting for her caravan to pass,
the wine jug is where we will meet

to improvise a hunting song writing it in the dust of the horse hooves,
expecting a gift from the emperor for it. Perhaps an estate

For the hunt I have chosen
the dog with the sharpest nose.

Repeat, Ibn Hani, in the pure cup I found the face
the face that pursues me.
And the hills are her thighs, her fragrance is the east wind
and my bed is a wilderness.
The way to the beloved is the closed door with the guard from Basrah.

. . . .

But in every tavern, in every willow,
there is some news of Jinan.

We follow her dancing caravan in a cloud of dust, never coming close.

. . . .

You were never two
how can you be one?

Her face fades in the last window of your rushing bus. Whenever signs say
she is coming, she disappears. Every Jinan disappears, wears her shadow,
becomes the escaping bird.

Every wilting rose is Jinan,
the ashes of the wind,
the dying flame, the dry grass

consumed by fire, lightning, glittering sand lifted by wind, the pheasant
in flight, Jinan. And so Ibn Hani, be what you like,

a wave, or a sail
to the Hakaman of sorrow.
Be our Magi huddled in a tavern.
Be the confidant of gilded dolls,
or the beggar at the door
of her gruff master.

Songs are the horses tamed at the gathering of deaf men. Be a stone or an echo. Be space or dew waiting for Jinan's caravan. Be a face or its shadow on the jug. The night is a drum. And though you are slapped and whipped, the Babylonian star fades in its dome, longing for your face and your songs. Surrounded by your drunken friends the light of the dawn turns into a lavender in your hands. The wine skin is empty, your coat frayed, and your face the object of snickers. Be the flame or the ashes.

Jinan means eternal waiting.
Jinan is defeat.
Jinan is suicide.

Translated by Diana Der Hovanessian with Salma Khadra Jayyusi

——Al-Rumaila: a village in the South of Iraq

——Abu Nuwas: famous early Abbasid poet who wrote much on wine, love, but also other formal topics. He was bisexual, but his unrequited love for the beautiful slave girl, Jinan, was made famous through his poetry about her.

——Jinan: see Abu Nuwas.

——Ibn Hani: another name for Abu Nuwas

——Hakaman: the name of the palace of Jinan's master.

Salma Khadra Jayyusi (b.1926)

Palestinian poet, critic, and anthologist. Born in Salt in East Jordan, she spent her childhood in Acre, then lived in Jerusalem where she finished her secondary education. She graduated in Arabic and English literature from the American University of Beirut and, later, obtained a Ph.D. from the University of London. Her doctoral thesis, *Trends and Movements in Modern Arabic Poetry* was published by Brill, Leiden, in two volumes. She has traveled widely and has lived in many places in the Middle East, Europe, and the United States, first as a diplomat's wife, then as professor of Arabic literature. She has taught at the Universities of Khartoum, Algiers, and Constantine, and in America at the Universities of Utah, Washington, and Texas. She has published her poetry and critical writings in many journals in the Middle East and abroad. Her first collection, *Return from the Dreamy Fountain*, was published in 1960. The June 1967 war made her suspend publication of her second *diwan*, and since then she has published little of the poetry she has written. Shocked at the fact that very little Arabic literature has been translated into the leading modern languages, in 1980 she founded PROTA (Project of Translation from Arabic), which aims at the dissemination of Arabic culture abroad, and to this enterprise she dedicates her full time and energy. In addition to the present anthology, she has finished editing two others: *Modern Arabic Fiction and Drama* (forthcoming, Columbia University Press), and *The Literature of Modern Arabia* (forthcoming, Kegan Paul International). She has edited several single-author books and collections, and is now working on an anthology of Palestinian literature and, with Roger Allen, an anthology of contemporary Arabic theater.

SCRAPPING LIMITS

Did I do it
> step over the line?
>> yes
> do my lovers know
>> how   I   prayed   God

                        I would
                                stretching
                                        beyond sky
                        to shatter wall
        after wall
                                        in my way?

Scrapping limits
        I crossed to a world
    where lovers never sleep
                                they are so far gone
                into each other
        leaping fences
                                I abandoned my sleepy fountain
                where I loved and drowsed
        completely
                                quiet and content.
I found fire's seed and entered
        watching the innocence in my dreams
                        die
                hypocritic standing guard
                                eager to become my tyrant

High noon sun blaze
        I pass the impassable
                        desire ending my journey
                        deserting the twilit world herded
                                        gulled by the shadows
                even moss casts
                on the walls that hem me in

Spotlight I can't get out of
        I won't strip for you
                        reveal myself
        I love dark corners
                with their wrap-around night
                I love staying home nights
                with   one I love
                to be strange
                        the stranger at the crowd's heart

No Salma there's no turning back
                harden now your tired heart
     and push on
              you completely the creature
                      of the noon-day sun

Where you were before   is a chasm now
         column of salt, body nailed to the gibbet
               going bare discloses
           loving heart's courage

Eyes ahead go on the way you came
        humble road's steepest
               walk up the stairs of hell

When you're there
       at your feet a spring
              gushes free of the rock

Translated by the author and Charles Doria

THE SHIP OF LOVE

Love, hide me in your breast.
No one is looking.
Don't even let the perfume of air
come between us,
one breath from the past
that could stir painful remembrance:
now that sky is ours,
I want to forget all earthly care.

Star of those who have lost the way,
rain down your light on me,
shine into the shy center
of my labyrinthine soul
the years have made dark
and be my sure-footed guide.

Dream, envelop my heart
in imaginary finery
while my rose of desire

pours forth her ardent perfume.
I am become passion.
Enfold me, heavenly wings,
lift me beyond the clouds.

This is bliss.
My heart can hold no more.
Call to me the wretched of the earth,
those who tried love and lost,
who flowered in hell,
for I would tell them
of the mountains we have climbed,
you and I, my love, together
how we made paradise home
and found the lighthouse
beaming us to snug harbor.
Yes, call to me
all who have lost.

Here my heart overflows its banks.
River, swathe me in your currents,
drown me in my own longing,
shade my breasts with your dark water,
pull me from the abyss
where my swamped ship slowly dances,
tugged this way and that,
on your sunless sandy bottom,
where the watchmen of my heart
fell asleep a long time ago
till you woke them with love's cockcrow!

Love, let me share your breast and hide.
I shall bestow my love on all creatures
Take me to the fountain of despair,
I shall summon it to new life,
recalling dead vision to fresh joy
by the ecstasy just conceived,
welling up in my heart
until it can no longer be contained.

You dreaming on the road,
go sleep somewhere else

and leave it to those
who purely mad sweep the sea of life,
who share the mad whispers
of the heart prompting love.

My ship splits the sea's waves,
rocking on his noble flanks,
he flows alone, alone!
with the ocean's roar,
the bubbling tides,
never awakening,
never falling asleep,
sways, floats, sinks
into the dark deeps.

O tent of those who've lost the way,
invite me to your shade,
there's no place here for the unhappy,
for the frowning face—
    Let me be free!
I was born on briny whitecaps,
I found where the sun shines,
how the Pleiades glow at night,
how the heart of loving day
is made resplendent by our devotion.
    Let me be free!
Venus' star is on the rise,
I surrender to the wind,
lighter than it I am carried aloft,
clasping the secrets of true love,
I know how to see truth in things.

Translated by the author and Charles Doria

APRIL WOMAN

Poem to My Son

I am an April woman:
December ash that consumes itself
                frightens me

My son, hide me while you rocket to the stars
spreading over the earth like grass
Winter thunderstorm will drink down
my river flowing with love's secrets,
muffling that music in whose echoes
                    you were born.

But you shrug your shoulders:
            "This woman is planted in time
            she bridges the air like a dove
                    a thousand years old.
She is a willow, I know her:
            bend her—she springs back
She is a palm tree, I know her
            pick her fruit—she makes more
                    honey and dates
She is a cypress tree, I know her
            she never loses her leaves
What do December storms mean to her?"

Yet the winter winds do howl, my son,
night and day I yearn for you
for your sweet sarcastic voice
your voice wise and cruel, innocent and selfish.

Night and day I miss you
We both live in space, in the wind and the rain
Each of us drinks his own wine
            each of us is poured in his own glass
for you were made of my elements.

I gave you:
            my impetuous soul
            my constant disappearance
                    flitting far away across the world
            my chronic elusiveness
            a will like rock, loyal
                    as the true stars
                    in the sky's valleys.
And I gave you:
            love's ecstasy

the will to conquer
passionate devotion
and the enchantment of the spirit
    in the presence of holy fire.

Should I blame you?

And you gave me:
    a promise and pledge
    security forever delayed
    love that's here and is never here
Should you blame me?
    I am a wild gazelle
    you are rock
    My head is bloodied.

Translated by the author and Charles Doria

ON VISITING THE M.D. ANDERSON

(In memory of Anne Royal, who translated this poem three years before her tragic death in 1985)

I saw you in Houston, waiting for the verdict
to decree life or death for you, one foot rooted
in death row, beating out an even song:
"Drive this death from me, scatter
these thousand seeds of death
from my tortured blood, those seeds
that dropped a steel anchor
deep into my heart's heart."

Where, stranger, did the crab monster strike?
Your face pale as bloodless wheat?
Where has his stinging tail
plunged into your flesh?
Tomorrow drink the cup of bitterness
and slowly watch the horrors of the battle
you must wage with this beast of many tails:
Watch and tire, tire and rest, then fight again, again.

Life here is a dagger: honed and sharp;
Here fellow bodies await the knife—twisted flesh,
half-slit veins, bloodless, dwindling sacks of bones,
chancred, chopped, flayed, hairless . . .
(these bald heads the beacons of this battle,
gleaming under the pitiless neon
that glazes their eyes,
grieving eyes whose hopes the beast has wounded,
eyes still brimming with the will to live).

For tomorrow, silent stranger, my countryman,
you will drink the bitter worm and the still more bitter cure
soon you will join the ranked heroes,
the legions of those who fight back.
For, yes, you are one more hero,
Your body made nothing, drowned in frothing quicklime
Now that that eight-armed demon makes your flesh burst
with alien cells that wall you in,
Jailing you in ransom to death . . .

You are one more hero who dared enter the wolf's lair,
selling him slices of your corpse: arm, leg, breast, neck,
letting him rape you head to spine to feet,
Giving him your body to mar
(the way he will my sister
who stands here beside me like a fallen queen).
But you will not yield!

You are one more hero who mocked the hyena's slashing laugh
He who tears you to shreds indelibly
But you will fight, fight him in an equal fight.
Life is the terrible sword shall contest
death and all his minions.

This is the war that only lovers,
consumed by love of life, will wage.
This is the war that flies
a single banner: "Live or die!"
a war where all: captive, victim, warrior—are one,
The enemy the crab tyrant of a thousand claws
a million poisoned cells.

This hollow crab, stranger friend,
where did he sting you?
I see you before me possessing that calm
those lambs display who climb
Mount Arafat for their sacrifice.
For you are the best of heroes,
of those who decline the victim's part,
You who crossed oceans
to slay the crab within
and then return.

And then return?
I hope
I hope!

Translated by Anne Royal and Charles Doria

——M.D. Anderson: the famous cancer clinic and hospital in Houston, Texas.

——Bitter cure: in Arabic it says "the CMF," which is the medicine given to cancer patients to arrest metastasis. It can cause great nausea and loss of hair.

——Mount Arafat: the mountain near Mecca where the Muslim pilgrimage ends and animals are sacrificed.

Shafiq al-Kamali (1930–1984)

Iraqi poet. He studied first in Baghdad, then went to Cairo to pursue studies in literature at its university. Early in his youth he entered the political struggle in his country and was imprisoned many times, but later, with the change of rule, he was given many important responsibilities, serving as Minister of Youth and Information and as head of the Union of Arab Writers for many years. He has published three *diwans: The Departure of Rain* (1972), *Marwan's Worries and His Tall Beloved* (1974), and *Sighs of the Arab Prince* (1975).

DISPOSITION NO. I

I loved you,
Many others were crowding
The way to your heart,
Yet still you appeared,
Lips thirsting,
The fear of slander
Kindling a glint in your eyes—
Casting a shadow, damp and slippery,
Over the pathway

I tell you
It is hard to reconcile opposites,
It is hard to love you
You who want to be crossing the distance
Under a canopy of fear—
Go back,
It is not possible
To be born without pain;
All fountainheads of light
Reveal truth in purity,
But hide your true feelings
Under the forms, and you shun
Naked truth

Do you know that the beaches
At night are a world
Of depravity? That affairs there
Grow in secrecy, words are caverns
Dripping with lies?
You desire
    but a timidity dragging
Through age after age
Hobbles your steps—
    You've grown accustomed
To being submissive, to blandishments
To content in a harem:
Rebellion—
        You are not equal to it,
Give it up.

I no longer remember,
Being accustomed to bitterness,
The thrill tasted on the lips
Of a woman desired, her scent
When she abandons herself
In the flow of passion.
You who desire
But fear to give
       wake up—
Time will snatch the rose of sweetness
From your cheeks and fly away with it.

Translated by Sargon Boulus and Christopher Middleton

CODA

They say in my village
I was born
With one hand placed
Over my heart
The men said
This child will live
With the heart of a prophet
And the women of the tribe

"Rejoice!" they said
Hailing the future lover
But the old men
Were holding back their tears
                and keeping calm

Translated by Sargon Boulus and Christopher Middleton

THE HARVEST

I came as a question
In infancy I knew the malice
of time, a child sacrificed
on the threshold of the house
having lived the beginning and the end
I was the amulet and the eye
the holy sepulcher
and the altar
with open jaws
Sated with the wisdom
of the old ones, I raised
over a tangle of crossroads
the banner of exile
I knew maidens
both fair and dark
and hoarded in jars
the honey of lips
wine of a nipple
and the wine that I pressed
and the wine that I sipped
and the wine that I dripped
on the velvet of the body when aroused
I was a fire inside her eye
where distances interlace
the wick and light
night, the voice and silence
the thing, its opposite
everyone and I
My blood was the harvest.

Translated by Sargon Boulus.

'Abd al-Karim Kassid (b.1945)

Iraqi poet. He studied first in Iraq and then in Syria, and taught in both Iraq and Algeria, where he learned French. He traveled to Paris many times, came to know modern French literature, and translated several books of French poetry into Arabic. He later went to Yemen, where he worked in literary journalism. At present he lives in Damascus. He is an innovative and experimental poet who writes in a style of his own, mixing a robust modernity with an inherent tenderness. Through a chain of colorful images, he creates a vivid picture of a world where people live, die, and interact. Kassid has published three *diwans: The Suitcases* (1975), *Knocking at the Doors of Childhood* (1978), and *The Gravestone* (1981).

THE GRAVESTONE

(Elegy for my father)

You leaned in your wooden chair
the women around you
imploring you to rise
and a leaf fell on my cheek . . .

And each time the cover is lifted I come near.
Did you want me closer in death? Did you fear my visit
and see my shadow passing among the women?
Did you share my happiness
my voice filling the small rooms—"They have come"—
the noise of my table
and my whispers filling the small rooms,
and the mail,
and the sheaf of papers,
and my pulse beating like thieves on the roof,
and the knocking at doors?
You were to me the humble one living close with the neighbors . . .
you became my distance and I ran . . .
you became my ceiling and I took shade . . .

you became my open space
                        I did not rise up
my gaze wandered shyly across the walls . . .

You bequeathed me what is left to the living:
the tears of a blind man
and your beautiful patience . . .
              —who will come with a breeze from you?—
your ample contentment with little
and a black sheet
they threw across the coffin
decorated with your flowers . . .
(who will take from my eyes his white hair, his calm face,
          on the abandoned shelf?)
You bequeathed me your green branches in the garden of the house—
let your branches stir for those who come . . .
It is your last celebration.

You bequeathed me your poverty, O impoverished one

A dock laborer who never rode the sea,
loading wagons in rooms which surrendered him to the streets.
Between the sun and the thunder of the trains
he uncovers on the gravel his bundle of food,
the floor covered with paint . . .
A worker in the reed huts who loaded his days onto crates,
scattered them like fodder to the beasts of burden,
piled them up in logs
and burned them in the smoke
(when he saw me once cheating the scales he caught me,
then taught me to be hungry)

Kassid . . .
To those who seek books (he did not read), to the one who keeps watch
near the ruined wall of the abandoned widow, to the one standing behind
the chair like a maid, to the condemned and the police detachment (Kassid
will not bear false witness, let him be chained till dawn), to the one de-
tained whom no brother bailed out, to the kinfolk, to the house mute and
the teapot (like a child he carries it to friends), to the pains of the night, to
doors closed by sorrow, to forgotten ones asleep on the water, to a family
that clasps branches and emigrates, to the thief crying before him, to an

idiot hiding his eyes in the palms of his hands, to the one who bleeds and
is drenched in his own blood, to the one who knocks at the door pierced
by a star, to the dead who appeared in the night, to poverty howling in the
four corners.

Kassid . . .
He was not perturbed when the guests scattered and returned in the dark
demanding hospitality.

Translated by Lena Jayyusi and Anthony Thwaite

TALES ABOUT MY FATHER

PROTEST:

Once he asked me:
How is it that these return after a few years
with titles and white collars
and slimly built . . . ?
And when I answered him tersely
he shouted at me:
But you read night and day
night and day.

HISTORY:

I said to my father one day:
There are many who enter history
as a whore enters the bed.
There are even more who exit history
as a whore leaves the bed.

But he did not understand.

AFTER THE BURIAL:

Between one day and the next
he would sit in his usual corner
shaving with old implements he acquired—perhaps before I was born.
And when he died
and I carried him with these two hands
and buried him under the earth

where my mother calmly knelt as though addressing one alive
I returned to find him in the house
in front of his small mirror
shaving, still shaving
with his old implements
his implements he acquired before I was born.

Translated by Lena Jayyusi and Anthony Thwaite

THE SUITCASES

Why do we draw the chains tight across thousands of miles?
Rest in rooms through which thousands of people have passed?
Glimpse our faces in the faces
And depart . . .
So that in the evening we can brush the dust off the suitcases?

Why the suitcases?
Three years, and every morning they wake us up
So we rise from our beds in pajamas, extinguished,
Leap up and carry them, then fall back to the door
    to wipe from our palms the dust of the suitcases.
Why the suitcases?
Madly they travel at night . . .
               then calm down amidst the noise of the ships,
               rest silently
         between my tormented face and the sea,
across the luggage racks of trains . . .

—Is my lady afraid of the suitcases
Rocking across the racks?
—Look, the sea beyond the window travels without suitcases
—Everything travels behind train windows except the suitcases
Fearfully then she touches her hair
               her lover's arm embraces her head . . .
—Look, the suitcases have jumped onto the pavement
They are vanishing now behind thousands of hurrying feet, they
               seem to be standing
—Aah . . . Where did I see you?
               Do you remember the suitcases?

—Do you travel without suitcases?
—Then who shakes off their faces the dust and the silence?

They hate to wait
and the chains across thousands of miles . . .
            I have hidden the chains in the suitcases
My mind clamors, the chains clamor within it . . .
—Rose, drink the wine
—I have had enough . . .
                  I shall wipe the dust from our two flowers
                  I shall wipe the dust from our lips . . .
And we shall move on . . .
—And where, Rose, shall I leave the suitcases?

The flowers fall wilted across the suitcases . . .
The flowers are silent in the damp hotel . . .
                  the suitcases float between the ships and the bridge
I carry them to the pavements . . .
—Open your hands to the sea, the pigeons will come hurrying,
All the ships will come
—Look, the sea turns down its hands to the birds
            the pigeons fall, they come here in the trains . . .
—In St. Germain people carry dead pigeons in suitcases
They stand there over the bridge
Shall we cross the bridge?
All the suitcases cross over
I cross the bridge packed with suitcases
The shadow escapes, the suitcases escape from our hands,
they line up among the faces of passport officials,
                  open their bowels
                  multiply among the many faces . . .
Suddenly a newcomer closes them.
—They are mine—smiles apologetically and departs
            and I smile apologetically and depart.

So that I can throw them across the luggage racks
The passport officials wake them up in the morning
the passport officials wake them up in the evening
They are opened . . . closed . . . closed . . . opened
            they enter soft-voiced

clutch their entrails with their hands
rush terrified into the streets
vomit up their chains . . .
then sit, cold, at my weary feet,
the suitcases.

Translated by Lena Jayyusi and Anthony Thwaite

Yusuf al-Khal (1917–1987)

Lebanese poet. The son of a Protestant minister, he grew up in Tripoli in northern Lebanon. He had an intermittent higher education, graduating in 1944 from the American University in Beirut with a degree in philosophy. His active working career took him to America, Libya, and Geneva. He finally returned to Lebanon in 1955, and in 1957 founded *Shi'r* quarterly, a magazine devoted to poetry. In 1957–1964 and 1967–1969 *Shi'r* was the forum for experimental poetry and for the dissemination of ideas on change and modernism in literature. Al-Khal also founded the Shi'r Publishing House, which brought out several avant-garde books of poetry and fiction, and Gallery One, for graphic arts exhibitions. After 1970, al-Khal devoted much time to a new translation of the Old and New Testaments. He has also translated into Arabic works by Pound, Eliot, Sandberg, Frost, and Whitman. He has published several volumes of poetry, of which *The Deserted Well* (1958) and *Poems at Forty* (1961) embody the bulk of his experimental poetry. Al-Khal was decorated with the Lebanese Medal of Merit just before he died.

CAIN THE IMMORTAL

When you turn at the road's
last bend
you eat the distance with your eyes
as if it were an idol raised to heaven.

You can't go back,
you will wither and fall
or reach the crossroad
until some oracle appears
like an image on the wall.
Perhaps the oracle is nothing
but the fist of God
dropped open with a sign?
               No,
you are leafed with worry,

devoured by stares.
Grumbling, you pierce the dust
with a curse
like Adam's rib,
                    and wander off
into forbidden grounds
into a cleft between
two shores—
the region of your death.
                    Not knowing
where you belong.
Your pallbearers are carrying
no one in your coffin.

Cain cannot die.

Translated by Sargon Boulus and Samuel Hazo

THE WAYFARERS

This house is closed to neighbors
open to wayfarers.
A fierce winter has left a gap
in the fence.
Every rainstorm now dislodges
a rock or two,
weakening what's left
of the foundation.
                    Dawn
glides from its edges and rests,
and suddenly leaves.
Dusk happens, and light
turns inside out in silence
to show its darker, its more
mysterious memories.
This house harbors just a few
who awaken to not so scanty a share
(one veteran of a hard voyage,
a seatamer; and a forest marching out to combat)
their aim to tear off the mask (it was
a rock).

       Having erased all the past
each wayfarer walks as if on air
or like a glinting dagger in the dark:
No cry for help
from the side of the road
there is no blood
it has now turned into wine.

They are clay, these wayfarers,
and they'll pass as breezes pass.

Translated by Sargon Boulus and Samuel Hazo

THE DESERTED WELL

I knew Ibrahim
my dear neighbor
from way back. I knew him
as a well overflowing with water
which people passed by
without stopping to drink
or even to drop
a stone.

"If I were to sail again
with my forehead a mast of light . . ."
says Ibrahim, on a piece of paper
stained with his blood,
"Would the stream change
its course, would
branches knot their buds
in autumn, would fruit ripen
and stones grow leaves?"

"If I were to live and
die anew, would the sky
unfold its face
and vultures stop circling
the caravans?
Would factories laugh
with smoky voices,

and noises subside
in the fields and the streets?
Would the poor eat their daily bread
with the sweat of their brows,
instead of humiliation's tears?"

When the enemy aimed
its cannon of death
and the soldiers rushed
under the hailstones of bullets
They heard,
"Retreat ! Retreat!
In the shelter behind you
is safety from death and shelling."
But Ibrahim kept on marching,
his tiny breast filling
the horizon, marching forward—
   "Retreat! Retreat!
   In the shelter behind you
   is safety from death and shelling!"
But Ibrahim kept marching
as though he didn't hear.

They said it was madness.
Maybe it was madness.
But I had known my dear neighbor Ibrahim
from way back. From childhood I knew him as
a well overflowing with water,
which people would pass by
without stopping to drink
or even,
even to drop
a stone.

Translated by Sargon Boulus and Naomi Shihab Nye

AFTER THE FIFTH OF JUNE

Two battles, hundreds of years ago—
remember Yarmouk? Remember Hittin?
The people are all there
waiting in the station of return.

They'll rise up, every one of them,
each wheatstalk worth a thousand stalks,
and what else?
Fighters are never vanquished.
They may be defeated—
they point a blow to the enemy
and fall,
but they do not resist
when resistance does not avail

For a long time we have not seen our feet.
We walk like a crippled forest of heads.
It is possible we might bend over the road
and see it,
that we might take off our old skin.

Woe to those who carry mountains
and topple under them,
to the angry who raise banners
and fall—
their shadows are heavy.
It would be better for them to sleep
in a palm forest, drink
the blessed waters
of its shade.

Woe to everyone who grips
the edge of day,
who clings to the last thread,
who believes in the final wall.
It would be better for them to
climb to the stars in a poem,
in a holy verse,
in a tune or sigh,
collecting the winds
in the suitcase of departure
away from the shores
and shapes of wounds.

Woe to them:
if only they would saddle their horses
and come down,

come down,
come down,
they might burn
and the ice return from the old wilderness
to obliterate these tombs.

Translated by May Jayyusi and Naomi Shihab Nye

——The fifth of June: reference to the Arab-Israeli War of June 1967.

——Yarmouk: a river in old Syria (now in Jordan) where the decisive battle of Yarmouk took place (636) in which the Muslim Arabs defeated the Byzantines.

——Hittin: famous decisive battle in which Saladin defeated the second crusaders in May 1187 at the Horns of Hittin near lake Tiberius. The victory at Hittin led to the capture of Jerusalem from the crusadors in October 1187.

'Ali 'Abdallah Khalifa (b.1944)

Bahraini poet. He has been active in the literary life of his country and has helped found the Union of Bahraini Writers, which he headed for three years. He also founded a publishing house and in 1976 the literary review, *Kitabat* (Writings). During the last few years he has helped found the Center of Folk Culture for the Arab Gulf States in Qatar, where he still works. His poetry stems from the very heart of his Bahraini experience, employing images from the surrounding landscape. He has to date published three collections, of which his last, *Illuminating the Memory of the Motherland*, reflects his developing technique.

THE CLOVER FLOWER

I hold your love up as a lantern. The blackness of night
hurts my eyes. The windows of the tower are locked
against my heart.
The lovers' caravans are leaving. My black tents
remain, though the well's dry, the valleys
never turned green this year,
and the desert was not a witness of our wedding.
At dawn, the cooing of pigeons is a torment,
the face of the wind dusty,
taking me by surprise, and snatching away
a memory that began to wake.
I carry her, my beloved, in my heart
where she moans, wounded . . .
And the clover flower complains . . . Nobody
will bandage its cheeks in the meadow;
the lookout men were watching open-eyed
from behind the fence of thorns
and nobody's left -
only seven slaughtered years and
the flash of a star.

· · · ·

My hands grope on the rocks, which out of the sea water
they rise,
the waves gasp. On the tower top
a lookout coughs and leans
gazing out placidly at the far-off rim.
Because the sea has no
key to the iron coffins
and the rocks are fixed to the sea bed, and the poor
exhausted lie in their first sleep,
the clover flower is calling, breathing fragrance
out from inside the walls.
The hunting hawk unties his leather mask,
terrifying his master,
and soars off beating at the distances,
daring the wilderness. The season
of the hunter has not come.
Instead all creatures are as marks for lightning;
in the crane a forgotten promise stirs again.

Translated by Lena Jayyusi and Alistair Elliot

ON SAYING GOODBYE TO THE LADY IN GREEN

When the tide smothers you
and asphalt laps across your name
and you've been buried in the brown
earth like a dwindling vein
you'll serve as a memorial
to a million tall ladies,
queens of all trees that nourish us

Once you were wife to the sea
where melting with love onto his knees
he kissed your feet and went away
and rushing back brought you his salty tears to drink

You were the servant who supports
the house of man, you were
the tired traveler's resting-place
standing as mother for the poor
in the expansive desert

Deeply fingering earth and fumbling sky
you gathered the berries of rain clouds
with friendly messages from streams
and seas and orbs that roll the sky

What can I tell the child asleep in my lap
if he should glimpse at the field's end
the rays of a palm-frond, somehow left,
if he should sing the passionate
qasidas of the olden days?

What can I say to him, my lady of green?
I see the land strip its green badges off
and forget the feasts and festivals of harvest
The world has swallowed its nostalgia
and calls to the hollow men:
"Come here -
bring all the tar and concrete you desire."

Translated by Lena Jayyusi and Alistair Elliot

Khalil Khouri (b. 1934)

Syrian poet. Born in Damascus, he studied law at the Syrian University. He worked as a teacher and civil servant, but lost his job several times because of his political convictions. At present he works as a consultant at the Ministry of Information in Iraq. Proficient in French, he has translated many books into Arabic, including the entire works of Rimbaud. Khouri is one of the earliest poets to experiment with the "continuous" poem, written with no caesuras. Among his many works in Arabic are three plays and seven collections of poetry. The two volumes of verse titled *Prayers to the Winds* and *No Pearls in the Oysters*, both published in 1963, contain some of his best poetry.

THE CRIPPLE

The gloomy cripple with his empty eyes
Has died. There was his funeral, but no -
No bells, no mourners at his obsequies;
Even the wind forgot to howl and blow.

The horses of the sun behind the door
Whirl him away, having him in their charge;
Their hooves on the horizon madly paw
The sog and flickerings of the mirage.

But when I open up the door to let
The sunlight in on what he left behind,
I see big flies that buzz over a pit;
His corpse watched by a crow is what I find.

Translated by Sharif Elmusa and Christopher Middleton

ANTS AND THE SUN

Sun at zenith; the sun-cross is hoisted; the sun-octopus with its million spears never ceases its warfare.

The sun shines over the ant kingdom and gives the ants over to the wilderness. The wilderness is a pit of dense silence, snake's coil, bottomless well, but light carries the promise of shade. Whoever sees the shining light will see the shade. In the wilderness the ants are watched over; but the ice of silence presses deeper and deeper into the heart.

The sun is far, the sun is near. It moves over the ant kingdom but we do not see it; the sun is a brazier whose flames are felt by the terrified ants, but they do not see it; the sun strides proudly but its creeping is not felt; only the echoes of its stride are felt, in the valleys of the ant kingdom.

And there is no way out. The ants are held together by questionings. They mill around and around, multiply, grow tired, melt with the heat, yet the road to the wilderness dissipates the efforts that are tinged with blood.

The sun is a cauldron, seething. The ants cross over, dazed, passive, naked, bloodied, their road spiked with thorns. They sink in the sticky night, their eyes wounded, clogged with sand, exploring the pit of the desert, heart of the wilderness, fatigued, thirsty, panting as they search for a seed with which to bribe their torturer, the sun, but there is no way out.

No deliverance, no way out . . .

Tammuz, stabbed in his parent heart, lies prostrate before the spears that engage the ant kingdom

And the bottom of the cauldron gulps whatever the octopus hunts, whatever lies in the folds of the wilderness crowded with dry logs . . .

There is no way out . . .

Translated by Sharif Elmusa and Christopher Middleton

——Tammuz: see the note under A. al-Bayyati

Muhammad al-Maghut (b.1934)

Syrian poet and playwright. Self-educated, he has lived in Damascus and Beirut and spent a few years in the Gulf, where he was in charge of the cultural section of the periodical *Al-Khalij* (The Gulf). His two plays, *The Clown* and *Hunchback Sparrow* (both 1973), were widely acknowledged and have been performed throughout the Arab world. His prose poetry, written in a simple and modern language, is highly allegorical and symbolic. It is rich in metaphors that reflect horror and anguish, but it sometimes reflects the comic and ironic. His main concern is with the problem of freedom and justice in the Arab world. He has published three *diwans: Sorrow in Moonlight* (1960), *A Room with a Million Walls* (1973), and *Joy Is Not My Profession* (1973). A selection of his poetry is being prepared in English translation by PROTA.

SHADE AND NOON SUN

All the fields of the world
At odds with two small lips
All the streets of history
At odds with two bare feet.

Love,
They travel and we wait
They have gallows
We have necks
They have pearls
And we have freckles and moles
They own the night, the dawn, the afternoon sun and the day,
And we own skin and bones.

We plant under the noonday sun,
And they eat in the shade
Their teeth are white as rice
Our teeth dark as desolate forests,

Their breasts are soft as silk
Our breasts dusty as execution squares
And yet, we are the kings of the world:
Their homes are buried in bills and accounts
Our homes are buried in autumn leaves
In their pockets they carry the addresses
of thieves and traitors
In ours we carry the addresses
of rivers and thunderstorms.
They own windows
We own the winds
They own the ships
We own the waves
They own the medals
We own the mud
They own the walls and balconies
We own the ropes and the daggers.

And now beloved
Come, let us sleep on the pavements.

Translated by May Jayyusi and John Heath-Stubbs

THE ORPHAN

Oh! the dream, the dream!
My sturdy gilded wagon
Has broken down,
Its wheels have scattered like gypsies everywhere.
One night I dreamt of spring
And when I woke
Flowers had covered my pillow.
I dreamt once of the sea
And in the morning
My bed was full of shells and fins of fishes
But when I dreamt of freedom
Spears were surrounding my neck
Like the morning halo.

From now on you will not find me
In ports or among trains
But there . . . in public libraries
Falling asleep over the maps of the world
(As the orphan sleeps on the pavement)
Where my lips touch more than one river
And my tears stream
From continent to continent.

Translated by May Jayyusi and John Heath-Stubbs

AN ARAB TRAVELER IN A SPACE SHIP

Scientists and Technicians!
Give me a ticket to space
I've been sent by my sad country
In the name of its widows, its children and its aged
To ask for a free ticket to the sky
I don't bear money in my hands . . . but tears

No place for me?
Put me at the rear of the ship
Outside on top
I'm a peasant, used to all that
I shall not hurt a single star
Nor offend a single cloud
All that I want is to reach God
In the quickest possible way
To put a whip in His hand
That he may rouse us to revolt!

Translated by May Jayyusi and John Heath-Stubbs

THE TATTOO

Now,
At the third hour of the twentieth century
Where nothing separates the corpses of the dead
Form the shoes of the pedestrians

Except the asphalt
I shall recline in the middle of the street like a bedouin shaikh
And will not rise
Until all prison bars in the world
And all files of suspects
Are gathered and placed in front of me
That I can masticate them like a camel in the open road
Till all truncheons of police and demonstrators
Escape their hands
And once again become blossoming branches
In their forests.
I laugh in the dark
I cry in the dark
I write in the dark
Until I can no more distinguish my pen from my finger
Whenever there is a knock at the door
Whenever a curtain twitches
I cover up my papers with my hand
Like a prostitute caught out in a raid

Who gave me this terror for an inheritance?
This blood fearful as a mountain panther?
Whenever I see an official paper on the doormat
Or a helmet through the crack of the door,
My bones rattle, my tears race one another
And my terrified blood scatters in all directions
As if the eternal police squads of the ruling class
Chase it from vein to vein.

Ah, my love,
In vain I regain my courage and strength
The tragedy is not here
In the whip, the office, the warning siren,
It is there
In the cradle . . . in the womb
For I was not tied to the womb by the umbilical cord
But by the noose.

Translated by May Jayyusi and John Heath-Stubbs

FROM THE THRESHOLD TO THE SKY

Now
As the sad rain
Covers my sad face
I dream of a ladder of dust
Of hunched backs
Made up of palms of hands pressed on knees
On which I'll climb to the topmost heavens
And find out
Where our sighs and our prayers have gone to
Oh, my love!
All those prayers and sighs
All those sobs and groans
Unloosed
From millions of lips and breasts
Through millennia, through centuries
Must have gathered, like clouds, somewhere in the sky
It is even possible
That my words are now
Adjacent to the words of Christ
Let us wait then for the sky to let fall its tears,
Oh my love!

Translated by May Jayyusi and John Heath-Stubbs

TOURIST

My childhood is a long way off
My old age is a long way off
My country, my exile, a long way off.
Tourist!
Give me your binoculars
Perhaps I might glimpse a hand or a handkerchief
In this whole world
Waving at me
Take my photograph as I weep
Crouching in my tatters on the steps of the hotel
Write on the back of the picture

"This is a poet from the East."
Spread your handkerchief on the pavement
And sit beside me under this tender rain
Let me disclose to you a great secret:
"Go dismiss all your guides
Throw to the mud . . . to the fire
All the notes and impressions you've written
Any old peasant in this land
Can tell you with two verses from our sad 'Atāba songs
All the history of the East
As he rolls his cigarette in front of his tent."

Translated by May Jayyusi and John Heath-Stubbs

——'Atāba: a sad folk song full of nostalgia and often expressive of deep sorrow for the separation of lovers. It is a kind of *muwwal*.

Sami Mahdi (b. 1940)

Iraqi poet. Born in Baghdad, he studied economics at the university there and has worked mostly in literary journalism. He is now editor-in-chief of the daily *Al-Jumhuriya*, one of Iraq's leading papers. He has published five collections to date, the most famous of which are *The Questions* (1979) and *Sunset* (1981). His work is versatile, simple, and direct, a departure from the prevailing style of contemporary Arabic poetry, which is dominated by ambiguity and complex imagery.

ON DETAILS

you're fond of details
while the changing world neglects them
what good is a book you've already read
a corner you've hung out at
a bartender, a dog, a well-dressed man . . . ?
Details are beyond your embrace
forgotten on the shores of a changing world
so memorize some
her body for example
something she said
a word, a whisper
for on the shores of a changing world
you must summon a memory
that won't let you down

Translated by May Jayyusi and Charles Doria

AWAKENING

Darkness slowly lifts
the yawning street
shakes off the remnants of long sleep

garbage still heaped at the corners
the shops still closed
and little trees search for their reflections
in the shining window panes.

Now the houses begin to show some movement
a window opens here
a balcony there as a lovely shadow
emerges with the morning light
A little while, then quickly
the earth goes crazy
a bus appears,
then another,
then another,
and people rush forth in every street and alley.

Translated by May Jayyusi

THE INHERITANCE

Between the earth and the sky
I draw a map for a newcomer.
Before I die
I give him his inheritance:
the glow of love
a ladder
and a living room full of friends.

Translated by May Jayyusi

WORLD OF FANCY

A man must tempt his heart with fancy
for in the darkness of this night
in the crowds of those who live and die
the heart and spirit suffocate.
Those who brave the dark need some fancy
to give them courage to march on
and a new fancy when the first one fails . . .

Such is the way with those who lose direction
and fall fatigued on the road
they go from fancy to fancy
until the hour of dawn.

Translated by May Jayyusi

THE MISTAKE

This is the hour of reckoning
Let me ask myself where I went wrong:
Was it in the studying
or the experience?

Translated by May Jayyusi

'Isam Mahfouz (b. 1939)

Lebanese poet, playwright, and critic. He studied at the École des Haute Études in Paris and is now literary editor of the daily *al-Nahar* and Professor of Dramatic Arts at the Lebanese University in Beirut. He has published four collections of poetry, among which are *Summer Grass* (1961) and *Virgo and the Sword* (1963), a volume which had an immediate impact in avant-garde literary circles in Lebanon. He has also written six plays and several books of literary criticism.

WEARINESS IN THE EVENING OF JANUARY THIRTY-SECOND

At your door
I left everything—
the house-mermaids, the psalms,
the kites and paper boats.
I left everything at your door
when I left you
yesterday.

The deeper I go
the longer grow my hair and fingernails.
The deeper I go
the more often I see
your shadow behind me.

The earth revolves
like a winter or summer fruit.
Before my eyes, sun and autumn happen.
Before my eyes and the gold
of the whole world—
only you
with me.

Between you and me—a sign,
a theater on tour,

a silver sword,
a lost crow.
Between you and me—a rainbow.

Your lovers are many and do not know me.
Your things are everywhere—
your trophies,
your medals,
your servants,
your shoe-shiners,
your plantations,
your compatriots,
your books,
your streets,
your statues.
I see them and forget them.

When demonstrations roar,
when armies are crushed,
when screams and words of justice fill the air,
I know you are near.

When there is weeping, when bread is trampled
and roads are deserted
and the Marseillaise begins,
I hear your voice.

When I hear your voice,
when I hear the horns of hunters,
I hear your silence.

When ships waver
and hotel sign-boards flash
and exports and imports cross
and throats are parched,
I glimpse your body.

When I undress before a mirror,
when I laugh or frown,
when I cover my hand with my hand,
when I drown in a mirror,
I see you.

When singing possesses me
on white evenings,
when, before I sleep,
I travel road after road
I feel your panting breath.

Even when I tire of talking
and the road is short,
I feel you behind me.

I lose you in days of work,
but still you find me.
I bury you in strolls
or in words
or in conversation,
but still you lift up your head.

I scatter you in laughter and gestures,
among plates of meat and vegetables,
among headlines and projects,
but still you appear before me.

I hide you among papers and letters,
I hold you in my arms
or between my lips.
Yet between one twitch and another
you expose me.

I crucify you with luck,
with all the numbers that lose and win,
and you stay near me.

I imprison you in safes
or in the boxes of my sorrow,
and still you escape.

I enter with you.
I exit with you,
and still you lead me on.

I betray you in public squares,
in cafes,
at the movies,

at celebrations,
in congregations,
inside shops and markets,
with people or without people.

I trade something for nothing,
and still you forgive me.

There is no way to escape,
no place, no time.
Even the planets are no refuge.

I stand on a summit.
Between the earth and myself,
there is space enough for murder.
Between the earth and myself,
there is time enough for hatred.
Between the earth and myself,
there is you.

Will you push me from the summit
with just a touch of your hand?
Will you push me?
Will you?

Translated by Sargon Boulus and Samuel Hazo

Muhammad al-Mahdi al-Majdhoub
(1921–1982)

Sudanese poet. Born to a prominent family in Damir, in the northern Sudan, with their own sufi *tariqa*, or mystical order, he had a religious upbringing and his early education was obtained at the family religious school. He then went to study at Gordon College (now the University of Khartoum) in the capital, where he remained, working as a civil servant, until his death. His abundant body of verse is one of the most important expressions of Sudanese poetry, reflecting the spiritual conflict of a lover of life and an heir to strict Islamic traditions. It is characterized by a terseness of expression and a great originality of diction and imagery. He has published three collections, of which *The Fire of the Majadhib* (1969) embodies his more public and nationalistic verse. His most boldly experimental poetry had not been published when he died.

THE RAIN

The night trembles in the black storm
My door moans like a victim
In my hands the embers of a fine wine
Peer into my soul's cellar
Where a wizened Old Man Fate
Bends over my many wounds.
I am the lonely and wretched man
But my heart celebrates all that's lovely
My gaze bound by subtle beauty
Too pure to be possible
Perhaps a certain fresh face
With its noble charm can kindle desire.

As night slept I passed a mosque
That fear of God had kept awake
No one there but the lonely and the blind

A beggar, a vagrant, one stricken with sickness
They don't care about dirt or disease
Oblivious to the winds of sorrow
Nothing matters if there's a breath
To stand up to sterile hope.

I said I'll go and slay my sorrows
They'll die the death of noisy wine
Between the banks of black dread
And a damned desire to be embraced
My body warmed with love of pleasure
And sharpened taste I'm urged on
My feet persisting drive my dreams
My mind frozen fast in chains
Brow down, I could see faint manshadows
Darting discordant in the alley
As ships in fog catch sight of light
That's lost between the eye's edges.

The frail night in the flooding rain
Soaked and broken like an old sieve
I walked the alleys absent-minded
My steps swallowed up in mud
I saw nothing but blind desire
Put in my mind a lit boudoir
With Raqqash waiting velvet veiled
Drunk with beauty and regret
Between the warmth of waiting and wine
And ecstasy's quiet delirium.

A picture of the cross above us
Its bitter pardon swallows sins
Sweet scent from the outcast soul
A pure and melancholy breath
Drops in glasses like tears in eyes
This is where hearts dissolve

Light and shadow meet over wine
In the glass sun's gentle death
Tell me, woman, why do you smile?
I'm not rich and I'm not your lover

It's only that your helpless face
Mirrors this soul where a stranger moans.

My heart heeds nothing now
But this body falling rising
Two arms hard about my neck
I awake amazed and dazed then doze
Lips on my lips
Stay sucking eagerly.

In the whole house of my black mistress
There's no paper to write these lines
I turned and tore the label off
A bottle of imported wine
I concentrated, pen in hand,
It flowed and heard my hidden visions
But impatient to write down my thoughts
I shouted out, "Pour the wine girl."

We were drunk, there was nothing more
Either sad or splendid to await
When we broke out our hearts were empty
As faithless as the night was silent
Slumber come and gone so sly
It spared the lash but struck the eye
The pillows, sheets, the lit lamps
A memory made of fading memories
It was a break in time the night can't bind
Its scope the morning fails to fathom
Where winds won't blow but only fear
And ruin and death. And madness.

Translated by Matthew Sorenson

BIRTH (AL-MAULID)

Hand on the Prophet, God
look not upon my sins
but help me to greater repentance!
For those alive with me
love the forbidden.

We used to go the unguided road
without God's hand showing the way,
and so we quarreled, we fought
on the purposeless path so long
we didn't care since we were living death
if we were going toward peace
or lost ourselves in void.

Can good combine with evil?
Power spring from the atom?
Pregnant with death's cypher
can it slay war and escape with peace?
Can weakness be upright and just
as strength so that we can pursue it?
Will Earth return to love and joy?

Praise to You, God!
Powerful Willful God,
You sent us a herald,
a warning sign of light,
a great flame to guide us,
a messenger of Your Eye
without whose light
we wouldn't have seen you,
the Maker of all things,
in so many of this world's things:
yes, Your Prophet
who made death hope
and deathlessness a tree
whose flowers refusing to wither
never die.

Hand on the Prophet, God,
On the Prophet, the best among us,
who on the night of Hirā'
saddled a moon,
flower of the full moon in the sky,
by whose light we read life's wisdom,
the secrets of permanence,
thanks to a God who guides us,

teaching with the words of his pen
what we did not know.

Hand on the Prophet, God:
overlook my sins,
help me to greater sorrow for them!

Maulid Night
secret of all nights, of all beauty,
spring enchanting me with virtue's charm
tonight my Muslim land burns bright
with the works of imagination
it circles the *shaikh*'s pillar,
blossoming with cluster lights
like Pleiades' light,
unveils woman's magic luster
in countless ways,
her loveliness fashioned by light
light reveals.
On 'Abdul Mun'im's Square
(who loved the people—
rain fall on his grave and bless him!)
the thousands who meet here
only on this holy day rejoice,
their painted tents granted
this one passionate night.

For it's here an old man
rocks to and fro, circling,
pounding the *nuba* dancers
keep circling, bowing,
like waves, back, forth,
up, down, their leaping
filling the night
under the long banners
that float from tent poles
like a drunken ship
on the mountain sea.

They meet, join souls
hand on shoulder greeting, feasting

they dance! they dance!
finding they drink together
the taste of joy:
eager feet stepping in,
treading out the dance!
so swift they move like birds,
kicking up *jallabies*,
dervishes turning,
never stopping spinning!
feet jerking, swaying
in the nets of their robes
like fires of flame!

Karir drum beats louder
than *nuba's* echo,
each dancer rippling, bubbling,
rising like a fountain!

Now a moment of peace
quells the ringing dance,
now body forgets self,
spirit radiant with light
relaxes, the old man's eyes
close on a universe still
dreaming its great dream.

The *muqaddam*, that great *shaikh*,
raises his voice in song,
drawing near he pounds the sweating drum,
from his mouth scattering
the holy words of the rites:
everywhere the circle of his dancing
bending where he bends,
his drum a fire on fire!

        • • • •

Hand on the Prophet, God
Help and support me with him
who speaks for the people
on Judgment Day—
with him who drinks pure water
from al-Kauthar, Paradise river.

On the square's other side
clear light spreads
a rainbow of hope and joy,
a spring flowing through
the darkness of night,
dance driving souls here
slowly one moment,
another faster than breath!

Here a girl dark as
the shadows her veil draws
sways on young hips
shyly, modestly, possibly
saying hello, calling you
with the fringe of her *thaub*
In chains, she is free,
in harmony, she is chaos.

But see there,
that pretty Maulid candy doll
vendors hawk, that princess
robed in hue of every color
A little thing, but how pretty!
Braced there on her throne
in the carnival high above
islands of sweets,
that seem to the eye
mythical treasures of imaginary pearls.

Though she does not
her downcast eyes speak!
Children turn around her,
dark eyes glinting rainbows
beam their hopes for her,
joyfully misted in tears.

God! How their poverty wastes them!
The tiny children who come here
on Your Prophet's Birthday,
longing for joy, but went home,
taste of dust in their mouths.
Weep for the mother

who'd give them stars
if they asked! Yes,
weep for her:
she carries nights without sleep
all through the brightness of the day.

God! You sent an orphan child
into the world to stand up
for the right, for what is just.
He was kind to us,
we remember him tonight.
Aren't we here to honor in mind
all those without a thing in the world?

In the people's market on the other side
of the square there's trumpet and drum
shouting up hunger and its cure,
a tiny kingdom revolving
around its famous kettle of stew
which grabs our eyes
and steals away thought:
and why not? tell me,
pleasure of the night
mistress of attraction?
From where he stands
the stall-owner looks around,
a barker, a pitchman,
at the huge crowd
sniffing up the meat smoke
whirling from his fiery grill:
O! a flame that found
none of us disobedient when it
called us to the dinner
it laid in our thoughts.

All around king chef
stately braziers fumed,
putting up with skewers
strung with meat cubes,
fat and dripping.

It was a kitchen
we'd entered
busier, noisier
than a prince's court,
its substantial owner
so full of good wit
one circle of diners
after another visited him.
We ate and were at peace,
we drank and felt so full
eating and drinking
no longer made sense.
Then we left and walked,
sleep dragging at our heels
if only we felt like this always,
how we'd thank fate!
And so the night went by;
bed called me and I obeyed,
leaving feasting behind,
and the thousands who hoped
for life's full food:
but no rains came,
each soul faint,
thirsty in the dust.

Echo recalled distant drums
like a crying child
all alone at night.
A snatch of song flew into my ear,
in the darkness already signifying
new dawn on the horizon,
new promises coming true tomorrow!

In my Muslim land, God,
we have returned to You;
depending, O my God, solely on You,
we remember tonight the Chosen Guide
who filled our spirit
with his purity and patience.

Hand on the Prophet, God,
look not upon my sins
but help me to greater repentance!

Translated by Salma Khadra Jayyusi and Charles Doria

——*Hirāʾ*: Ghar Hirā; the cave where the Prophet Muhammad hid in his flight from his hometown, Mecca, and from his own tribe of Quraish, to Medina (or Yathrib). Followed by Qurashite horsemen, he hid in this cave with his companion Abu Bakr. A spider is said to have miraculously woven a web at the mouth of the cave, which dissuaded his enemies from entering to look for him since it gave the impression that the cave had been long abandoned.

——*Maulid Night:* the birthday of the Prophet Muhammad is celebrated by festivities, especially at night, that vary from one country to the other. It entails great festivities in the Sudan, especially by the mystic dervishes.

——The *Nuba* Drum: a huge drum used in festivals and in *Sufi* circles.

——*Jallabies:* the long and ample robes worn by men in the Sudan and other Middle Eastern countries.

——*Karir drum:* a large drum used to accompany *Sufi* chants and dancing.

——*Muqaddam:* the *shaikh* who heads the dervish dance.

——Al-Kauthar: the river of paradise in the Muslim religion.

——*Thaub:* the traditional dress worn by Sudanese women. It is uncut and has no sewing, but is wrapped around the waist, on the shoulders, then over the head, and can be very attractive and elegant.

Nazik al-Mala'ika (b. 1923)

Iraqi poet and critic. Born in Baghdad of a literary family, she attended the
Higher Teachers' Training College in Baghdad and Princeton University,
where she studied English literature. She has also taught at several institu-
tions of higher learning in Iraq and Kuwait. She was a major pioneer of the
free verse movement, which she backed with both poetry and critical writ-
ings. The movement was launched formally with the appearance of her
second *diwan, Ashes and Shrapnel* (1949). Her poetry is characterized by the
originality of its thematic variations and of its use of imagery. Since the
seventies it has acquired an ardent tone of Islamic piety, rare in the contem-
porary period. She has published several collections of poetry. Her *diwan,
The Trough of the Wave* (1958), was one of the most important volumes of
poetry published in the fifties. She is also a major critic of poetry, and her
book, *The Case of Contemporary Poetry* (1962), was one of the best critical
contributions of the period.

LILIES FOR THE PROPHET

The sea   love song
the sea   blue   the sea
flow of a child's hair
to the dawn behind its eyes
dawn that is breaking
    dawn that flickers
        dawn catching its breath

The sea plays
       with dolls of water
mist   spread the fog wings
these sea brides have flung away my being
made of me a ship of desire
       thirst
     in the silver waves

sea brides make of me
     froth and cloud
       a moth

Filling my spirit
  all face of my beloved
canticle star his breath cool
face of my beloved
    vaster than the sea's everlastingness
blocking its blue
    domains
      but its birds
but its surging but its dreams
       hidden
     • • • •

  O sea tell me
where does this face end?
Where do you begin This face of sea
I am lost in it
   the lights are out
in every port
     his eyes
where do you think they end?
     • • • •

Heart of mine
   it was floating in a deep
mirror, prolific, reflections
      surge
  a daze and a wilderness

In a dream of love lost in fields
of long eyelashes
searching the big seas for the snow pearls
they have the heart my beloved has
pure
a bright fragrance of secret
    melody of wind's warmth
mystery
with a fountain a murmur in it

southern gale gliding
         I was on the sea
the sea brimmed with my desire . . .

Ahmad had ocean eyes
watering the wastes of What Is
they would exude perfumes

      Sprout in the stones
         a field of daisies
river of saffron flowing
Ahmad young like new vine shoots
Ahmad the smell of my earth, taste
of my river
Ahmad fragrance of my soil
         has given me his light to drink
Ahmad
has gone through my meadow of praise
       his wings are scattering me
       his wings are gathering me

From endless light came Ahmad
from forest of sparrows and fragrance
over the essences of the Qur'an
over the recitation and the fasting
Ahmad
     radiant from depths of memory
              my hidden years
in the cypress tree
from scent of poppy and almond
the face of Ahmad

O bird of dawn O wings of white lilies
you
life of mine

O apricot guise supplying the time
across my life's river
in my words
Ahmad Ahmad

Color   deep chasms   cheek of the secret
my escape
from frozen forms of self, from the chains
from the snows of me

You
bird of silence and mystery you smooth candlestick
the range you are and the ascending
the beauty and the abundance
Ahmad   my rose   harvest of my life
You
total past
you
all that is to come

Ahmad pure like March rains
first mercy season snow
                Ahmad shimmer of star
eyelash
   Ahmad   O shore
of eternity, across lilac sky
the spirit of stillness drinks
                my interior mists

Ahmad me and you
nature
the sea   atmosphere
of a temple
          candle of promise
In the wish of the wise
          God is kindled
God in our dream
     a window of gold

a window of gold
                    • • • •
The birds flew in the morning
        a whole-hearted flight
playing with cloud and wind
            shaping the light
above endless ocean

Ahmad never flew but came
closer and closer
        in the shadow of clouds
Stained by brightness
            we sang to the sky and the sea
two full sails
            two wanderers we were

A pair of prodigals lost
        in a forest of song
in our song the sun was broken
            eternity, the harbors

Broken our laughter, broken
        our desires
Till the tale is told and the tide
            to the feet we stand on
streams with its kisses and breaks
        Ahmad Ahmad us and you and me
this height where night and the silence
            have set us

And in our spirit
    Allah
    is
        Song

Translated by Matthew Sorenson, and modified and abridged by Christopher Middleton

THE VISITOR WHO NEVER CAME

The evening has passed and the moon will soon vanish
We are prepared to bid another night farewell
Witnessing how happiness can leave us
You did not come, lost instead with other dreams
You left empty your chair
Engaging our dull circle
In clamorous questionings about
                A visitor who never came.

I didn't know your disappearing all these years
Would leave your shadow in every sense of every word
And all dreams in every corner, every curve
I didn't know how you could overpower these people here
A hundred guests lost
In a moment of desire
As it ebbs and flows in yearning for
                  A visitor who never came.

If you came, if we sat with all the others
As conversation gains its power among friends
Would you just become another guest with evening at an end
Both of us, our eyes turning, still in search?
We'd ask the empty seats about
Those we missed at meetings past
Crying out that among them was
                  A visitor who never came.

And if you came one day (it's better that you don't)
The fragrance of that flowering world would leave my memory
The wings of wonder would be clipped and my songs sad
My hands would hold the fragments of my innocent hope.
I love you as a dream
If you come as flesh and bone
I still would dream of the impossible
                  The visitor who never came.

Translated by Matthew Sorenson and Christopher Middleton

LOVE SONG FOR WORDS

Why do we fear words?
They can be rose-petal hands,
Cool, fragrant hands stroking our faces,
And sometimes cups of refreshing drink
Sipped in summer by thirsty lips.

Why do we fear words?
Some words are secret bells, the echoes
of their tone announce the start of a magic
And abundant time

Steeped in feeling and life,
So why should we fear words?

We took to silence
We did not want our secrets to pass our lips
We thought that words amassed an unseen monster
Pent up inside the letters, hiding from the ear of time
So we battened down the words
And did not let them spread the night for us
With a pillow of music, fragrance, hopes,
And warm cups.

Why do we fear words?
They are a back door of love through which
Tomorrows come, uncertain
Let us raise from words the drape of silence
They are a window of light in which appears
All that we have hidden and kept covered in our depths.
When will this tedious silence ever find
That now we love the words again?

And why do we fear words?
They are the friends that come to us
From distant spaces in the soul
They surprise us, catch us unaware,
And sing for us, and a thousand ideas are born
Ideas that were dormant in us, never before expressed
But the friendly words, the words
Offer them as gifts:
Why should we not love words?

        • • • •

Why do we fear words?
Yesterday their thorns may have wounded us
But often they have taken us up in their arms
Perfuming with their sweetness our desire
If they stung us
If they left us cold
How many times did they touch us with a promise
Tomorrow they will lavish on us life and roses
Ah! Let them brim, our cups, with words!

One day we will build a nest of dreams with words
High up, a trellis for the ivies
Fed with poetry
Watered with words
We will build a balcony for modest roses
Its pillars made of words
And a pathway floating in the deep shade
Shielded by words.

Our life in innocence we dedicated
A prayer
To no one but to words.

Translated by Matthew Sorenson and Christopher Middleton

SONG FOR THE MOON

Are you a glass of milk, rich and cold?
Or a stream flowing with mother of pearl?

Or a white ripple of the twilight time
Sweetly crossing the face of night?

Or a jar, colored and dewy
A honey jar for all who are hungry?

Or are you a cheek of fragrant lilies
Dozing over grass and fallen leaves?

Or are you silver, lightlike and supple?
Ah, the glow of my old enchantment!
                    *
What are you? A vessel of light
A blending of stars out of the dark

Oh, kiss of lilies pouring out clear
The honey of a perfumed evening

You are a refuge and a haunt for beauty
A bouquet of lilies clasped by the sky

Your lips of light have come so close
To caressing the face of these fresh arbors

Oh pool of goodness and perfume
Sloping to the horizon, a basket of jasmine
    *
The lovers' ferry bears them beyond
The lazy ocean and the sea of dream

On your nimble feathery wing
Strewing the path of passion with hope

Your spring spills slumber on any eye
Made sleepless by a lover's longing

You nourish those soft eyes with visions
Tilting your cup of toxic sleep

Oh, your finger, caressing wounds
Sowing songs and sprinkling kisses!
    *
An island in the gloom, suspended
Dawnlike its propitious shade

Floating over an ambrosial stream
Flanked by magic starry shores

Light has frozen on the shore
A cradle of silk, a crystal treasure

Oh, penitence of ugliness, Oh sail
of love, colorful and finely featured

The dark's heartache, the night's regret
Oh, atonement of the storm clouds!
    *
Melt the fragments of rays and visions
at night, immerse our roofs in silver

Shake your tender wings in space
And the colors flow from the butterfly

Thanks to you the shadows dance
And the frail lilies' cups are cooled

You wove our dreams and suckled us
With your sweet flickering flashing light

You are dawn's window when night is spent
You feed the flowers that fill the meadows

*

Stay as you are, a secret world
Not such a thing as a soul discerns

Spinner of poems, the last muse
In a world whose mirrors are all dimmed

What song did not flow with honey
If you were to smile your praise upon it?

Joy was granted to song by you,
You, the weighted weaving pulse

Stay beyond life, in dreams, with love
Stay with poetry, and with God above

Translated by Matthew Sorenson and Christopher Middleton

Khairi Mansour (b. 1945)

Palestinian poet. Born in Dair al-Ghusun in Palestine, Mansour lived on
the West Bank and studied in Cairo. In 1967 the Israeli authorities deported
him from the West Bank and he went first to Kuwait, then to Baghdad,
where he still lives and works as a literary editor of *Al-Aqlam*. Mansour's
poetry reflects, on the personal level, a great preoccupation with age and
the passing of time, and, on the communal level, the sorrows of the Pales-
tinian experience, as well as the faith and hope that have dominated much
of the poetic expression of Palestinian poets in recent times. He has pub-
lished two collections of poetry, *Gazelles of Blood* (1981), and *The Seas are
Narrow* (1983).

DAY

Still asleep his body wakes from sleep
only his watch has slept
    from which the sun rises
    for he eats not when he is hungry
    but when his watch tells him
    only enjoying his siesta
    on the same terms
    he is his watch

the day's cycle begins
    "morning"
    "morning"
    "tea?"
    "you?"
    "coffee please"

wipes his glasses
lights a cigarette
pages through the papers

The room is long and narrow
the three of us read yesterday's papers
hearing the silence that builds on the ceiling
    "reading something interesting these days?"
    "just a book with nothing to do with poetry"
the greyhaired woman
fills her water glass
walks back and forth
holding the glass half-empty in her hands
    "please close that door"
    "I'll close it partway"

At the table faces
growing long and sleepy
as day begins its round
only growing round and alive
when day ends
a hidden light sparking
in the ashes of our eyes
we leave, moving to where
day begins a second round

Noon and time slumps
the vast square crowded with the same faces
that thronged there in the morning
everybody knows him
a woman used to his face might look back
and search his face with her eyes
on his way home or in the store
meeting those faces he almost greets
but when his eyes meet theirs
they look away staring instead
at a pair of breasts passing by
or a fruit juice stand
evening and time falls
sticky, heavy with the day's dust
    "will you eat or rest?"
he sags into a long wooden chair
the garden path is empty
at the sound of his steps

sleeping weeds stir
    "eat or rest?"
he sinks into his glass
remembering how flies buzzed
hither thither, then died

Night and time slip past
like a shadow stealing its way to bed
every corridor shuts its door
streets empty going nowhere
day concludes the second round

this is another day
    gone
we lost it
   it lost us
days are the footsteps of death

Translated by Lena Jayyusi and Charles Doria

FROM: NIGHTWATCH

I see trees breaking off their branches
    I glimpse the branches fleeing toward the desert sands
I see a river expell its waters
    I glimpse the branches fleeing toward the desert sands
I see a river beg for a drop of water.

Translated by Lena Jayyusi

ʿAbd al-ʿAziz al-Maqalih (b. 1939)

Yemeni poet and scholar. He completed his higher education at Cairo University and became very active in the literary life in Yemen, both as a writer and lecturer on literature and as director of the Center for Yemeni Studies in Sanʿaa. He is now the President of Sanʿaa University. In addition to several books of criticism on Yemeni and Arabic literature, he has published seven collections of poetry, including *A Message from Sayf Ben Dhi Yazin* (1973), which made his reputation in the Arab world. Much of his poetry derives from the rooted and "different" experience of Yemeni life and history, and combines the Yemen's rich heritage with a new and modern outlook. His work also reveals a great involvement in Arab life and experience in general, expressing anger, frustration, and grief at Arab political experience in the contemporary world. In October 1986 he was awarded the Lotus Prize for Literature.

TELEGRAMS OF TENDERNESS FOR SANʿAA

FIRST TELEGRAM

As I retire, each day, with myself,
lay down the burdens of self
and hoist the sail of memory,
I see you rising like blood in my veins,
like trees in my blood,
and I see the siege-wall that separates us
disintegrate,
our arms intertwine,
our bodies embrace.

SECOND TELEGRAM

Every evening when night retrieves the substance of our longings,
the bird of yearning steals out of my body,
departs alone toward Sanʿaa,
returns just before daybreak,

eyes wounded by the dust of separation,
in the heart a bloodied face,
vessels filled with the ashes of tenderness.

SEVENTH TELEGRAM

The day recedes,
gathers up its white robes,
here is the face of evening knocking at the windows,
stretching out in the long passageways,
lanterns can't stop the night from sleeping in the streets
and spreading over the city,
across its rivers, naked.
Wish I had a moon from the mills of your eyes
to expel from my world the seasons of darkness.

NINTH TELEGRAM

The trains roll over my heart
when they run South
and my bones are littered over the Northern rocks.
Why, when I yearn, do the trains' eyes become my window,
the sound of the train my tears?
Why should I be torn apart,
then tossed away by exile?

TENTH TELEGRAM

I wish I had a boat,
and this darkness coming between us
I wish it was a sea,
so I could visit you.
I am the prince of lovers, mad about you,
I love you, can you deny my voice?

Can you deny my face?
Deny it, if you can—
my poems hung in the windows
along the housefronts
are aflame on the lips,
alive in the mountain springs.

THIRTEENTH TELEGRAM

The faces that stab the eye are familiar,
Familiar the faces that carry warmth to the heart.
How can I reconcile the faces that stabbed me
and those that have preserved me?
And how to fight those scalpel faces making polite talk with me?
You, heart's homeland, like me
you lose your way in the crowd of faces,
bereft of understanding,
unable to choose.

FIFTEENTH TELEGRAM

The birds that migrated,
that migrate every day,
spoke to me of their love,
of their longing for the trees, their home,
of their fear of the dust of distances
and of the bitter season.
Once night has come do you hear the weeping of birds
do you hear it when the window of dream darkens on the shores
and the face of day burns out in the mirrors?

SEVENTEENTH TELEGRAM

Your weeping gray streets
inhabit my memory
and go with me to the cities where glory is,
they cry when we see the clean-washed streets,
the glad houses,
ask me:
How will our people
and our roads emerge from the age of tears?

NINETEENTH TELEGRAM

Love has changed the face of distances,
we have grown closer, blending into one another.
Your bosom has long been the place I wander in,
you have dwelt in my soul,
so come run with your barefoot children in the streets of my heart,

burn away every sea that separates us,
all the sands that besiege us.
You are the heart's homeland, its history—
remove
the last mark of the ancient royal wound
from your face.

TWENTIETH TELEGRAM

Ah my city, my lady,
the night of mourning has been too long
in your heart, the palm trees of love have withered,
sorrow has flowered,
the purest of your children have died
or live in exile.
When will the migrant day return, city of my heart,
when will we drink a toast to "Al-Tawil" and " 'Aiban,"
eat spring cakes,
play with roses on a night in April,
when will joy's river wash our tears of exile away?

Translated by Lena Jayyusi and Christopher Middleton

CHOICE

Between grief on my knees and death on my feet
I choose death:
between a safe silence and a voice that's bloodied
I choose the voice:
between a slap and a bullet
I choose the bullet:
between the sword and the whip
I choose the sword:
This is my destiny and my glory,
this is the longing of man.

Once God was love, a plentiful cloud,
daylight at night,
a song extended
over the hills of grief,

a heaven that washed with green rain
the furrows in the earth.
Where did the ship of God go? Where the song and man's rebellion?

Now God is ashes, silence,
a terror in the executioners' hands,
an earth swelling with oil,
a field where rosaries and turbans grow.

Between God the song of revolution
and the god coming from Hollywood
on tapes, in stacks of dollar bills:
I choose God the song, I choose God the revolution.

Love was a springtime for all seasons,
a lovely girl whose supple feet
rested on the sea, whose palms
touched the sun.
Her braids spread over the green hills of poetry,
she had bread for her lovers,
the wine of luscious dreams was on her lips.

Now love's tree has grown old,
love's eyes are dull,
the leaves of poetry have been torched,
all seasons are winter,
love has become banknotes and the hearts of men
have turned to ice.

Between love the deal and love the poetry:
I choose love, I choose poetry.

Translated by Lena Jayyusi and Christopher Middleton

FIRST COMMUNIQUÉ FROM ONE RETURNING FROM THE ZANJ REVOLT

I was in the army of the Zanj
A slave fighting for a dream that glimmers across the sun's face
Across the blind Gulf
That sleeps, awakens,

runs forward, stumbles
And when my dream and the dream of comrades faltered,
I carried my sword under my arm, and said:
The South is my sky, my face,
I have comrades in the South
With their dreams they went before me to the port of the sun
they are drowned in its radiance
after their bodies' fragrance had burned out
in the prison of the Imam
After dawn had died in their withered eyes
under the invader's alien whips,
After dawn had died in heads held high
that gave of their fire generously.
No, they are not defeated
The dream remains still, fertile with love and light
Here is one comrade
And there is another
My hand can almost touch them who departed with the dream
Touch the soil's wound
And when I went down the Gulf to the Great Water
I was smitten with the first longing
My feet burned
I did not pause to weep
I reined in my tears,
and loosed my voice to the wind,
took up the art of wistful song
I sang for the country whose blood was licensed to be spilt
I held the wounds of the people in my breast
From the bones of the fallen I fashioned flutes
And songs flamed out in the veins of the day
And now I knead the earth into my language,
offer it a cake for multitudes
for the child at the breast, for the father,
for the hawk, for the dove,
for the sword, for the flower.

Enter my garden safely, you poor of the North
Cast off your hunger at my door
Here is where the dream begins:

The face of distances approaches
The fountain draws near
In the age of love water and fire mingle
and sun and earth
All beings unite
The seasons of revelation are at hand
And the hour of Union approaches.

Translated by Lena Jayyusi and John Heath-Stubbs

——Al-Tawil and ʿAiban: two mountains in the vicinity of Sanʿaa in North Yemen which were strongholds for the Yemeni revolution.

——Zanj (The Zanj Revolt or Black Revolt): see note to the poetry of Adunis under ʿAli ibn Muhammad.

——South: a reference to what the Yemenites feel are different revolutionary attitudes and developments between North and South Yemen. The South was a direct British stronghold, while the North was the royalist stronghold of the Imam, the hereditary and traditional ruler of Yemen. The revolution of 1962 was able to get rid of all forms of undesired rule, spreading to Sanʿaa, the capital of the North, which after a long siege fell to the republican army in 1969. The South revolted in 1963 and won its independence in 1967. The North remained a nationalist republic while the South became a Marxist state.

——Imam: the rule of the Imam has become one of the major themes in contemporary Yemeni literature, both prose and poetry. It has been a symbol of the extreme oppression, exploitation, and ignorance which have caused nationwide suffering among the Yemeni population. Imam Yahya died in 1948 and was succeeded by his son, Imam Ahmad, who died in 1962. His son, Imam Badr, lost the royalist battle and now lives in exile.

Muhammad ʿAfifi Matar (b. 1935)

Egyptian poet. Born in Ramlat al-Anjab in the province of Manufiya in Egypt, he studied philosophy at Ain Shams University and, after teaching philosophy for a few years, worked in literary journalism. He subsequently moved to Baghdad as one of the editors of *Al-Aqlam* literary review. His poetry has grown in complexity and he is now one of the most difficult poets in contemporary Arabic, using many allusions and images from his Arab, Egyptian, and contemporary local heritage. Among his collections are *From the Notebook of Silence* (1968); *Features of the Empedocesian Face* (1969), *Engravings on Nocturnal Crust* (1972), and *The Silt Speaks* (1977).

RECITAL

This sun wears a live chemise of blood.
A wound gapes from its kneecap, wide as the wind
And horizons gush blood-springs revealing birds and palmtrees.
  Peace, it stays until nightfall . . . Peace
The river women rise:
  Anklets of grass twist circlets of
  Silver and silt, desire wet with the water's foam;
The river women call to the birds,
With shawls wipe the glass horizon.
They weep, they shed newly warmed sorrow.
  Peace, it stays until nightfall . . . Peace.

The fields folded their knees.
The ploughsocks softened, relaxed.
The serpents slept.
A pall of peace piles up: Downy hay and plume.
The bulls, standing, slumbered.
In their absent phosphoric eyes, night stars shatter.
  Peace; that mask of merciful night.
The living half unawakened, the mortal half slept.
This earth seemed empty.
When the night's prayer was recited and the dream angels came,

When sleep like the sun rose with its green radiance of rebirth, its sign of illumination,

Then, by His mercy, I shed the diurnal limbs and opened a window in the mortal half;

I enfolded myself in the living half

And the vision erupted:

I stepped out of the sheets' patterns and the pillows' perfume.

Have the covers left their bold arboreal designs on my face?

My face's become flying leaves, falling fruit, sprouting twigs.

An imperial mare rises in my father's house:

Space is folded for her.

The silver, the flashes of her hoofs are the lights of Granada and those lands beyond the River.

The mercury and kohl of her eyes mirror a blaze of royal ruins.

My form floats from my dream's body. I glow.

Trees spread through my face like traceries,

Freshly green tears inscribe springs and crescents of water on my features.

My form floats from my dream's body:

The star Canopus looks a trembling flower in the eyelet of the heart.

Life's blood-dimmed springs are loosed.

Horses rise from the *Amma* of the Book,

The circumference of the earth expands.

Peace, it stays until sunrise . . . Peace.

My knees grip a lodge on the horizon's ledge.

In my face crowd the lightning of writing, green leaves and water.

(The letters, a nation among nations, are addressed and entrusted.)

The birds broke out from the dome of the wind as a well breaks out.

I remember . . . it's the horizon's divan.

My body is a lodge. I reign in what's not mine, what's not others'.

I remember . . . beneath me runs that river of living images;

And the springs sported as I wished.

I remember . . . the earth's globe approached and the heavens came to me. They exchanged garments.

The mixing of memory's creatures and the marriage of what's not male with what's female; what's not female with what's male,

And the joys of earthly powers

Gave me the strength to conjure with the sources of memory's shattered images.

I conjured delicacies, images and chants as I wished.

The pause in the *Be* of the Book lingered.

Joy filled with tender questions,

And the foliage of the face dropped with fresh fears and the buds of discovery's bewilderment.

I knew I walked the way of Ascension. I dwelt in the lodge of ultimate certitude.

The circumference of the earth expanded.

The heavens appear as garments ripping at the waistline of the living river,

A window beneath the garments of the oceans gapes open.

The Oriental Sages, the Hermetists and Gnostics partake of the banquet of luminous dialogue.

Al-Suhrawardi breathes in the fullness of space, divides bread and the silvery fish of the Nile. He eats in the plenitude of anarchy and drinks in the profusion of ceaseless emanation.

The Hermetists weave the cape of chants and enchantments. They unfold it for the noble tribe, the beasts and the birds as a resting, sheltering space for initiating and linking creatures twice, thrice, four times and up to the last number memory may retain.

Rising from sleep the river women reveal bronzed legs, silt and earthy grass.

      Peace, it stays until sunrise . . . Peace.

A mare whinnies in my father's house.

My father's house is a nomad in my dream's body.

The two Euphrates read like a book of rising blood

And the Nile is a book.

The Ocean pulls off the garments of diffused blood.

Then the desert's dressed, the large land and the cracked ruins adorned by the splendor of lightning, by the green life of fire.

The sun penetrates the flanks of night with purple gloves and stockings of hammered and unhammered gold.

It rises and falls.

He descends to the murmur of vermin, the clinging of insects, the slither of reptiles.

The steps shorten.

I wrapped myself in the tatters of the diurnal half.

The smell of nocturnal sleep spread

And the woolen covers heaved.

The wet cotton covers collapsed.

Peace, a spider of blood, clothed by the features' similarity . . . Peace.

Water drains from the body.

Memory drains from the water.

Translated by Ferial Ghazoul and Desmond O'Grady

——Al-Suhrawardi: Shihab al-Din Yahya ibn Habash, known as "The Slain." He was a famous mystic of the second half of the twelve century, who lived in Baghdad and then Aleppo, where he was under the patronage of its viceroy, al-Malik al-Ẓahir, son of the famous Saladin. However, al-Ẓahir eventually put him to death when al-Surawardi was only thirty-six, because his original mysticism rendered him suspect to orthodox believers. Al-Surawardi believed in the agreement of all religions and all philosophies, which, he insisted, express only one single truth. He was a student of the major Greek and other philosophers before him. The most characteristic attribute of his work was his metaphysics of spiritual light, which he regarded as a symbol of emanation and as the fundamental reality of things. He even based his proof of the existence of God upon this symbol.

Orkhan Muyassar (1914–1965)

Syrian poet and critic. Born in Istanbul to an old Syrian family, he moved with his parents to Aleppo when he was fourteen. He studied first in Aleppo and Lebanon, then in Chicago, where he studied both literature and science. The last period of his life was spent in Damascus, where his house was a meeting place for poets and intellectuals. A highly cultivated man, he was fluent in Arabic, French, English, and Turkish. He authored three books of criticism, many articles, and in 1946 coauthored a collection of prose poetry, *Siryal*. He was influenced by the surrealist movement in Europe and spread its ideas in his critical writings. An iconoclast and a lover of innovation, he exerted a deep influence on several Syrian poets in the forties and fifties, including Adunis.

THE WALL OF TOMORROW

They feed on shadows
breathe back what they should breathe out
and deck the tables scrapped by hunger
with their nights and days.
Having gazed so long at nothing,
their eyes behold mere holes of light
and all they hear is the hoarse trumpet
and noise of all the factories on earth.
Their hands flutter like gills,
and their feet imprint the ground.
The prayers they utter
on the premises of time's cemeteries
hover nimbly on the zenith
of a spider's web
suspended from tomorrow's wall.

Translated by Lena Jayyusi and Samuel Hazo

RACE

Even though it's dark,
lights bewilder me.
I see a race of images,
colors fading and glowing,
lines becoming curves
that narrow and thicken
minute by minute
into a compass
where entire oceans contract,
and a stream widens
as it flows.

Translated by Lena Jayyusi and Samuel Hazo

TRANSFORMATIONS

Echoes are soundless.
Memories have no memory
except for those
who hear sounds in echoes
and discover memories in memory.

Translated by Lena Jayyusi and Samuel Hazo

GRAVES

Without a pickaxe to my name
I dug the graves with my fingernails
and buried there
the lures of all horizons.
Later in what seemed
but a pause of moments,
I returned to my cemetery
and found between two graves
a grave I never dug—
as if it held
the wanderings I never made
between one grave and the other.

Translated by Lena Jayyusi and Samuel Hazo

THE STATUE

You, my statue, why do you torment me?
Everything is as clear
as though I were my yesterday, my today, my tomorrow.
You have the power and the mystery,
so let me enjoy for a while
what little trifles you have left me.

Translated by Lena Jayyusi and Samuel Hazo

LOST

This god who has gaped ever since we created him
and shrined him in the sky
I wish he had never spoken
but only opened his heart and arms
to embrace those
who created him
and made him a legend.
I wish his shadow had stayed
uncolored by the world
his silhouette had remained
untouched by motion,
his words had lasted
without being eaten
and re-eaten.

Instead he mutinied against his creator
wanted him to be the created
and man was lost between two creations—
        his creation of the god
        and the god's creation of him
still, creator and created
became a single destiny,
marching as one
toward a new creation
that is still beyond us.

Translated by Lena Jayyusi and Samuel Hazo

Huda Na'mani (b. 1930)

Syrian poet. Born in Damascus, she studied law at the Syrian University and then studied literature, sufism, and Islamic studies at the American University of Cairo, where she was living with her husband. The family eventually settled in Beirut. Na'mani writes prose poetry of a mystical nature, and her poetry is an original expression of Islamic piety reflecting a universal spiritual attitude. She has published several volumes of poetry to date, among which are *To You* (1970), *My Fingers Did Not* (1971), *Love Poems* (1973), and *I Remember I Was a Dot, I Was a Circle* (1978).

LOVE POEM

In your quest or request God is remote.
Yet He alone can be your anchor and your space,
the pulse and the parts,
the vine and the separation.

If God were a man, I would touch His robe
and burn into Him.
If He were a man, I would kiss His feet
and kneel or lie before Him.
I would cry, bleed, die . . .
But He is not a man,
not a body.

You yourself are God because He made you,
classified you, gifted you and sailed within you.
You yourself are God because He sees you,
knows you, speaks to you,
enlightens you, bears you,
throws you, treads on you,
scatters and sunders and bolts with you.
You yourself are God because you exist.
The world is a moth in God's hands,

and the moth is greater and more beautiful
than you because it is
smaller and larger than you.

Between you and God are time and light.
Between you and God are sun and stars.
Between you and God are heaven and all
created things.

But God is not you, and you know best that God is not
because you are naked without God.
His fingers stretch from your head to your heart.
His hands are in your blood.
Your face and all the seas are but a bit of sand.
Yet you say you are God!
Do you dare to say that you will kiss God's robe,
God's chest, God's feet?
Do you dare to say that you are God, and God is you?
Do you dare?
Do you dare?

Translated by Lena Jayyusi and Samuel Hazo

TO YOU: THREE POEMS

I

Why do the sun rays laugh across the swamp?
Because they carry water's jewels to the sky
and return them like dewy pearls to the lily
while the black weeds remain at the bottom?

2

You sever a hand
to plant a tree
You stay a ship
it escapes the storm,
You demolish a wall
to conceal a treasure
for a future day

You strike a nation
it becomes a giant,
This is Your nature.

3

A blind man asked me
why do I say I cannot see the sun
when I feel it?

I almost kissed his hands.

Translated by Lena Jayyusi

BOTH EARTH AND HEAVEN

How would it all end?
When we hate so much?
To be whole, what we hate is that which we should love
Where do we start from when we think that we hate?

To all who are terrified:
From sin came Adam. From the deluge came Noah. From disease came
Job. From questioning came Abraham. From the wilderness came Moses.
From the cross came Jesus. From illiteracy came Muhammad. From inno-
cence came ʿAli. From self-destruction came Socrates. From despair came
Plato. From exile came al-Mutanabbi. From darkness came al-Maʿarri.

To all those who are terrified:
From weakness strength comes. From night the day.
From division comes unity.
To all those who are frightened: do not fear!

Every morning when we read
Most of what we read we should not read.
We should only read about love.

What is history?
What is man?
How do we embrace history?
Like a child on its mother's knee.
We must be this mother.

Most of those who wrote history were old. They hated death and did not
know God. They were against history.
Most of those who wrote history were dead. And they wrapped us round
with the garments of death.

He who knows God knows colors, trees, letters; knows good and evil;
knows creation. They all came from the same rib. He who knows
God knows that all belongs to God.

Is God tiny fragments we could share among ourselves?
Or is He a cloak that we can wear, and that we can cast off?
That is the difference between seeing nothing but desert or living within
sight of eternity's sea
That is the difference between life in death and death in life.
That is the difference always between being earth and being heaven.

There is much speech in silence.
What does the Jew say? I alone have the truth.
What does the Buddhist say? I alone.
What does the Christian say? I alone.
What does the Muslim say? I alone.
What does every sect within a sect say? Alone.
What does every province within a province say? Alone.
What does every living creature say? Alone.
What does every family say? Alone.
What does every individual say? Alone.
This pride, this ignorance, how do we transform them into love?

That is why God is the one who speaks most: Let us be still; let us be still
and listen!

How long has civilization gone on? Five thousand years.
How long has the destruction we should claim gone on?
Five thousand years.
Ten thousand.
Has man learned anything from these words, from this silence?
He has learned nothing!

What is the secret of this strife then?
The ego.
Is there a cure for it? Knowledge.
What is knowledge? Other people.

We return to the primal silence.
Strife with others. Is it not a strife with one's self?
The self that we know. The self that we do not know.
The self that should be purified every moment.
The self that every moment should dwell in God.
Where does God dwell?
Does He dwell among us? This is blasphemy!
Does He not dwell among us? This, also, is blasphemy!

What is history? It is man, and it is God.
Where should we start from?
Where we think that we hate.
Where we think that we hate.
With other people who are the self which we ignore
Therefore God is all.

Is there no shore? The shore which is the sea?
What is the sea?
It is within the soul and beyond it.
It is today and it is yesterday.
It is the point and the circle.
It is all parts of one whole
It is where we start from and we do not end.
It is where we love and do not hate
It is where we live and do not die
It is where there is a shore and no shore.

Translated by Lena Jayyusi and John Heath-Stubbs

——‘Ali: ‘Ali ibn Abi Talib, the Prophet's cousin, who married his daughter, Fatima. He is
revered by all Muslims as a great and courageous man, with absolute integrity and faith in
men. By the Shi‘as, however, he is regarded as the head of the Shi‘a faith.

——Al-Mutanabbi: see note under ‘Abdallah al-Baraduni.

——Al-Ma‘arri (973–1057): the famous blind poet of al-Ma‘arra in Eastern Syria, and one of
the greatest poets of the Arabic language. He was an ascetic who spent most of his life in his
birthplace. Aside from his poetry, he is the author of *Epistles of Forgiveness*, a treatise in fine
Arabic prose about the poet's imaginary visit to paradise.

Amjad Nasir (b. 1955)

Jordanian poet. Born in al-Turra in Jordan, he obtained his primary and secondary education in the town of Zarqa. He worked in Jordanian television from 1975 to 1978, then in journalism. After that he moved to Beirut, where he edited the cultural section of the Palestinian review, *Al-Hadaf*, which had been founded by the famous Palestinian writer Ghassan Kanafani. During the Israeli siege of Beirut in 1982, he joined the group of young Arab writers who were broadcasting the Voice of the Palestinian Revolution. Today he edits the cultural section of *Al-Ufq* review, which is published in Cyprus. He is one of the young experimental poets who are trying to find new avenues for modern Arabic poetry. However, his verse has been able to retain great authenticity and a firm link with his roots in a yet unindustrialized society, demonstrating the great capacity of modernist poetry in Arabic to reflect various aspects of reality in modern terms. Nasir has published three collections of poetry to date, the last of which, *Shepherds of Solitude*, appeared in 1986.

EXILE

> you see
> we haven't changed that much
> perhaps not at all
> our words are still
> strong, clear
> the way we Bedouins talk
> long embraces
> asking after family and herds
> laughing thunderously
> the scent of old wood
> stored in barns
> still breathes from our clothes
>
> you see
> we haven't changed that much

perhaps not at all
we still squat on the earth
washlines still block
the doors to our houses
our children covered with dust
while in the evenings over mint tea
we exchange gossip
that refreshes
we still avenge our honor
our blood
has not changed to water
we live
as if still living in al-Mafraq
or Salt, Karak or Ramtha
as if we hadn't crossed
northern borders
to big cities and coasts
where cruel war rages
and a great sea roars
where strangers clutch at each other's shirtcollars,
from balconies
shoot bullets through washlines

Translated by May Jayyusi and Charles Doria

LONELINESS

at night
yes night
when walls start breathing
and concrete fogs spread
seeping between fingers, into nostrils
when we find no one to talk to
when in vain we search out wrinkled faces, scarred hands
when in rooms hermetically sealed we scream
where echo does not echo
when we raise our hands and no shadow falls
when at the door we hear no knock
and none pass beneath the window

when we hear no marmots gnaw in the cupboard
or love groan in the next room
when we rush to the dresser drawer
but fail to find the family photo album
when we look for a gun, knife or rope
yet hit only plaster wall
which in total silence cracks
when we think of our names but do not think of them
when all this happens alone at night, God,
in a sealed room
what shall we do?

Translated by May Jayyusi and Charles Doria

BENT BRANCHES

I want to clear my head
of the bric-a-brac of sermons and kind words
I want to purge my heart
of young love's heartbreak
and slivers of tinted glass
from my eyes I want to wash
life's shredded nets
and curtains behind locked windows
I want to clear my voice
of songs' acid
and those melodies that come
all wrapped up in shiny ribbons
I want to free my shoulders
of birds' nests
and morning's silent birds
from body I want to strip away
the raiment of war and peace
and the powder of conquests in reverse
I want to purify my soul
of obedience's thoughtless assent
and the overrripe grapes of forgiveness
from my face I want to banish
the aristocrat's pedigreed hauteur

and his multibranched family tree
from my page I want to chase
the nonsense of poetry
and the futility of meaning
I refuse to play any more roles
That're not clear and well defined
or be exposed to harmonies
that are not real
All I want to hear
is the universe shudder
while it batters my heart
and watch light dissolve
in eye's still water
I want to walk alone
closing behind me
the door of the ancestral house.

Translated by May Jayyusi and Charles Doria

Salah Niyazi (b. 1935)

Iraqi poet. Born in al-Nasiriyya in Iraq, he studied in Baghdad, then did his postgraduate work in London. He worked as a teacher and broadcaster in Baghdad before he moved to the British Broadcasting Corporation in London, where he was promoted to head of the Arabic Talks section, a post he held until 1984. He has published several works of poetry. His best known are the long poem, *The Thinker* (1976), and the collection, *We* (1971). His poetry reflects his intellectual interests as well as his anguish at the social and moral shortcomings of society.

HAMEED

In the sky
Your flock of birds
circling your reed house
swim in ecstasy
waves of colored silk
You atop your cart
a fallen knight, neck broken,
circle under them in silence
going from house to house
collecting garbage here, there
Your eyes inflamed, festering, gloom-filled
are fixed on the trash heap
while in the sky flocks of birds
create waves of pure color.
You gag, almost spitting blood
. . . the horse wearies . . . how many times
it dies on its rounds
like a captive
while you circle,
circle,

and the flocks of birds
you do not see
circle.

Translated by Lena Jayyusi and Charles Doria

UM HAKEEM

She cannot read or write
she does not understand
the radio's bulletins:
victories here, marches there,
thundering drums,
this bridge crossed, that overwhelming advance
while the wheels of another war
that never leads to victory
grind continually
in the head of soldier Hakeem.

Beginning of the month
she awaits for it to end
and dies thirty times.
One pound in his letter:
on one pound a month
who can survive?

No one drops by
but she backs him into a corner
has him read her Hakeem's letter.
Quickly her eyes fill with tears;
she does not understand what it says
yet from the first word she weeps.
"Hakeem says he is well
and enjoys good health,
when night and the night's ghosts come,
he remembers his aunt: 'Lord, won't she recover?'
Remembers his sister: 'Why was she divorced?
She is so good!' "

She listens, she cries,
she awaits each month
and dies thirty times.

Translated by Lena Jayyusi and Charles Doria

——Um Hakim: the mother of Hakeem. Arab women in many Arab countries are called by the names of their first born child, the male being preferred to the female.

Nizar Qabbani (b. 1923)

Syrian poet. Born to a well-to-do Damascene family, he studied law at the Syrian University and entered the Syrian diplomatic corps, representing his country in various European and Asian capitals. His first collection, *The Brunette Told Me* (1942) was published when he was nineteen years old and it was an instant success, arousing a popularity which has only increased with years. Qabbani, certainly the most popular poet in the Arab world, has published to date numerous collections of poetry, concentrating mainly on two themes: first, the man-woman relationship in all its dimensions, particularly love, which he expresses exuberantly; and second, an outspoken criticism of Arab political and social life and a great celebration of resistance in the face of the various types of oppression of human freedom and dignity. Qabbani, moreover, has been instrumental in modernizing poetic language and imagery, proving that accessibility is no deterrent to poetic excellence. Among his collections are *Poems from Nizar Qabbani* (1957) *Poetry is a Green Lamp* (1964), *The Diary of a Blasé Woman* (1968), *The Book of Love* (1970), *A Hundred Love Letters* (1972), *Outlawed Poems* (1972), and several others. A collection of his poetry is being prepared in English translation by PROTA.

POEMS

Between us
twenty years of age
between your lips and my lips
when they meet and stay
the years collapse
the glass of a whole life shatters.

·

The day I met you I tore up
all my maps
all my prophecies
like an Arab stallion I smelled the rain

of you
before it wet me
heard the pulse of your voice
before you spoke
undid your hair with my hands
before you had braided it

                    .

There is nothing I can do
nothing you can do
what can the wound do
with the knife on the way to it?

                    .

Your eyes are like a night of rain
in which ships are sinking
and all I wrote is forgotten
In mirrors there is no memory.

                    .

God how is it that we surrender
to love giving it the keys to our city
carrying candles to it and incense
falling down at its feet asking
to be forgiven
Why do we look for it and endure
all that it does to us
all that it does to us?

                    .

Woman in whose voice
silver and wine mingle
in the rains
From the mirrors of your knees
the day begins its journey
life puts out to sea

                    .

I knew when I said
I love you

that I was inventing a new alphabet
for a city where no one could read
that I was saying my poems
in an empty theater
and pouring my wine
for those who could not
taste it.

•

When God gave you to me
I felt that He had loaded
everything my way
and unsaid all His sacred books.

•

Who are you
woman entering my life like a dagger
mild as the eyes of a rabbit
soft as the skin of a plum
pure as strings of jasmine
innocent as children's bibs
and devouring like words?

•

Your love threw me down
in a land of wonder
it ambushed me like the scent
of a woman stepping into an elevator
it surprised me
in a coffee bar
sitting over a poem
I forgot the poem
It surprised me
reading the lines in my palm
I forgot my palm
It dropped on me like a blind deaf
wildfowl
its feathers became tangled with mine
its cries were twisted with mine

It surprised me
as I sat on my suitcase
waiting for the train of days
I forgot the days
I traveled with you
to the land of wonder

.

Your image is engraved
on the face of my watch
It is engraved on each of the hands
It is etched on the weeks
months years
My time is no longer mine
it is you

Translated by Lena Jayyusi and W. S. Merwin

TWO AFRICAN BREASTS

Let me find time
to welcome in this love
that comes unbid.
Let me find time
to memorize
this face that rises
out of the trees
of forgetfulness.
Give me the time
to escape this love
that stops my blood.
Let me find time
to recognize your name,
my name,
and the place
where I was born.
Let me find time
to know where I shall die
and how I will revive, as

a bird inside your eyes.
Let me find time
to study the state of winds
and waves, to learn the maps
of bays . . .

Woman, who lodges
inside the future
pepper and pomegranate seeds,
give me a country
to make me forget all countries,
and give me time
to avoid this Andalusian face,
this Andalusian voice,
this Andalusian death
coming from all directions.
Let me find time to prophesy
the coming of the flood.

Woman, who was inscribed
in books of magic,
before you came
the world was prose.
Now poetry is born.
Give me the time to catch
the colt that runs toward me,
your breast.
The dot over a line.
A bedouin breast, sweet
as cardamom seeds
as coffee brewing over embers,
its form ancient as Damascene brass
as Egyptian temples.

Let me find luck
to pick the fish that swim
under the waters.

Your feet on the carpet
are the shape and stance
of poetry.

Let me find the luck
to know the dividing line
between the certainty
of love and heresy.
Give me the opportunity
to be convinced I have seen
the star, and have been spoken to
by saints.

Woman,whose thighs are like
the desert palm where golden
dates fall from,
your breasts speak seven tongues
and I was made to listen
to them all.
Give me the chance
to avoid this storm,
this sweeping love,
this wintry air, and to be convinced,
to blaspheme, and to enter
the flesh of things.
Give me the chance
to be the one
to walk on water

Translated by Diana Der Hovanessian
and by Lena Jayyusi (first translator)

POEMS

Disrobe, my love.
Since it has been such
a long time since the time
of miracles. Disrobe.
And let miracles begin.
I am speechless
before you.
Your body speaks all languages.

I am afraid to
put my love into words.
Wine loses its bouquet
when poured out of its jug.

       ·

You ask for the date
of my birth?
Write this down.
It was the day you loved me
and gave me our first kiss.

       ·

EQUATION

I love you
therefore I am
in the present.
I write, beloved,
and retrieve the past.

Translated by Diana Der Hovanessian
and by Lena Jayyusi (first translator)

I CONQUER THE WORLD WITH WORDS

I conquer the world with words,
conquer the mother tongue,
verbs, nouns, syntax.
I sweep away the beginnings of things
and with a new language
that has the music of water the message of fire
I light the coming age
and stop time in your eyes
and wipe away the line
that separates
time from this single moment.

Translated by Diana Der Hovanessian
and by Lena Jayyusi (first translator)

FOOLISHNESS

When I wiped you from
the book of memory

I did not know I was striking
out half my life.

Translated by Diana Der Hovanessian
and by Lena Jayyusi (first translator)

LANGUAGE

When a man is in love
how can he use old words?
Should a woman
desiring her lover
lie down with
grammarians and linguists?

I said nothing
to the woman I loved
but gathered
love's adjectives into a suitcase
and fled from all languages.

Translated by Diana Der Hovanessian
and by Lena Jayyusi (first translator)

CUP AND ROSE

I went to the coffeehouse
intending to forget
our love and bury
my sorrows, but
you emerged
from the bottom of my
coffee cup,
a white rose.

Translated by Diana Der Hovanessian
and by Lena Jayyusi (first translator)

TESTAMENT

You want a guarantee
of love
signed in bold letters?
Yes, I can promise that

you will be the last woman.
But what good is
the sea's guarantee of
an island's boundaries?

Translated by Diana Der Hovanessian
and by Lena Jayyusi (first translator)

INTRODUCTION TO *PAINTING WITH WORDS*

Twenty years on the road of love
but the road is still unmapped.
Sometimes I was the victor.
More often the vanquished.
Twenty years, O book of love
and still on the first page.

Translated by Diana Der Hovanessian
and by Lena Jayyusi (first translator)

THE CHILD SCRIBBLES

My fault, my greatest fault,
O sea-eyed princess,
was to love you
as a child loves.
(The greatest lovers,
after all, are children)

My first mistake
(and not my last)
was to live
in the state of wonder
ready to be amazed
by the simple span
of night and day,

and ready for every woman
I loved to break me
into a thousand pieces to make
me an open city,
and to leave me behind her
as dust.

My weakness was to see
the world with the logic of a child.

And my mistake was dragging
love out of its cave into the open air,
making my breast
an open church for all lovers.

Translated by Diana Der Hovanessian
and by Lena Jayyusi (first translator)

FRAGMENTS FROM *NOTES ON THE BOOK OF DEFEAT*

If an audience could be arranged
and also my safe return
this is what I'd tell the Sultan
This is what he'd learn:
O Sultan, my master, if my clothes
are ripped and torn
it is because your dogs with claws
are allowed to tear me.
And your informers every day are those
who dog my heels, each step
unavoidable as fate.
They interrogate my wife, at length,
and list each friend's name.
Your soldiers kick and beat me,
force me to eat from my shoes,
because I dare approach these walls
for an audience with you.
You have lost two wars
and no one tells you why.
Half your people have no tongues.
What good their unheard sigh?
The other half, within these walls,
run like rabbits and ants,
silently inside.
If I were given safety
from the Sultan's armed guards
I would say, O Sultan,
the reason you've lost wars twice

was because you've been walled in from
mankind's cause and voice.

*Translated by Diana Der Hovanessian
and by Lena Jayyusi (first translator)*

FROM *THE ACTORS*

(1)

When ideas, when thought itself,
flattens out, in a city,
and curves like a horseshoe,
when any rifle picked up by
a coward can crush a man,
when an entire city becomes
a trap, and its people turn
into mice,
when the newspapers become mere
funeral notices,
everything dies
everything is without life—
the water, the plants,
voices and colors.
Trees migrate, leaving their roots.
Geography is wrested
from its place; place escapes
and we the end of man.

(4)

When a helmet becomes God in heaven
and can do what it wishes
with a citizen—crush, mash
kill and resurrect
whatever it wills,
then the state is a whorehouse,
history is a rag,
and thought is lower than boots.

When a breath of air
comes by decree
of the sultan,

when every grain of wheat we eat,
every drop of water we drink
comes only by decree
of the sultan,
when an entire nation turns into
a herd of cattle fed in the sultan's
shed, embryos will suffocate
in the womb, women will miscarry
and the sun will drop
a black noose over our square.

(9)

The June war is over.
It is as if nothing happened.
Faces, eyes are no different.
The courts of Inquisition reopened
and the inspectors, the Don Quixotes,
are back with their malignant conclusions.
People laugh
because it is past crying
They laugh because
it is beyond tears.
And we are content,
content with war, with peace,
with heat, with cold,
content with sterility, with
fertility, and with everything
in the Book of Fate
in the Heavens. And all we can say is
"Unto God we shall return."

(10)

The stage is burned
down to the pit
but the actors have not died yet.

Translated by Diana Der Hovanessian
and by Lena Jayyusi (first translator)

———The June War: the six-day war in 1967 between Egypt, Syria, and Jordan on the one
hand and Israel on the other. It ended in a disaster for the Arabs which aroused the concern
of poets all over the Arab world.

Samih al-Qasim (b. 1939)

Palestinian poet from Galilee. Born into a Druze family, he was educated in Rama and Nazareth and took up a teaching position in an Israeli public school, from which he was dismissed because of his political views. He has also been imprisoned and held under house arrest several times on account of his poetry and political commitment. By the age of thirty, al-Qasim had published six collections of poetry, widely read throughout the Arab villages of Galilee and eventually throughout the Arab world. His poetry deals mostly with Palestinian captivity and struggle. His current concern is to establish a Palestinian theater with a high artistic and intellectual mission. His most recent *diwans, The Dark Side of the Apple, the Bright Side of the Heart* (1981), *The Dimensions of the Spirit* (1983), and *Persona Non Grata* (1986), reflect his continuous experimentation with language and tone.

GIRL FROM RAFAH

The acacia is drooping
Rafah's gates are sealed by wax
and locked by curfew
The girl's job:
Carry bread and bandages
to a wounded fighter
who'd come home past midnight
She had to cross a street
watched by foreign eyes,
tracked by gunsights,
by the wayward wind.

The acacia tree is drooping,
the door of a house in Rafah
opens like a wound
She leaps into the courtyard's lap
A second leap:
a palm tree embraces her

on terror's pavement
Another leap:
a patrol
Another leap:
a flashlight
"Halt! Who goes there?"
Five guns
She stares wide-eyed
Fuve guns!

The acacia tree is snapped in two
In the morning
a court is held in session
for the criminal
For Fatimah
Child of eight!

Translated by Sharif Elmusa and Charles Doria

FROM: AFTER THE APOCALYPSE

I feel my limbs,
but cannot find them.
I implore my sense of sight,
but see nothing beyond a neutral grey.
Suddenly, warm radiates through the sand
crowding my spirit.
I discover my hands and legs,
there they are, familiar limbs,
assembling themselves into a heap of sand!
My body sees me.
Here I am, creating myself in my own image.
Here I am, the first human on another planet called:
Dayr Yasin,

One could say then that humanity
reconsiders itself,
reconsiders the laws, and the laws of the laws,
takes phenomena seriously,
in anticipation of what surprises the future holds

in the galaxy's enchanted whirl,
orbited by earthly satellites
gushing from wombs of volcanoes
to be grabbed immediately
by space scientists
who bless them with the loveliest names:
Lidice
Kufr Qasim
Sabra, Shatila,
My Lai.
One cannot help being astonished
at the breakdown of norms and mores,
at the simultaneous fall of all equations,
let alone fig trees, bonds, travel tickets, house arrests,
school and marriage certificates,
let alone global conventions: the Third World,
European Common Market, the Stock Market,
Alignment and Nonalignment, Nuclear Weapons, Disarmament,
and documents of death,

Come with me, bedouin girl,
you who have not yet spoken,
come, let's give names to new things,
they may give us back our own names in return.
In my name you rise from the dead.
In your name I make death acceptable,
a familiar morning greeting,
a bending over the neighbor's fence
to pluck a little rose for a tired lapel.
O virgin bedouin girl, with lips open,
but silent, you see everything
through the transparent wall of Apocalypse,
you bear on your shoulders the burden of everything:
storms, bloodstained hands, children's lips
still clutching their mother's severed breasts,
everything: trees twisted in the mud,
tall blackened buildings, broken windows,
charred skeletons sitting cross-legged
cigarette in hand, watching the TV set

continue its broadcast (live under the rubble)
of the emergency session
of the United Nations . . . etc. etc.

You see through the transparent wall
of Apocalypse sound mufflers on secret guns,
nickel handcuffs, police billy clubs, tanks,
tear gas bombs, demonstrations, burning car tires,
and bullets fired into the air,
apologizing to angels,
making their ways straight
to the school girls' breasts.

At this, international agencies would hurry
to quiet reactions and rumors
while the doleful, angry chorus
exercises its absolute freedom
in the biggest armed robbery
in history.

The present is an innocent lie.
To see the future we must consult the past—
a past ever-present before our eyes,
a mammoth octopus.

O virgin desert!
Here we are, sent by the heart and mind
on an official mission
to build the world anew.
To prepare it once again
for another Apocalypse!

Tree trunk against tree trunk,
stone next to stone,
thus the relationship takes form.
We begin from here
though doubts sometimes assail us.
Sometimes we'll miss one another,
but we won't be afraid to look behind.

Later,
new children will be born,

they'll ask their fathers sternly:
Why? For whom? When and how?
There won't be anyone to answer

except the ground waters singing:
I am grief! I announce my innocence!
I am desire! I enforce my authority!
I am love! I spread my sails on land
and scatter my seeds in the furrows of the sea.
I am hate! Your fire, your sacred fire!

Nothing remains the same.
In the long run, motion asserts itself,
erects new rules over the pure sands
now subject to factories' oil,
fires, the vomit of the sick,
and the wretched human din.

But after all this
there must be some recompense
for the children are about to go to school.
So let the storms subside a little
and the darkness lift itself off part of the road
for their sakes, for their sakes only,
for the sake of the children
going to school
after the Apocalypse!

Translated by Sharif Elmusa and Naomi Shihab Nye

——Rafah: southernmost town of Palestine in the Sinai, occupied since 1967 by Israel. A town with a large refugee camp, it has always shown resistance to Israel and, in the fifties, was a center of the early Fida'i movement. It was bombarded by Israel in 1956 and 111 people from the camp were killed.

——Dayr Yasin: a village near Jerusalem whose population was massacred by the Irgun terrorist faction led by Menachem Begin. The tragedy took place on April 9, 1948, and was meant to terrorize the Arab population in other parts of the country.

——Kufr Qasim: a massacre committed by Israeli soldiers in 1956 against the inhabitants of the village of Kufr Qasim. While the villagers were out in the fields, the Israeli authorities imposed a curfew. The soldiers stationed around the village shot returning villagers even though they were aware that they could not have known of the curfew.

——Sabra and Shatila: two Palestine refugee camps in West Beirut which were attacked by Phalangist forces in September 1982, during the Israeli occupation of the city. Numerous civilians were slaughtered in cold blood, and many whole families were wiped out. The two camps have become symbols of atrocity.

——My Lai: the massacre in the Vietnamese village of My Lai conducted by the American Lt. William Calley and his military unit on Vietnamese civilians and unarmed soldiers in 1969. The verdict of guilty was given against Calley. He subsequently lost an appeal and the case was closed.

Sayf al-Rahabi (b. 1956)

Omani poet. Born in Masqat, Oman, Rahabi studied in Cairo, specializing in journalism, and now works as a journalist in Paris and the Gulf. He is a promising young poet whose poetry, all written in prose, sets out to show the unity of contemporary Arabic culture and the shared aspirations of Arab poets everywhere for internal order and external liberation. He has published three books of poetry: *Sea Gull of Madness* (1981), *The Green Mountain* (1982), and *Bells of Estrangement* (1983).

ENTERING THE GARDENS OF DOOM

I know I'm more alone than ever.
My life's a rainy ending.
How can I watch time
with all its strength drag sheep
in broken chariots?
How can I see rivers of blood flowing
from the skulls of infants
just before they sleep
or wait for years to heal
the festering Arab wound?
or blunt the sleepless thorns
that crucify my brain?
In all that I remember
there are dancers planting the axes
of war against those cultivated murderers,
those civilized bulls
that are the judges of our courts.
I feel in my blood
like hurt birds
the presence of shepherds and evenings.

I stand in God's creation
like a sun wrapped in grief.

I receive telegrams of tragedy
that must be answered.
There are no seasons anymore,
just life.

Who knows how rocks stand guard
like flowers from the tropics
around the field of massacres?
Who understands the dialects of sorrow
that survived when Cordoba was slain,
and now Beirut?

The princes are recovering from colds
they caught in the brothels of politics.

Leave me to sadness.
The clouds have broken many a man with rain,
and winter is a snake among the tatters of the poor.
Leave me to find some sweetness
from the spirit of aging serpents.
Leave me to the nothingness of sip after sip
of coffee.
Distance has destroyed us,
and a single bird keeps vigil
over bayonetted bellies
like a laurel of havoc.

Translated by Lena Jayyusi and Samuel Hazo

Fu'ad Rifqa (b. 1930)

Lebanese poet and scholar. He studied in Lebanon and Germany, where he obtained a Ph.D. in philosophy. He has taught in various universities in Beirut and, in 1976–1977, at Indiana University. He is now Professor of Philosophy at Beirut University College. He has translated selections of the poetry of Rilke and Hölderlin from German. His first collection, *Anchor on the Bay*, appeared in 1961, and he has published four more since. In 1973 a discourse titled *Poetry and Death* was published. A lucid but highly symbolic diction and imagery, a subdued and wistful tone, and a spirit of gentle alienation characterize his poetry.

MIRRORS

Always these gallows,
this crowd, the eyes
that meet and turn away,
these daggers of defeat
that hide in the bricks of this house,
in seasons to come,
in the very seeds of fruit.

Always these cafes,
these wounding tongues
that articulate through smoke
like eyes that search and search.

In eyes, in shivering hands,
in laurel, in mirrors—
always the face of death
masked like a prince of the heart,
a knight who comes
to awaken your feast.

Translated by Sargon Boulus and Samuel Hazo

THE THRESHOLD

Having crossed the threshold,
you leave your house to itself.

You pass the end of the fence
and make all distance near,
and nearness distant.
The slope and all you loved
are like a face in the past.
You yield to memory.
You scale mysterious mountains.
You climb the castle of the dead
and forget your losses.
You come to a valley,
and you feel that terror within you
when everything is memory
and you can't save yourself
and there are no thresholds
anymore.

Translated by Sargon Boulus and Samuel Hazo

THE ULTIMATE DISTANCE

You will not travel
the ultimate distance
nor witness the harvest.
Snow barricades your door,
and your silent fence confines
no more than poetry.

There are seasons in your body's cells—
seasons and gleaming shores.

Soon they will vanish
as will the sign that followed you
from towers to mountains
where you explored temples in ruins
and noon's high wound.

You will spend tonight here.
The stars will keep their distance.
You will not witness the harvest.
Snow barricades your door,
and your silent fence confines
no more than poetry.

It is enough to know
that there remains an ultimate distance
like a thread from here
to anywhere.

Translated by Sargon Boulus and Samuel Hazo

THE FORTUNE TELLER

She points to a star
that shows you your other shadow.
You see in a single poem
the fact of God, the fact of earth
and everything between the two.

You see a dove
that sleeps like any vagabond
in crevices, or rides the lightning
until it rests in a blue cloud
moored on its own seas.

You seek a new map.

Translated by Sargon Boulus and Samuel Hazo

Su^cad al-Mubarak al-Sabah (b. 1942)

Kuwaiti poet. Born to the Sabah family, rulers of Kuwait, and married to one of their prominent members, she distinguished herself in her own right not only through her poetry but also through her active participation in several pan-Arab organizations for freedom, human rights, and Arab unity. She has also supported several literary activities, sponsoring recently the republication of all forty volumes of the prestigious *Al-Risala* literary review, which was at the heart of the Arab literary movement in the thirties and forties. In 1982, she obtained her Ph.D. in Planning and Development from the University of Surrey and has recently published several books in the field of her specialization, including *Kuwait, Anatomy of a Crisis Economy* (1985, in English). Her poetry, which began along conservative lines, underwent a great change both in technique and content, now reflecting wit as well as anguish, deep joy in life's gifts of love and friendship, but also great anger at the plight suffered by her fellow Arabs. She has published two volumes of poetry, *A Wish* (1972), and *To You, My Son* (1982), on her young dead son. A new volume containing her recent poetry is now in publication.

MAD WOMAN

I am quite mad and you are wholly sane
From the mind's paradise I've sought to flee
You are all wise, yours are the summer months
So leave the winter's changing face for me.

I'm sick with love and I'm past any cure
Oppressed in body, that is woman's plight
My nerves are taut and should you only whisper
Into the empty air I would take flight.

I'm like a small fish lost in the great ocean
When will you lift the siege? You've hidden away
The key to unlock my house in your own pocket
And enter my life's details day by day.

O love, my passion whirls me dizzily
Gather my scattered soul whose fragments fly
For you are standing at the frozen pole
And I beneath an equatorial sky.

O love, I stand against the ten commandments
History behind is only blood and sand
To love I owe allegiance. Lemon trees
Within your breast my only native land.

Translated by May Jayyusi and John Heath-Stubbs

FREE HARBOR

Many ships have asked for sanctuary
In the harbor of my eyes
I refused asylum to all of them
Your ships alone
Have the right to take refuge
In my territorial waters
Your ships alone
Have the right to sail in my blood
Without prior permission.

Translated by May Jayyusi and John Heath-Stubbs

YOU ALONE

You alone . . . control my history
And write your name on the first page
And on the third, and the tenth,
And on the last.
You alone are allowed to sport with my days
From the first century of my birth
To the twenty-first century after love.
You 'alone can add to my days what you wish
And delete what you wish
My whole history flows from the palms of your hands
And pours into your palms.

Translated by May Jayyusi and John Heath-Stubbs

A WILD CAT

Your love lurks in my veins like a bandit
Commits arson, shatters lanterns
And skulks in the corners of my veins
Like a wild cat with sharp claws
Alert to hunt moths
To pounce on birds
And I lie awake at night waiting for it to come forth
From my blood.

You came with your conquering army, and caused an upheaval
That changed my life
You sequestered all my possessions
Bound me with chains of gold
And put me under house arrest
Within the limits of your eyes
You locked me in the cell of love
And took the keys away with you.

Translated by May Jayyusi and John Heath-Stubbs

THE PIT

You madly kiss my lips—I seem to see
A dreadful pit that's gaping wide for me
For you are a professional in love
Amateur I, in my simplicity.

Translated by May Jayyusi and John Heath-Stubbs

Kamal Sabti (b. 1958)

Iraqi poet. He was born in al-Nasiriyya, Iraq, and obtained a degree in cinematography. He worked in literary journalism until his conscription into the Iraqi army, where he fought at the Persian front. Sabti is one of the young generation of Iraqi poets who have been building on the traditions established by the older generation that includes Hameed Said, Sami Mahdi, and Sa'di Yusuf, who, although deeply committed to the political scene, have been able to see life in all its dimensions. Sabti shows great promise, and his poetry reflects an early maturity and a capacity to experiment in technique and imagery. He has published three collections of verse, *The Rose of the Sea* (1980), *The Shadow of Something* (1983), and *Jungles* (1984).

POEMS FROM *JUNGLES*

4
What remains in the hands
except for the poem?
No one is left in the land
who can steal the flame
carry it toward the fear of saddened faces
No one is left in the land
who can haul the rock
of questions and torments

so who are you
        to bear the rock?
            the fire?

Who are you . . .
language uttered in alien deserts
panting naked
without a body
to gather sleep
from a dying wakefulness?

6

The echo of the minaret crumbles within us,
a speechless language
It dissovles in us and we in it
in order to say
the resounding echoes are questions
Within the questions
lies a guillotine

8

When the others abandon
the two of us in the wilderness
and a grave materializes, pursuing us
like a snake, and we flee far into the distance
only to find that grave advancing from the horizon
When we are wounded, trapped
between two graves, we will cry,
cursing our luck . . .
then . . .
then . . .
do not say goodbye
It is I, my friend,
who will cry out:
Earth,
do you see this?
We are approaching our end . . .
when will you approach yours?
There

      in that distant land, she embraced
      two questions, and she died.
      Who, by the way, was she? Who, by the way, were you?

9
      Will you stand tall?

His feet are neither attached to land
to sea nor to sky . . .

      Will you stand tall?

He bends down, a corpse in the darkness
far from his kin,
submitting to strangers,
their joints chilled,
their vision stunted

      Will you stand tall?

He bends down, a form
slackening . . .
disintegrating bit
              by bit
He treads the earth with his head
weeping
        Will you stand tall?

where are his feet?

13
Lifeless birds
migrate to you
Women come to you
but they are deserts

Then you have died

14
Is it because childhood is a neglected ship's mast
that the sea fumes,
dismembers it?
Is it because childhood
      is a refuge for a lovely day
that terrors and guillotines
multiply beyond its fancies?

Everything
scattered across your traps . . .
the voice could no longer remember its objects

Could no longer build for itself a garden
              of echoes
              a garden of messages

We took
    everything
        —empty or full—
        to the forest of fire
Nothing remained to meet their gaze
except our nakedness before the swords!

Translated by Lena Jayyusi and Naomi Shihab Nye

Hameed Saʿid (b. 1941)

Iraqi poet. He studied Arabic literature at the University of Baghdad and worked for some time in teaching, then went on to be editor-in-chief of the daily *Al-Thaura*, Iraq's major newspaper. After heading the Radio and Television Broadcasting System for several years, he was reappointed editor-in-chief of *Al-Thaura*. A dedicated Baʻthist, he is one of the few committed poets who has also written on the experiences of his own life, merging the national with the personal in a highly symbolic fashion. He has three collections to date: *An Eighth Reading* (1972), *Book of Gypsy Songs* (1975), and *The Fires of Presence* (1978).

DYING AT THE EDGE OF DEATH

To Ghassan Kanafani, the Witness

Here is the scene: She follows him.
He follows her. The soldier patrols
the square. And the gypsy man shudders.
          She continues her watch.
On the road perhaps he will be waylaid.
But he was made to take this role,
the part of him who pursues the dream.
The royal guards must detect him.
          He is lost, and
          he is lost to her.

In the streets of Madrid, Jerusalem removes
her blouse. She is naked and hungry.
Looking out the windows in the evening
Madrid recognizes her and closes
          all the doors.
Fear drinks the glass of sweet wine.
And Madrid drinks the blood of her own children.
          He is lost. And she walks.

But the birds fear her
since her loss, and curse
their own nests.

Wherever he has been she follows now
to ask about him.
                    Any distinguishing marks?
Oh, don't you know? He crossed the sea
without a ship. He burned all his cards.
He died. And no one in al-Sumainah grieved.
No one wept for him. No one dug his grave
with spearheads. The spearheads lie mute
in the museum showcases.
He sinks his eyes into them.
The spears turn into books.
O Arab homeland, chained with sands,
take a page out of this book of spearheads
and ward off the Mongol horses that stand ready.

I gather your letters and scatter them.
I see you hesitate,
postponing your promises.
Come toward me.
I will show you the boundaries,
the edges of your hands,
of your chains.

Those who wake up with her
wander with her from coffeebar
to coffeebar.
In the night they wipe her face,
scent it, and sleep beside her.

Translated by Diana Der Hovanessian
and by Lena Jayyusi (first translator)

DAILY DELIGHTS

Tell this poem
that delights never end
they stand between our joy and morning office hours
between reality and mystery.

Tell this poem
    to continue its manifestations, its dialogues, its presences
to learn the delights
    the family knows:
the son speaking boldly, "Take me to my grandfather's house."
the daughter laughing at false pretexts.
In the morning family demands
are accompanied by chiding
At noon the family
is afraid of pretended anger, of gloom.
Evening, all is forgotten,
these are the waters that take hold of your time
the sweet fatigue,
and that's a wise wife you have.

Why does this poem announce its mutiny sometimes,
and elude you,
why does it do what your beloved sometimes does,
and suddenly attack?
Ah, you wanton poem!
What do your tired green orchards
have to do with us?
Your raw face came to me when I was a little boy,
accompanied me in youth
and claimed me in manhood
You belong to a family from the land of the *jinn*
from the celebration of roses
the angels of my inspiration do not fight
    a family of your stock
they've surrendered to the fire of your fragrance
and on the pages of expectation laid down the arms
I had intended to fight you with.
Fear has its own climate,
    just like courage.
I fear you when you are near,
    and when you are far,
in the roses, and in the sand.
This is what gave your empty spaces their greater distance,
awakened a mare in its sands

where between the echo of its hoofsteps
and your enchanting expanse
the dilemma lies.

In your golden gardens
we planted flowers once
why did those flowers
        which accompanied us to you
block our way?
Did our gardens block *your* way?
We told you: enter in peace . . . and we said
enter by force
our gates are flung open for the fires,
        for love and water.
You were never anything but the desired, frolicking elf,
the docile one
An unexplainable drive
        pushes us toward your land
        where your obtrusive conquests reach
and is caught in the net of your mirrors
Now my body celebrates your joy
is crowded with your delights
made whole by your glow
crowned by your glow
You are an onerous tempter
    and I'm a man who never tires of the chase
I burst a queenly language
in the rose of death
and erect for it a kingdom.

Translated by Lena Jayyusi and Naomi Shihab Nye

EMANATIONS

I reclaim the moment . . . call the madness madness
birds will not abandon their habit of chirping
Let us call things by their names.
                    They were no homeland, those trees
                    that pretended youthfulness

And you were only the beginning
Enchanting homeland . . . fragrant waters
I testify that you gave me the sea
So then confess:
                    You are suspended in my blood
                    Caught up in the tide
                    and when waters retreat,
                    they leave you
                    Then with the tide you come again.
Let us say that what is between us
is a youthful passion
Will we spend the vacation trying to awaken?
Birds will not abandon the habit of chirping
and gardens do not know heresy.

I reclaim the moments . . . madness
awakens . . . you become the beloved
whose seasons I can discover
They were no homeland, those trees
                            that pretended youthfulness
Birth seems more splendid
when one is dying
Language's barrier will not touch
this vigilance between us
Have we awakened? I asked myself
How did I find you? Does birth have its secrets?
A firechild dances within me
I wonder:
            whether a firechild dances
within a woman
                whose face is inhabited by the sea
                from whom poems emanate
I turned round and cried out
to all the women of the city . . . "There is one
                among you
                who can impose madness"
Why among all women must you be my chrysalis
and must you be my gate?
I wonder: Does the sea offer medals to lovers?
Dates remain forgotten

O Sea!

       Extinguish your lanterns. The kindly guards
       are asleep
       Did the shores tell you of two passersby
       whose faces are shadowed by sorrow
               and savage happiness?

They awaken

       they are from countries
       who teach their lovers to lie.

The cities have changed from what we remember
The streets open their shirts to the stars
The light falls down
across the brow of the woman
       whose face the sea inhabits
       from whom poems emanate.
The streets laugh . . . and depart in the swell of passion
I read in your name

       who are you?
       who are you?
       who are you?

Many birds of grass between you and me
knock at my door at dawn
Once the night approaches
they come and settle in your dream
Are you dead?

       How is childbirth in the state of death?
Let me confess:

       You were burning
       But I did not bless your flames
       The birds that accompanied me to you
       threw themselves

               down between us

They burned
and I burned

       and what was left between the sheets was only my ashes

I reclaim the moments
My memory awakens
the songs that have aged recollect
their childhood

and the noble madness returns
My memory journeys to the cities of earth
You are now with me
Place has become time . . . and
                this is *your* time
Where time is . . . there you are
All the destruction that afflicted the soul
                recedes now
Happiness besieges me . . .
                  sadness besieges me
This is a crucial time when the poem
may once again be hammered and formed
It emerges naked and prays for the woman
whose face the sea inhabits
from whom poems emanate

Of which night do you want me to speak?

My memory awakens
                Were you with me that night when
                the crimson moon approached me
                and demanded the Euphrates?
                Were you with me when the sea
                embraced me
                and shared my shirt?
                Were you with me the night I
                distributed my sadness among the palm trees?
My memory awakens   Madrid — Baghdad
                How beautiful night is when
                you are tired and sleep in my arms
                The rain wakens you . . . the thunder . . .
                you press close to my skin
Words desert us
The birds that take refuge in the bowers of your hair
                forget the songs
and remain a witness at whose doors
                confession knocks.

Translated by Lena Jayyusi and Naomi Shihab Nye

——Al-Sumaina: a place in southern Iraq.

——The Mongols: the Tatar hordes that swept over Persia and the Arab lands from the thirteenth century, destroying much of the thriving civilization of the Islamic empire, massacring people, and burning whole libraries. Because they caused a great decline in the Arab world, their invasion has not been forgotten and is mentioned in many poems and other literature.

Yusuf al-Sa'igh (b. 1933)

Iraqi poet, short story writer, and critic from Mosul. Educated in Iraq, with a Master's degree in Arabic literature, he has worked as a journalist and lectured on Arabic literature. Active in the Union of Writers and various cultural organizations, he has also cultivated a keen interest in painting. He was one of the editors of the prestigious literary monthly, *Afaq 'Arabiyya* (Arab Horizons), published by the Ministry of Information, and is currently an editor at the daily, *Al-Thaura*. He has four collections of poetry, including *Lady of the Four Apples* (1976), which mostly contains elegies on his wife, and is one of the most original works in contemporary Arabic poetry.

SUDDENLY

Her hand in my hand
her hair on my shoulder
and the road flying by
                quickly, quickly

Her hand in my hand
her head on my breast
I kiss it there
while she touches me
                finger by finger

There we were together
the road unreeling, spinning by
                quickly
when the sudden beast of the road pounced
and our vehicle spun
                turning us around
                spinning with it
one moment
and then

her hair
her head
her body
her hand
her fingers   in the dust
waving goodbye
    finger by finger

Translated by Diana Der Hovanessian with Salma Khadra Jayyusi

IS THIS ALL THAT REMAINS OF LOVE?

This midnight brings a moonless,
glossless dark, leaving our dew unlit
and mysterious in the grass.
My lady
begins as usual to cross
the gloomy path,
barefoot over grass and I
shall see her face
framed in my window's glass.
And inside her wild eyes
the illusions will break.
There—
the dew changes
her ebony hair to green
and a damp lock clings
to her brow. Now she stretches
out her hand without a word
(lovers need none) to show where
the golden band of love has been removed
leaving a white circle of skin
like an old scar. She smiles
at me like this. A quick glance,
and leaves. She's gone,
disappearing beyond
the fogged glass. I gasp
with unkissed kisses
and turn to search the pillow perhaps

for a hair, one left behind.
Already her perfume bottle top has dust.
I clasp her nightgown with its woman's scent.
And this is all that's left? of love?

Translated by Diana Der Hovanessian with Salma Khadra Jayyusi

A STORY

Two silhouettes
at the night express:
a man and woman.
They meet. They kiss.

In the next window
a man sits alone.
A gypsy, hand on his face,
sullen as stone.

Next scene: A cafe.
The man and the woman laugh,
pour wine into two glasses,
share an apple cut in half.

At the next table
the gypsy. He also splits
his apple in two; wine in two
glasses and sips.

Last act: A hotel window shows
gypsy and woman embracing now
In the other window our hero alone,
wild and wild-haired, silent as stone.

Translated by Diana Der Hovanessian with Salma Khadra Jayyusi

WHY

Usually
you wake first
get up naked from your bed

and in my dream I imagine the dawn
I open my eyes
and let the flavor of water wash my consciousness
the beautiful feminine wetness.

Usually
you come home before I do
and I know you are here
                windows are open
                the garden is watered
                flowers are on the table.

Usually
we go to sleep together
now you have gone before me
                        why?

Translated by Diana Der Hovanessian with Salma Khadra Jayyusi

WET

It has rained
and the moon twitches under moist clouds
I put on my slicker
                to walk
through empty streets alone
                you, at my side,
                my soul, walk too
                with me, damp with rain

Translated by Diana Der Hovanessian with Salma Khadra Jayyusi

ANTS

A thread of red ants
moves between the door and my bed.
I rise from sleep and grope,
then crush the ants
and sleep again and wake
                to find the thread

      of red ants between bed
      and door has grown
      to a thick rope

Translated by Diana Der Hovanessian with Salma Khadra Jayyusi

HAIR

Five months have passed
and my beloved's hair has grown
but is not washed
but is not combed
but is not set
with jasmine blossoms
like this, next to her part
          on the right.

Translated by Diana Der Hovanessian with Salma Khadra Jayyusi

Laila al-Sa'ih (b. 1936)

Palestinian poet. She studied psychology and philosophy at the Arab University in Beirut and has worked as a freelance literary journalist in Kuwait. She writes her poetry in a prose medium that reflects her sensitive approach to major events pertaining to the Palestinian experience, but also writes on love and the liberation of woman's spirit and mind. Her collection of prose poems, *Copybooks of the Rain*, appeared in 1979. A diary on the Israeli invasion of Beirut is in publication.

SEA DESIRES

Every evening before the sea departs from Beirut
he leaves a desire with her,
an apprehension. Like any little boy,
the sea dreams that what besieges
Beirut and bursts in her heart is
nothing but a fleeting passion;
nothing but a nightmare born
in her bed and gone scurrying
through her streets and hotels,
pausing at the harbor and
melting in every atom of the air.

Every evening the sea sends her his good wishes
and letters;
when roused by the sound of guns
and roaring tanks, he
is overcome by surprise or terror
seeing the stiff corpses on the ground,
in the corners and curbs.

The sea is naive, stands
on the shore staring at Beirut
wet with fire, water, smoke,
then hoards his desire and sleeps.

In Beirut man borrows the sea's waves
but not his naiveté
and in one fleeting moment spans
the years of life and discovers
that everything changes,
that everything is bathed in
a vision of destruction; he thinks
of Parliament, State, the national flag
and the South.
When did they all exist?

He thinks that
the abandonment of the old happiness
the familiarity
the friendly faces
now takes place
in the firelight
of bombs and shells
along shadowed streets
lined with corpses.

He contemplates:
return is impossible
to what came
before the beginning.

Translated by Patricia Alanah Byrne with the help of the editor

———The South: the south of Lebanon, an area of fighting and Israeli skirmishes which in 1982 culminated in the Israeli invasion of Lebanon.

Saniyya Salih (1935–1985)

Syrian poet. Born in Misyaf in northern Syria, she lost her mother at an early age, an event which had a permanent impact on her life and work. She married the poet Muhammad al-Maghut, and they lived in Damascus and Sharja, where her husband worked in literary journalism. She wrote a prose poetry that reveals a deep perception into the plight of women in the Arab world, and conveys a message of love that is sometimes tinged with despair. Her first collection, *Straitened Times*, appeared in 1964, and her second, *The Ink of Execution*, in 1970.

GOODBYE, ZENOBIA

In the end darkness drowned Zenobia
while the horsemen shouted for joy,
the oceans roared in a way
that had nothing to do with the pain
you etched in my heart, Zenobia.

    I shall continue to disappear into history
    careful the invading horses do not tread upon me
    Perhaps then I can reach you
I, the primitive woman, and you the dust.

Homeland falling to pieces, scatter like leaves,
I am your frail moon, the bridge built
from your children's bones . . . cross over,
catch up with the Romans as they nip at Zenobia's heels.

Homeless, lost, Zenobia wanders, limbs turned to stone;
outside, winds blow, horsemen destroy our homes.
She lies cold with fear while her heart's flame warms the invaders.
    In silence I built you a fortress palace
above the rocks, Zenobia; Palmyra your kingdom of
velvet moss, a capital that was
a butterfly of frost: by night

the water carriers' torches reflected
off your fabled palace until
it was mantled with stars.
That wounding winter, your windy season,
hurled the lost and defeated like strangers
into the desert. That season of winds
is no longer yours, you who once perched
like a dove on top of all your victories.
Even the poor and rejected broke their promise
and betrayed you. Later, oppression
made them cry and they are remembered
in the ledgers of failed storms. Waiting
for their glittering dream to come true,
they aged and vanished like a handful of dust.

For you the dream ended
on the streets of Rome,
where they carried you in triumph, a lamb slaughtereed in front of
the shamble house of justice.
In Rome's bitterblue sky
what did you see, your heart
swollen with rebel reverie,
as they slipped the grey cord
around your neck?

Whoever ascends the palace becomes king!
Behind him history and time fall away
Where can you find song now
that time weighs you down so?
        Hello vagabond time!
        Hello stars:
        Up there in your lofty heights
        what did you do?
I watch on history's shores
to return to Zenobia perhaps
        but an army of mistresses, whores
        and courtesans charges,
        with them the butchers come.
I shut my door in fright.

Zenobia! The desert has turned its poisonous back on you;
the problem was easily disposed of.
    My tears are full of dust,
    there isn't one clear glance
    of love: Zenobia, the world
    is lit with the fire of dogs!

Translated by Patricia Alanah Byrne with the help of the editor, and Charles Doria

——Zenobia: Queen of Palmyra and one of antiquity's most famous heroines. She was the remarkable wife of Odainatti, ruler of Palmyra. At his death, she took the reigns of government since her son, Wahab-Allath, was still a boy. Her ambition was to make Palmyra the capital of the Roman Empire in the East. The Palmyrene army occupied Egypt in 270 under the pretext of restoring it to Rome, and reached as far as Chalcedon opposite Byzantium (Constantinople) in Asia Minor. When Aurelian became emperor of Rome in 270, he feared Zenobia's ambitious policy and led an expedition against her, defeating her finally at Emeso (Homs). Aurelian captured her and reserved her for his expected triumph when he returned home. It is said that Zenobia was led in a cage through the streets of Rome and died humiliated and persecuted, but this story has not been substantiated. However, it fits the poem presented here.

Mai Sayigh (b. 1940)

Palestinian poet and writer. Born in Ghaza, Palestine, she graduated from the University of Cairo with a B.A. in sociology in 1960. She has dedicated her life since to the cause of freedom, particularly the women's movement. Since 1971 she has been president of the Union of Palestinian Women and has served on numerous panels at feminist meetings the world over. She has published three collections of poetry: *Garland of Thorns* (1968), *Love Poems for a Hunted Name* (1974), and *Of Tears and the Coming Joy* (1975). She has also written a prose account, *The Siege*, on the Israeli invasion and siege of Beirut in 1982, forthcoming.

LAMENT

Those we love die like birds
mourned by orange trees which never wither
tomorrow when birds return to Ghaza
to peck at your blue window
while narcissus perfume is everywhere
and jasmine fills the air
the henna tree will still stand
alone, a stranger to the world

On dark alley walls
our comrades' deaths are announced
posters show their smiling faces
The usual way we learn
one has fallen on the long road
We discovered in blood's path
           that death is life continuance
life deeply rooted in death
Yet when they drank to you in the pine woods
I asked why
        a tear hesitated in my cousin's eye
the tear in her green eye

that told me of your death
          what a great poster that'll make!

I burn with grief
I am no stone
yearning is a burden
for you bridge my life and death.
On Omar al-Mukhtar Street
foreign helmets that sting like whips
block your funeral
pursuing your beloved name
wrapped in a coffin that rests on Ghaza's wounds
                    . . . .
I am no stone
you fighter up to the moment of bitter death
whose perfume time after time rained down
                    from your window
penetrating you three times
on the fourth time you fell
dissolving all memories in my blood
floating on the tree-lined road to the old graveyard
where the grass laughed at my childhood's shadow
                and accompanied me to your resting place
                    . . . .
I am no stone
so I welcome your magic footsteps
                    when they come
joy pours from my bosom
all doors open in my face
I blame myself
I pledge you will be my eternal shadow
                    . . . .
Did they kill you?
Your wounds pierce every city
          that lies dreaming in the summer
Trees bleed, bird wings break
          the scent of basil everywhere
          in the alleys
          although passers-by

                    do not even notice you
don't they know your name is hunted?
          That you are under siege?
                        •   •   •   •

I am no stone
is it because blood's gleam
is all that's hopeful in the world that
we write our own histories
draw our faces' features in it
fix our seal
on the brows of the motherland
                we love so well
building it anew?

In blood we appoint the time
                to sow
                for it is the secret to freshness
Is it because we refuse to multiply like weeds or seagrass
          that lack identity or form
          to define our origin
tears dance from me
my joy weeps
joy that stretches to include
the last arm hurling death
at the aggressor's patrol
that stalk your streets
     which God has forsaken?
                        •   •   •   •

Time never ends its moments
the pride of your grief purifies
all moments passing through
the mind of the stars
and the veins of the stones
No bullet will pass
                without changing faces in some new way

Time will never end
for you are a beginning that never ceases
all about you the strangeness of things vanishes

they enjoy again the innocence of their first beginnings
I learn to perfection the art of waiting
  on the sidewalks of love and fire

Translated by Charles Doria with the help of the editor

Tawfiq Sayigh (1923–1971)

Palestinian poet. Born in Southern Syria, he grew up in Tiberius, where his family had acquired Palestinian citizenship. He studied at the Arab College and the American University in Beirut before going to Harvard to study English literature. After that he went to Cambridge University where he taught Arabic. Between 1962 and 1967 he was editor-in-chief of *Hiwar*, a bimontly cultural magazine. He published three collections of poetry, *Thirty Poems* (1954), *The Poem, K* (1960), and *The Ode of Tawfiq Sayigh* (1963). When *Hiwar* was no longer being printed he went to teach at the University of California at Berkeley. He has published several translations from English literature, including T. S. Eliot's *Four Quartets*. Sayigh wrote prose poetry whose language and images have great precision. It reflects an anguished soul torn between the sorrow and alienation he experienced as a Palestinian refugee, his ungratified love for K, and his deep metaphysical conflicts, which produced some of the best examples of the Christian faith within Arabic literature.

OUT OF THE DEPTHS I CRY UNTO YOU, O DEATH!

Come near   come nearer
my white young filly
Come nearer   my strong delicious filly
Come nearer   my filly in season
        Your words are songs and hymns
I heard them before I was born
They lullabied me quietly to sleep
I heard them on wedding nights when the dancers sang
I heard them in church above choirs of chanters
I heard them from the lips of my beloved
        while we grappled in a tangle of bedsheets

Come nearer   let me leap on you
        Then kick the earth and scream in the face of heaven
stir up the dust and fill the world with clatter

and gallop   gallop and gallop and gallop
climb the mountain and ford the streams
race the wind and birds and light itself
and even the vows of lovers.
Let's gallop wherever we choose
Let's never stop even when the light turns red
Let's damn directions   and gallop
I'll spur your flanks and gallop and gallop and gallop.

Don't loiter in pastures soft with hay
sweeter than sugar in your mouth
Don't pause with me
in festivals of sickness
or in the still swamp of senility
where bodies are corpses
where childhood is not a dream of innocence
but just a prison for the simple-minded
where eccentricity is a disease
        exile—humiliation,
and madness, deviance.

Listen, I wouldn't have loved you
and chosen you to ride
had it been you and only you in the stables.
I wouldn't have loved you
if I'd been rotting in a swamp
and hated the universe without daring to spit
on everybody in it
or had waited with empty eyes
in an emptier existence
for an emptiness that you would bring me.
You wouldn't have been my mount
if I hadn't passed a thousand stables
packed with horse after horse after horse—
sorrels, palaminos, chestnuts, blacks
thoroughbreds and halfbreeds
racehorses and ploughhorses
pampered or overloaded
well-groomed or not
if I hadn't rejected them all

and yearned for you
saying   You are the one I love   You and you alone.

So come nearer   nearer
The sentence is clear
I'm nailed to the wall of my prison
Come nearer
I'd rather die than wait to die
Slow time bites like a whip

Come nearer   You are the one I want   Just you
You alone are my escape, my home, my Eden.
Come nearer
my help, my guide, my savior
my midwife
my mother
Come nearer   please

I don't know your name
your parents   or your country
(who cares about the kind of clay that is a statue
and who would send the beloved's bones to the laboratory?)
It's quite enough that you are beautiful
that your body is my "open sesame"
to life itself.
Tonight I must make a journey
that will break my father's heart   and gladden me
like a journey that broke my heart   and gladdened him.

Carry me now   and gallop.

Don't pause with me
beside the spring where you always drink
where I promised to meet you.
Don't stop with me
in the fields of blood
where life is paid for
by a medal, a leader's speech, a headline.
Don't ride through fields
where hate's perfume is fouled
with the stink of heroism and braggadocio and duty
where hate is saved for enemies alone.

Fields of my blood
I don't patrol you   I have no comrades here
Fields of my blood
Like guzzling mouths that are always thirsty
 for the frozen blood of old men
  the blood of young girls that blooms in their cheeks
   before the long monotony
  the blood of warriors
  the blood of healers
  the rich blood of healers
  the stained blood of syphilitics
  the blood of friends and neighbors
  the blood of my wife
   with a child in her arms
   and another she labors to bear.

Fields of my blood
Gardens fertilized with hatred
with utter, total hatred
for those there and those here
those I've seen   and those I haven't
with hatred
for you, and you and you, and even for me

Gallop with me
Fly without wings beyond the horizon
Flick at space and the world with your mane
Flick the sun
Drive it off as if it were a tick
glued onto your flanks.

I won't ask
where your hooves strike
where the road goes   where you spend the night.
I'm satisfied to ride you   to be riding you
playing with your hair
hearing you
and see the world bow low and disappear
before you as you gallop.

Don't swerve with me
into some Bacchanalian garden

where the stars are like so many eyes
where songs are the hisses of snakes
where flowers are only paper and ribbon
their colors mingled—
red and white and yellow—
the colors of blood and sperm and pus.

Don't take me
to a garden crowded
with circling dancers
whose arms and breasts   mummified centuries ago
seem mounted on bodies
that move them like machines
They jabber prayers
in foreign tongues
to an unknown goddess.

They dance and cavort
    machine with machine
They carry out their secret rites.
They mate until their climax sunders them
like a shedding of innocence
a baptism of sin and knowledge
a bond making the two one
and the one   nothing . . .

But with you a sweet song
rises and rises when you are near me
You are the queen that ends all festivals and rites
Strongly beneath me
you gallop.

So gallop with me
my new Shahrazad . . .
You who swallow every night
a new Shahriyar
gallop with me
and I'll gallop with you.
I breathe in what you breathe out.
I touch my feet to yours.
I'll pant with you

until we climb and search and then descend
the last horizon.

Gallop with me.
Falling, let's fall as lovers fall,
together.
Let's move in tandem
to the song we hear as one,
you beneath me,
I above.

Gallop with me.
The race is short,
and there is one goal for both of us.
Leap the last stream with me,
and when the last exhaustion topples you,
I'll fall beside you,
spent, transformed and still.

Translated by Anne Royal and Samuel Hazo

PHANTOM

This phantom who is always with me
(I've known him as long as I've known life),
Has he no land that beckons him to sleep
so he can leave me alone?
Is there no trumpet call he might obey?
No temple where he might put on priestly robes?
Is there no woman's form
that writhes for him in the night
so he might spend an hour there?

I tore my passport
when I saw his picture in it;
when he claimed my name was his I took another,
renounced my native land the day he joined a party there.
I ran away, I disappeared, I hid in caves by day,
slipped out into the wilderness at night.
I grew a beard, tattooed my face;

but as I lay in a foreign land,
stretched out, relaxed and smiling,
up he loomed before my eyes and laughed.

With me when I see him
With me when I don't
Like my hump, he is with me.

Shadow, tenacious Phantom,
where can I go?
I see you even in the middle of the day,
and I saw you, quietly waiting for me
in the ripples of the water
when I frantically sought refuge
in the hole-riddled rock.

Translated by Anne Royal and Thomas G. Ezzy

——Shahriyar and Shahrazad (or Sheherazade): Shahriyar was king and husband of the famous Sharazad, whom the legend has it was the one who narrated the *Thousand and One Nights* to the king. King Shahriyar had discovered that his wife had been regularly unfaithful to him during his absence from the palace. He killed her and was so filled with resentment against all women that he married a new wife every day, only to kill her in the morning. Shahrazad was the daughter of his first vizier or prime minister, and she worked out a scheme to save the remaining few women in the kingdom. She insisted that her father marry her to the king. Each evening she told him a story which she never finished during the same night but promised to do so the next evening. The stories were so entertaining that the king kept postponing the execution from day to day until he ultimately gave up his plan. Shahrazad had been used in Arabic literature as a symbol of women's cunning in their treatment of men.

Badr Shakir al-Sayyab (1926–1964)

Iraqi poet. One of the greatest poets in Arabic literature, whose experiments helped to change the course of modern Arabic poetry. At the end of the forties he launched, with Nazik al-Mala'ika, the free verse movement and gave it credibility with the many fine poems he published in the fifties. These included the famous "Rain Song," which was instrumental in drawing attention to the use of myth in poetry. He revolutionized all the elements of the poem and wrote highly involved political and social poetry, along with many personal poems. The publication of his third volume, *Song of Rain*, in 1960 was one of the most significant events in contemporary Arabic poetry. He started his career as a Marxist, but reverted to mainstream nationalism without ever becoming fanatical. While still in his thirties, he was struck by a degenerative nervous disorder and died in poverty. He produced seven collections of poetry and several translations, which include the poetry of Aragon, Nazim Hikmat, and Edith Sitwell, who, with T. S. Eliot, had a profound influence on him.

RAIN SONG

Your eyes are two palm tree forests in early light,
Or two balconies from which the moonlight recedes
When they smile, your eyes, the vines put forth their leaves,
And lights dance . . . like moons in a river
Rippled by the blade of an oar at break of day;
As if stars were throbbing in the depths of them . . .

And they drown in a mist of sorrow translucent
Like the sea stroked by the hand of nightfall;
The warmth of winter is in it, the shudder of autumn,
And death and birth, darkness and light;
A sobbing flares up to tremble in my soul
And a savage elation embracing the sky,
Frenzy of a child frightened by the moon.

It is as if archways of mist drank the clouds
And drop by drop dissolved in the rain . . .
As if children snickered in the vineyard bowers,
The song of the rain
Rippled the silence of birds in the trees . . .
Drop, drop, the rain . . .
Drip . . .
Drop . . . the rain . . .

Evening yawned, from low clouds
Heavy tears are streaming still.
It is as if a child before sleep were rambling on
About his mother (a year ago he went to wake her, did not find her,
Then was told, for he kept on asking,
"After tomorrow, she'll come back again . . .")
That she must come back again,
Yet his playmates whisper that she is there
In the hillside, sleeping her death for ever,
Eating the earth around her, drinking the rain;
As if a forlorn fisherman gathering nets
Cursed the waters and fate
And scattered a song at moonset,
Drip, drop, the rain . . .
Drip, drop, the rain . . .

Do you know what sorrow the rain can inspire?
Do you know how gutters weep when it pours down?
Do you know how lost a solitary person feels in the rain?
Endless, like spilt blood, like hungry people, like love,
Like children, like the dead, endless the rain.
Your two eyes take me wandering with the rain,
Lightnings from across the Gulf sweep the shores of Iraq
With stars and shells,
As if a dawn were about to break from them,
But night pulls over them a coverlet of blood.
I cry out to the Gulf: "O Gulf,
Giver of pearls, shells and death!"
And the echo replies,
As if lamenting:
"O Gulf,
Giver of shells and death . . ."

I can almost hear Iraq husbanding the thunder,
Storing lightning in the mountains and plains,
So that if the seal were broken by men
The winds would leave in the valley not a trace of Thamud.
I can almost hear the palmtrees drinking the rain,
Hear the villages moaning and emigrants
With oar and sail fighting the Gulf
Winds of storm and thunder, singing
"Rain . . . rain . . .
Drip, drop, the rain . . ."

And there is hunger in Iraq,
The harvest time scatters the grain in it,
That crows and locusts may gobble their fill,
Granaries and stones grind on and on,
Mills turn in the fields, with them men turning . . .
Drip, drop, the rain . . .
Drip . . .
Drop . . .

When came the night for leaving, how many tears we shed,
We made the rain a pretext, not wishing to be blamed
Drip, drop, the rain . . .
Drip, drop, the rain . . .
Since we had been children, the sky
Would be clouded in wintertime,
And down would pour the rain,
And every year when earth turned green the hunger struck us.
Not a year has passed without hunger in Iraq.
Rain . . .
Drip, drop, the rain . . .
Drip, drop . . .

In every drop of rain
A red or yellow color buds from the seeds of flowers,
Every tear wept by the hungry and naked people,
Every spilt drop of slaves' blood,
Is a smile aimed at a new dawn,
A nipple turning rosy in an infant's lips,
In the young world of tomorrow, bringer of life.
Drip, drop, the rain . . .

Drip . . .
Drop . . . the rain . . .
Iraq will blossom one day in the rain.

I cry out to the Gulf: "O Gulf,
Giver of pearls, shells and death!"
The echo replies
As if lamenting:
"O Gulf,
Giver of shells and death."
And across the sands from among its lavish gifts
The Gulf scatters fuming froth and shells
And the skeletons of miserable drowned emigrants
Who drank death forever
From the depths of the Gulf, from the ground of its silence,
And in Iraq a thousand serpents drink the nectar
From a flower the Euphrates has nourished with dew.
I hear the echo
Ringing in the Gulf:
"Rain . . .
Drip, drop, the rain . . .
Drip, drop."
In every drop of rain
A red or yellow color buds from the seeds of flowers.
Every tear wept by the hungry and naked people
And every spilt drop of slaves' blood
Is a smile aimed at a new dawn,
A nipple turning rosy in an infant's lips
In the young world of tomorrow, bringer of life.

And still the rain pours down.

Translated by Lena Jayyusi and Christopher Middleton

SONG IN AUGUST

Tammuz dies on the skyline,
His blood seeps away with twilight
In the dim cavern. Darkness
Is a black ambulance,

Night a flock of women:
Kohl, black cloaks.
Night, an enormous tent.
Night, a blocked day.

I called to my negro maid:
"Murjana, it's dark now,
Switch the light on. You know what? I'm hungry.
There's a song, I forgot, some sort of a song.
What's this chatter on the radio?
From London, Murjana, a
Jazz concert so
Find it, I'm happy, jazz,
Blood rhythm."

Tammuz dies and Murjana
Crouches cold like the forest.
She says, breathless:
"The night, wild pig,
How miserable the night is."
"Murjana, was that the doorbell?"
So she says, breathless:
"There are women at the door."
And Murjana makes the coffee.

Fur over white shoulders:
Wolf covers woman.
On her breasts a whole sheen of tiger skin
Filling the forest, stealing from the trees.
Night stretches,
Distraction, night
An earth-oven, radiant from ghosts,
Bread inhaling the night fires,
And the visitor eats, famished.
Murjana crouches
Cold like the forest.

The visitor laughs, she says: "Su'ad's boyfriend,
Been giving her a bad time, broke the engagement,
The dog disowned the bitch . . ."

Tammuz dies, never to return.
Coldness drips from the moon,
The visitor huddles at the fire gossiping, sharp-tongued.
Night has extinguished the coasts,
The visitor crouches, cold, robed
With wolf fur.
The fire she lit with bloody talk
Goes out.

Night and ice,
Across them a sound falls, clank of iron
Muffled by wolf howls.
Distant sound,
The visitor, like me, is cold.

So come on over and share my cold,
Come by God,
Husband, I'm alone here,
The visitor is cold as I am—
So come on over,
Only with you can I talk about everyone.
And there are so many people to be talked about.
The dark is a hearse, the driver blind
And your heart is a burial ground.

Translated by Lena Jayyusi and Christopher Middleton

JAIKUR AND THE CITY

The city streets coil around me:
thongs of mud bite into my heart,
a dull ember in it yields only clay,
cords of fire lash naked melancholy fields,
they burn Jaikur in the pit of my soul,
they plant in the pit ashes of rancor.

These are streets of which drowsy hearthside legends say:
From them no more than from the shores of death
has any traveler through night returned,
as if there

echo and silence were wings of the Sphinx,
two wings that jut from buried rock through the subsoil.
Who then shall let water gush to those streets,
that our villages may be built around them?
And God, who shall one day restore Him there?

Night, paradise
regained, when the rock
weaves across the streets a grill
of stony twigs, congregates
the lamps like flame apples
and prolongs
into the taverns a few leaves of the fig tree,
who shall kindle love, love
on every path, in every coffee bar and home?
Who shall change the human claw into a hand
with which the child can wipe his forehead?
Whose touch, whose
divinity of spirit shall bead the veins of stone
with dew?

Forenoon:
if the wheels milling copper into the merchants' palms
might sing in praise to the demon of the city,
with the voices of birds in a *sidra* tree
from which God creates the hearts of children,
millwheels that glisten
like Jaikur's fish and with a name that is manifold—
who then would hear the spirit? Who
spread a shade against the scorching blaze of gold,
who find his way to her across the icebound sea
and not possess the ship for plunder?
And Jaikur, who is it
has shut her doors
to her child who knocks at them? And the road to her,
who diverted it, so that wherever he goes
the city cranes toward him?

And Jaikur is green, dusk
has touched the crests of her palm trees

with its sorrowful sun.
Sleep
has paved me a path to her: out of my heart
it goes
through the city labyrinth, across the night, across
the fortified citadels. In Babylon
the dancers are asleep, asleep the iron they sharpen,
the gasping of gold they hoard glazes
the eyes of storekeepers: this
is the crop of famines from the city's
double Eden.

My path
crossed millstones of flame,
here are vineyards, their dead sprigs
veins of Tammuz crossing the city, veins that branch
through every home and prison, every coffee bar,
every prison and bar and every nightclub,
through all the insane asylums,
every whorehouse of Ishtar,
ignoble flowers
bursting into bloom like lamps whose oil does not burn,
where no flame touches,
and in every coffeebar and prison, whorehouse and home—
"This water is my blood, will you drink it?
This flesh is my bread, will you eat it?"
And the goddess Lat grieves for Tammuz.

First light, and she lifts up her lament,
lifts up her voice, like a sigh of trees:
"O Fate, engine, killing him
you killed the Spring and the Rain."
The *Times* and *Events* publish the news,
and the goddess asks the surgeon to help, to bring home
her son to her: his hands, his eyes, any trace of him.
She sends out her lament: "Cornblades of the moon,
my son's glass blood has been smashed in his veins,
the spark of our house has struck stone,
the city wall
crushed him, scattered him, flung him down in no time.

He wanted the light, wanted to disperse
darkness . . . and he was defeated."
She sends out her lament—
the voice fades, and the music.

And Jaikur is green,
the dusk has touched
the crests of her palm trees
with a sorrowful sun. My path
went to her, like a lightning flash
it showed and vanished, splendor returned, kindling the road
until it lit the city, and under the bandages
could be seen the wounds on my hand:
they were scorchmarks.

And outside Jaikur a wall has been raised up,
and a gate,
and a stillness envelops her.
Who shall pierce the wall? Who opens the gate? Bloody his
right hand on every lock? And my
right hand: no claw
to fight with on the streets of the city, no grip
to raise up life from the clay, it is clay only.
Outside Jaikur a wall has been raised up,
and a gate,
and a stillness envelops her.

Translated by Lena Jayyusi and Christopher Middleton

DEATH AND THE RIVER

Buwayb . . .
Buwayb . . .
Bells of a tower lost in the sea bed
dusk in the trees, water in the jars
spilling rain bells
crystals melting with a sigh
"Buwayb ah Buwayb,"
and a longing in my blood darkens
for you Buwayb,

river of mine, forlorn as the rain.
I want to run in the dark
gripping my fists tight
carrying the longing of a whole year
in each finger, like someone bringing you
gifts of wheat and flowers.
I want to peer across the crests of the hills,
catch sight of the moon
as it wades between your banks, planting shadows
filling baskets
with water and fish and flowers.
I want to plunge into you, following the moon,
hear the pebbles hiss in your depths,
sibilance of a thousand birds in the trees.
Are you a river or a forest of tears?
And the insomniac fish, will they sleep at dawn?
And these stars, will they stop and wait
feeding thousands of needles with silk?
And you Buwayb . . .
I want to drown in you, gathering shells,
building a house with them, where the overflow
from stars and moon
soaks into the green of trees and water,
and with your ebb in the early morning go to the sea.
For death is a strange world fascinating to children,
and its door was in you, mysterious, Buwayb . . .

Buwayb ah Buwayb . . .
twenty years have passed, each one a lifetime.
And this day when the dark closes in,
when I lie still and do not sleep,
and listen with my conscience keen—a great tree
reaching toward first light, sensitive
its branches, birds, and fruit—
I feel like rain the blood, the tears
shed by the sad world;
my death bells ring and shake my veins,
and in my blood a longing darkens
for a bullet whose deadly ice

might plow through my soul in its depths, hell
setting the bones ablaze.
I want to run out and link hands with others in the struggle,
clench my fists and strike Fate in the face.
I want to drown in my deepest blood
that I may share with the human race its burden
and carry it onward, giving birth to life
My death
shall be a victory.

Translated by Lena Jayyusi and Christopher Middleton

IN THE ARAB MAGHREB

I have read my name on a rock
here, in the desolation of the desert,
on a red tablet of fired clay,
on a grave. How
does a person feel when he sees his grave?
He sees it and is perplexed. Is he
alive or dead? For it is not enough
that he should be impressed by what he sees across the sand,
a dusty minaret,
a cemetery,
some vanished splendor,
a minaret from which God's name rang out again and again,
in which a name for God was cut,
and Muhammad was an inscription on a green clay tablet
shining at a great height . . .

Now dust and flame
feed on him,
conquerors kick him without boots,
without feet,
and wounds that give no pain, he
bleeds from them,
not shedding blood—
he has died . . .
and we have died in him, the dead and the living.

For we are all dead,
I and Muhammad and God.
And this is our grave: a dusty ruined minaret
where the names of Muhammad and God are written
on scattered fragments,
fired brick and clay.
So O grave of God
across the day lie shadows
of a thousand spears and elephants,
the color of Abraha,
and the guide points to another shadow,
the sad disfigured Kaʿba.

I have read my name on a rock,
on two graves, between them the spaces of generations
marking this as a pit for two:
my ancestor's, some sand only
and a black powder left in his grave,
and myself, his son in death
biting with him on clay.

And a cry would float from my ancestor
with the tide,
a cry to fill the shores: "O valleys of ours, arise,
rise up in revolt!
O the blood that rushes through generations,
heritage of our people, now
shatter and smash these chains,
and like an earthquake shrug off
the yoke, or smash it and smash us with it."
And proudly our God
swayed among the headbands of the heroes,
from wrist to wrist,
from banner to banner.

Yesterday at Dhu Qar
the mighty God of the Kaʿba
armed himself
with battle-dented armor marked with the blood of al-Nuʿman.
The God of Muhammad and of my Arab ancestors

appeared now in the mountains of Rif,
carrying the banner of the revolutionaries,
but in Jaffa the people saw Him weep among the ruins
of a house. One day
we glimpsed Him descending from clouds into our land:
He walked in our neighborhoods, wounded, begging for alms.
We did not bandage His wounds.
No believer among us
sacrificed more than bread and charity.

The voices of men at prayer tremble in His elegies,
when they kneel the blood oozes out,
lips are quick to put on the bandage:
with holy verses
dulled by the old wound
that heal our fearful understanding that we shall revive Him,
when the revolutionaries among us
joyously proclaim: "Him shall we redeem!"

A swarm of locusts swooped down out of darkness,
attacking our villages and setting fire to them;
by the waters of Tigris, where the swarm turned back,
with blood and with ink stories are told of it.
The swarm, was it fate that horrified women
big with child so they bore but ashes?
Hooves of the horses, were they not shod
with the crescents of minarets kicked and trampled?
Did the swarm not arrive in Damascus
trailing across her terrains the footsteps
of two lions that were hungry-hearted?
To the hungrier one, Christ it gave
and quenched its thirst at the font of baptism;
but the desert Orient, did it not arm for battle
when the swarm bit the Prophet of Mecca?

Because the swarm was defeated, has it now returned
to inflict punishment?
And because God endures in our villages,
because we have not killed Him?
Because we did not eat Him when we were hungry,

nor for money sold Him as they sold their god
whom they fashioned out of the gold we toiled for?
As they ate him when they were hungry,
the god we modeled for them
out of the bread that was soaked in our blood?

The whores of Paris
make their pillows from Christ's agony,
and in their bowels sterility implants
the dragon's mouth, loudly hissing,
hurling at our lands
armies of iron, horsemen without soul
that move toward Mecca, toward mountain
citadels we have built, or on the slopes
toward Medina.

I have read my name on a rock.
Between two names in the desert
the world of the living drew breath,
as blood flows from heartbeat to heartbeat
From a red tablet of fired clay
standing over a pit
blood
illuminated the features of the land
steadily
naming it
that it may take its meaning

So I know it is my land
So I know it is part of me
know it is my past
that without this land my past is dead
without this past I am dead, walking with her dead.
Is it ours, tumultuous valley teeming with banners?
Is this the color of our past
lit by the windows of al-Hamra
and by a green tablet of fired clay,
God's name on it, written by the lifeblood that remains to us?
Is this the sound of the dawn prayer
or is it the chant of the revolutionaries

rising from our citadels?
Earth has labored, graves have brought back to life
the dead in millions
and Muhammad and his Arab God and the Ansar all rose up:
Our God is within us.

Translated by Lena Jayyusi and Christopher Middleton

——Thamud: an ancient Arabian tribe described (with the tribe of 'Ad) in the Koran as having been destroyed by God as punishment for their sins. Their names are often mentioned in classical Arabic literature as reminders of the impermanence of human power and glory.

——Tammuz: the Phoenicean god of Fertility. See note to A. al-Bayyati's poetry.

——Murjana: a name usually given to slave girls, especially black slave girls, in old Arabic culture.

——Jaikur: the poet's village, which he immortalized in numerous poems of regret and nostalgia for the innocence, fertility, and freshness of his lost country life.

——*Sidra* tree: the tree supposed to be at the right hand of God in heaven.

——Ishtar: see note to al-Bayyati's poetry.

——Lat: the goddess Lat was one of the gods worshiped in Arabia before Islam.

——*Times* and *Events:* a translation of the names of two newspapers.

——Buwayb: small river that flows near Jaikur, al-Sayyab's village in the district of Basra.

——Abraha: king of southern Arabia in the middle of the sixth century. Originally an Abyssinian slave, he rebelled against Abyssinian domination of Yemen and made himself the king of San'aa, the capital. Tradition has it that he wanted to divert Arab attention from Mecca to San'aa and therefore waged war against the Arabs of Mecca c. 570, which ended in his defeat and the annihilation of his army.

——Dhu Qar: a watering place in Iraq not far from where Kufa is now. It was the site of an important battle against the Persian king Khusru II in which the Arab tribes led by the tribe of Bakr ibn Wa'il defeated the Persians, registering the first Arab victory against the Persian empire. Reference here is to the myth that grew around the invincibility of the Persian hordes which was dispelled in this battle, a reminder that modern Arabs, too, should take stock of this possibility against a mightier enemy. The battle of Dhu Qar was instigated perhaps because of the imprisonment of al-Nu'man ibn al-Mundhir, the Arab king of Hira, by Khusru.

——Al-Nu'man: al-Nu'man ibn al-Mundhir, king of Hira in Iraq from 580 to 602. He was a vassal of Khusru II, Emperor of Persia, but lost favor with him. Khusru imprisoned al-Nu'man, who died in prison. His death is regarded as the possible cause of the fight which broke out between Arab tribes and Khusru, culminating in the battle of Dhu Qar, above.

——Rif: a reference to the Algerian countryside where the war of liberation against the once intransigent French occupation was at its strongest.

——Mecca and Medina: the two holy cities of the Muslims in Hijaz, a province now in Saudi Arabia. Mecca is the original city of the prophet Muhammad where the holy Ka'ba is. Medina harbored the prophet when he fled his own tribe, Quraish, which persecuted him during the first years of his call. The Muslim calendar begins in the first year of the prophet's emigration (*hijra*).

——Al-Hamra: handsome palace of the last Arab rulers of Muslim Spain. It is situated on a hill in Granada, and is a great monument to the splendor of Arab civilization and art. It was from al-Hamra (or al-Hambra in Spanish) that the last Arab king left Spain in 1498.

——Ansar: the people from Medina who supported and welcomed the prophet on his arrival to their city from Mecca, which he fled in the first year of the Islamic calendar.

'Ali al-Sharqawi (b. 1948)

Bahraini poet. Born in Manama, Bahrain, he completed his secondary education there. He then studied science at the University of Baghdad, graduating in 1979. In 1981 he took a course in veterinary science in Britain and now works at the veterinary laboratory in Manama. He is one of the experimental poets of the Gulf area who has combined modern sophistication with a zealous commitment to the cause of justice and liberation. He writes in the new tradition of modernist Arabic poetry, using complex imagery and a difficult technique. He has had seven collections of poetry published, among which are *Thunder in the Seasons of Draught* (1975), *She Is the Obsession and the Potentiality* (1983), and *Psalm 23 to the Singers' Nectar* (1985). He also writes folk poetry and poetry and plays for children.

FROM: PSALM 23 TO THE SINGER'S NECTAR

(1)
I shall knock three times at the door
My mother will know me, will say
the absent one has returned.

He casts his blue-black eyes beyond the rim of vision
his eyebrow rises
and the heart is constantly watchful.
The street is wider than vision
The hollow feet of time have no edges
Hungry questions shower down
over the bags of relief agencies.
      —Who will come tonight?
      —How will I sleep?
      —Is solitude wide enough for the heart's song?
He stops
      Damn this gate!
Between the stab-wound and the blade he saw his blood

a bedouin child on whose lips the horses of daily blows
     rest their hooves
and the smell of death leaving its traces

Is there anyone who knows which seas inhabit
     the heart of a prisoner released in the fifth summer?

He turns around
and the gate stands asking
     four?
     two?
     three?

He stops.
The one who passes through this gate turns to stone
and the one who leaves may . . .
The fifth summer scratches the memory of the bedouin child—
the river had abandoned him, wild deer had nurtured him.
My heart is taut
My mouth constricts my tongue
and the street—how wide it is!
It stretches from
The tears of a mother's farewell
     to the artery of the fifth summer
I hear her ripe tears crying out
     —Who is at the door?
The fisherman kneeling over the carpet
     comes out to the broken steps
     —Here you are at long last!
I can smell the familiar pledges of neighborhood women.
My soul is contagious with questions
and my aging skin penetrated by new air.
     The gate crouches
        Do not say no.
        Do not say no.
        Do not say it.
He turns—
     what time is it now?
Feels his pocket, removes his watch, and laughs
     It's still telling the time of the first summer!

He puts his watch away
      Why the hurry?

(2)
Between the lover and love is a wordless road
crossed only by the spirit

(3)
How can I face my days?
How to live with them
      when the neighborhood is no longer a neighborhood
      a gray sea is buried in my glass
      and all my friends' concerns have changed.

(4)
From where has this tawny woman sprouted?
Radiant, she emerges from the sea's foam, singing
followed by waves and boats,
by birds escaping the cages of bewilderment,
and by the scorching summer.
Flaming pomegranate trees
      give praises at her feet
walking proud and disdainful as the sun moves over the bedouin map.
She swings her childlike laughter
    into the pastures of dream.
At dawn, where darkness threads with light,
      the lotus tree keeps her company,
      the bird gives her new words.

(6)
He stops, swallows his Adam's apple,
stares at the gate remembering slain comrades
      who tried to escape
He walks on.
His eyes see the cup of death in the guard's hands.
The cup will make its rounds,
and the axe's teeth will find the soil.
He walks on,
      inhaling and exhaling like other people,
but inwardly seething.
    No one recognizes me

> or if they do
> they may ignore me

I left my hands and followed her
I left my blood and followed her
till we met
and I planted my flaming years on her lips
   —Mujanar, is that you?
     Where are you going, Mujanar?
     —To where my love is
     —And where might he be?
She departed with violet fragrance on the wings of space
     —There, beyond wishes and prison songs.
And she bade me no farewell.

(9)
I perfect the dream and I know
that whoever perfects the dream of the sea
does not drown in a pool of water.

(10)
The street is congested with foreign languages
     hard on the ear
Has he taken a wrong turn and arrived at Babylon?
Understanding nothing, his steps are painful
as salt in a wound
He is afraid even of himself
     Am I really walking in the streets
     without a policeman?
Advancing gradually as an ant hauling a grain of corn
his feet stutter
A truck could run over him!
How comic death by truck would be
after five years of darkness!

(11)
I am a sand grouse
and the bustards hunt me
since the time I said the old passes away
and desert houses are made of glass.

(14)
He advances—
He imagines her preoccupied just now
Fancies possess him,
he follows her fearless steps
The deep waves know her
and the mountain tattooed with trees
She walks like the chant of seagulls
bound to the blood of sailors
She sits happily in the heart of things
On the lotus tree a sparrow
trills his moonspun joy
Mujanar is everywhere—in cells and mirrors,
in rivers and corners
Mujanar, walking in the dark
singing for the day.

(17)
Everyone races
Everyone moves like cats toward fish
Everyone munches from another's shoulder
Every step is compulsive
Be my companion, heart
Soften my questions
My memory has aged in the past four years
The muse ran away from me
    And what about the friends?
    Will they come tonight?
We can laugh at our old troubles.
Will my broken mother serve me joy
            baked with laughter?
Will my father tell the familiar story of his first voyage?
I walk forward through the neighborhood . . .
How often I repeated to friends
that I would walk barefoot on asphalt
crying, "Harbor of the world, I am the boat!"
I stare at things, the old playground speaks,
    —Have you come to break your hand a second time?
I walk on

Should I stop by the coffee bar?
Black tea used to be fragrant and full in the cups
Unrehearsed poetry gushed out from our lips . . .
But where *is* the coffee bar?

(18)

The fifth summer—questions feverish as typhus
Will I write again?
Where will I work?

(19)

I look for her arms
for her purity amidst questions and answers
I walk in the alleyways where children draw
with coal and almonds on the walls
fish-shaped stars
cloudlike words
At the end of the line she stood watching me
I approached like Solomon's hoopoe-bird
—Where are you going, Mujanar?
—To the sea, as close to me
as a mother's milk-rich breast
—And what is its color?
—The laughter of bedouin coffee
—Mujanar?! Perhaps we will meet again
—When you shall speak out!
And she bade me no farewell.

(21)

I befriended the darkness,
the moon inside a hole in the damp walls.
I advanced toward a group wearing bedouin clothes
but recognized no one.
One of them might remember me, I thought,
for my memory is weak in the fifth summer.
I raised my hand saying, "Greetings!"
swallowed my pain, and knocked at her door.

(22)

I await this maritime girl
to cleanse my bewilderment and outline my path

Who will extract her from my memory?
Who will implant her within my memory?

Translated by Lena Jayyusi and Naomi Shihab Nye

——*Babylon:* ancient city of Mesopotamia (Iraq in modern times) on the Euphrates. It became one of the most important cities in the Near East during the times of Hammurabi, king of Babylonia in the eighteenth century B.C. who composed the famous code of law. Legend has it that there were many tongues spoken in Babylon.

'Abdallah al-Tayyib (b. 1921)

Sudanese poet, scholar, and classicist. Another prominent member of the al-Majdhoub family of Damir and a cousin of M.M. al-Majdhoub, he studied in Khartoum and London, obtaining a Ph.D. from the University of London. Back in Khartoum, he lectured at its university, became dean of the College of Art, and eventually became the chancellor of the university. He was later a professor at the University of Fez in Morocco. Al-Tayyib has great love for and knowledge of classical Arabic poetry, which has been revealed both in his poetic style and in his erudite critical writings, particularly his famous *Guide to the Understanding of the Poetry of the Arabs*, published in two volumes in 1955. His first collection, *Echoes of the Nile*, went into several editions. He has published several other collections of poetry and poetic plays.

THE BREAKING OF THE GLASS

Friend, do you remember the time we went
into that lofty hotel, that grand hotel, in Leeds?
That spacious, that noisy, that solemn hotel,
that formidable, terrifying hotel, and the four of us
together: you and Ilyanus and his girl?
When all eyes
sent angry arrows at us,
remember?
First we sat in a far corner, then got up
and moved toward the center,
sat there under the full glare of the lights
drinking and chatting,
half serious, half amused,
discussing things,
remember? How we wanted to stay there all night,
ignoring the eyes around us,
how we shed our alien caution, though misgivings remained,

anxiety that wore a mask of calm
as a girl might, modest and intelligent, but shy,
who glimpses evil and looks away,
she walks on, alert, shaken,
on guard against attack, pretending to be calm.

Remember? I'll never forget that mood, our talk, our joy,
glasses brimming,
cigarette smoke floated above us, blurring the lights
and people sat together, drinking and conversing
And I'll never forget
how suddenly your glass
fell to the floor,
that brimming glass, how it spilled its contents
and was shattered in a million pieces,
how your face showed the shock, changed color,
how the world around you suddenly went quiet,
how that heavy awesome silence spread
and filled the place; and the doors, the lights, the ceiling
were all eyes,
a low whisper spread, the walls, the cops, the street
listened,
an annoyed whispering disclosing
human baseness, the camouflaged hypocrisy.
Remember how you stayed bravely sitting in your chair,
looked for excuses, whatever came to your mind,
referring the actual evil
to a metaphysical design,
proposing a theorem about
the treachery of Fate, the will of God
who defeats fantasy. O what excuses you invented
for the breaking of that glass
when it was shattered in a million pieces,
when the ceiling and the doors heard the crash!

Are they unteachable, those who know better?
Does one curse the malevolent? What good does cursing do?
Like fantasy your glass was gone, broken in that populous hotel,
that lofty, that awesome, that formidable, that noisy, that solemn hotel
in Leeds—

What a crash it made, a shrieking sound,
that echoed and echoed.
No! Don't curse Fate, what good does cursing do?
Like fantasy your glass was gone; your friends were consoling you.

That was a moment, buried in the past
Always, when I remember it, I feel
laughter filling my heart and soul.
Do you remember it?

Translated by Salma Khadra Jayyusi and Christopher Middleton

Khalil Touma (b. 1945)

Palestinian poet from Beit Jala near Bethlehem. Unable to complete a university education for lack of funds, he worked in a Jerusalem hotel as a receptionist. In 1966 he was elected to the administrative committee for the Union of Hotel Workers in Jordan. Following the Israeli occupation of the West Bank, he resumed work at the same Jerusalem hotel. In April 1974, he was placed under administrative detention by the Israeli occupation authorities. His first *diwan, Songs of the Last Nights* (1975), appeared while he was in prison, and during the twenty-two months of his imprisonment he completed his second collection of poetry, which was published in 1976 under the title *Star over Bethlehem*. A third collection of poetry will soon be published.

A SONG OF JOB

Night on the shores, your voice is no stranger,
your face is no stranger . . .
To keep all things from vanishing,
I tent the wind with pegs
and scream.
The wind cascades from hill to hill,
and I hold on to rocks, walls, grass and trees.
My soul will not sink to the dregs.
Strangers have kicked me from my home by inches . . .
I may be crushed or crucified or killed,
but my rebellion nothing can kill.
I swear no land will greet me but my own.

Night on the shores, your voice is no stranger . . .
You sped across the East a thousand years ago,
crossed mountains of snow
and roads banked in fog
until you disappeared,
but still the traces of your horses furrow my face.

Tyrants have jailed my green orchards.
My only sky's become a storm of foxes.
The Mount of Olive's changed into a minefield.
A dam's become a forest of spears.

Something's emerging from the ground,
something we call resistance.
It rises from the dust of dynamited houses
like a ghost from the ruins.
It rises from deserted wells.
It cannot sleep in the shadow of chains.
It rises from the earth in the form of shrapnel
or sparks of fire.
Something we call resistance
rises from the earth itself at midnight
to bridge the shores of a wound.
Blessed is he who can wait until morning,
and blessed is he who fights until morning.
On the final night
when everything becomes fire and light
in our captured land,
Those watching will not forgive
those who held back the procession.

It is said:
"A land gives of its bread.
Its depths can rage us into fire.
Its very stones can become sapphires.
Pure gold is not enough to buy it,
nor can its price be weighed in silver."

Translated by Lena Jayyusi and Samuel Hazo

Fadwa Tuqan (b. 1917)

Palestinian poet. Born in Nablus, Palestine, she was introduced to the art of poetry by her famous poet brother, Ibrahim Tuqan. Initially a Romantic poet skilled in the traditional forms, she turned to free verse at the outset of the movement, writing on a variety of personal and communal subjects. She was one of the first major poets to work toward emotional veracity, laying the foundation for feminine explorations of love and social protest. When her birthplace fell to the Zionists in the June 1967 war, resistance themes predominated in her work. Since the publication of her first *diwan*, *Alone with the Days* in 1952, she has published several collections of poetry, among which are *I Found It* (1958), *Give Us Love* (1960), *In Front of the Closed Door* (1967), *Horsemen and the Night* (1969), and *Alone on the Summit of the World* (1973).

IN THE AGING CITY

City streets and pavements receive me
with other people, the human tide rushes
me on. I move in this current, but only on
the surface, remaining by myself.
The tide overflows to sweep
these sidewalks and streets.
Faces, faces, faces rolling on,
dry and grim, they move on the surface,
remaining without human touch.
Here is nearness without being near.
Here is the no-presence in presence.
Here is nothing but the presence of absence!

Traffic light reddens; the tide holds back.
Bats flash across memory:
a tank passes, as I crossed in the Nablus marketplace,
I moved out of its way.
How well I've learned not to disturb

the path of traffic! How well I've memorized
traffic laws!
And now here I am, in the London slave market
where they sold my parents and people . . .
Here I stand, a part of the profitable deal,
carrying the brunt of the sin—
Mine was that I am a plant
grown by the mountains of Palestine.
Ah! Those who died yesterday are at rest now.
(I suspect that their corpses cursed me
as I gave way for a tank to pass,
then moved on in the stream.)
Aisha's letter is on my desk,
Nablus is quiet, life flowing on
like river water . . .
The prison seal is an eloquent silence
(A guard tells her the trees have fallen,
the woods are not set ablaze anymore.
But Aisha insists the forest is thick,
trees standing like fortresses. She dreams
of the forest she left blazing with fire
five years ago. She heard the thunder
of wind in her dream, tells the guard:
"I don't believe you, you're one of them,
and you remain the Prophets of the Lie."
Then she crouches in the darkness of prison, dreaming.
Shaded by her standing trees she is joyous at the sound
of the far forest rattling with swords of flame.
And Aisha dreams and dreams.)

The traffic light clicks green, the tide drives on.
My memory flits away, bats fall into a deep well.
A shadow changes direction, follows me,
sends out a bridge.
         —Are you a stranger like I am?
Two drops separate from the tide,
sit removed in a corner of the park.
         —Do you like Osborne?
         —Who doesn't?

—England's elderly and its officers
    setting with the sun of Suez . . .
—Who do you think will plant tomorrow's tree
    for this country?
—The hippie youth.
—You are sour, very sour.
The hippie tide passes by,
sweeping the city.
London keeps beat with
the toll of Big Ben.
    —Around the corner
      there's a pub and an elegant hotel
      with central heating—will you come?
    —Impossible!
A London lady passes, complaining to her dog
of arthritis and a pinched sciatic nerve.
    —Impossible!
    —Aren't you a modern woman?
    —I've grown beyond the days of rashness;
      sorrow has made me a hundred years old. Impossible!
I remove his arm from my shoulders.
    —I'm besieged by loneliness.
    —We're all besieged by loneliness;
      we're all alone, play along with life alone,
      suffer alone, and die by ourselves.
      You will remain alone here, even if a hundred
      women embrace you!
City streets and sidewalks swallow us with others,
a human tide sweeping us away in waves of faces.
We remain on the surface, touching nothing.

Translated by Patricia Alanah Byrne with the help of the editor, and Naomi Shihab Nye

IN THE FLUX

That evening
faces faded around us
The room was drowned in fog
Nothing lived

but the shining blue of your eyes
and the call in that
shining blue
where my heart
sailed, a ship
driven by the tide
     The tide carried
     us onto a sea
     without shores
     stretching
     limitless current
     and flow
     waves telling the endless
     story of life
     now abridged in one glance
     and the earth drowned in the rushing
     flood of winds and rain

That evening
my garden awoke
The fingers of the wind
unhinged its fences
Grasses swayed, flowers bursting,
fruits ripening
in the blissful dance of wind and rain
Faces faded, all else was a fog
that evening
nothing existed
but the blue shining light in your eyes
and the call in the shining blue
where my heart sailed
like a ship driven by the tide.

Translated by Patricia Alanah Byrne with the help of the editor, and Naomi Shihab Nye

FACE LOST IN THE WILDERNESS

Do not fill postcards with memories.
Between my heart and the luxury of passion

stretches a desert where ropes of fire
blaze and smolder, where snakes
coil and recoil, swallowing blossoms
with poison and flame.

No! Don't ask me to remember. Love's memory
is dark, the dream clouded;
love is a lost phantom
in a wilderness night.
Friend, the night has slain the moon.
In the mirror of my heart you can find no shelter,
only my country's disfigured face,
her face, lovely and mutilated,
her precious face . . .

How did the world revolve in this way?
Our love was young. Did it grow in this horror?
In the night of defeat, black waters
covered my land, blood on the walls
was the only bouquet.
I hallucinated: "Open your breast,
open your mother's breast for an embrace
priceless are the offerings!"
The jungle beast was toasting in the
tavern of crime; winds of misfortune
howled in the four corners.
He was with me that day.
I didn't realize morning
would remove him.
Our smiles cheated sorrow
as I raved: "Beloved stranger!
Why did my country become a gateway
to hell? Since when are apples bitter?
When did moonlight stop bathing orchards?
My people used to plant fields and love life
Joyfully they dipped their bread in oil
Fruits and flowers tinted the land
with magnificent hues—
will the seasons ever again
give their gifts to my people?"

Sorrow—Jerusalem's night is silence and smoke.
They imposed a curfew; now nothing beats in the
heart of the City but their bloodied heels
under which Jerusalem trembles
like a raped girl.

Two shadows from a balcony
stared down at the City's night.
In the corner a suitcase of clothes,
souvenirs from the Holy Land—
his blue eyes stretched like sad lakes.
He loved Jerusalem. She was his mystical lover.
On and on I ranted, "Ah, love! Why did God abandon
my country? Imprisoning light, leaving us
in seas of darkness?"
The world was a mythical dragon standing
at her gate. "Who will ever solve this mystery,
beloved, the secret of these words?"

Now twenty moons have passed,
twenty moons, and my life continues.
Your absence too continues. Only one memory remaining:
The face of my stricken country filling my heart.

And my life continues—
the wind merges me with my people
on the terrible road of rocks and thorns.
But behind the river, dark forests of spears
sway and swell; the roaring storm
unravels mystery, giving to dragon-silence
the power of words.
A rush and din, flame and sparks
lighting the road—
one group after another
falls embracing, in one lofty death.
The night, no matter how long, will continue
to give birth to star after star
and my life continues,
my life continues.

Translated by Patricia Alanah Byrne with the help of the editor, and Naomi Shihab Nye

I FOUND IT

I found it on a radiant day
after a long drifting.
It was green and blossoming
as the sun over palm trees
scattered golden bouquets;
April was generous that season
with loving and sun.

I found it
after a long wandering.
It was a tender evergreen bough
where birds took shelter,
a bough bending gently under storms
which later was straight again,
rich with sap,
never snapping in the wind's hand.
It stayed supple
as if there were no bad weather,
echoing the brightness of stars,
the gentle breeze,
the dew and the clouds.

I found it
on a vivid summer day
after a long straying,
a tedious search.
It was a quiet lake
where thirsty human wolves
and swirling winds could only briefly
disturb the waters.
Then they would clear again like crystal
to be the moon's mirror,
swimming place of light and blue,
bathing pool for the guardian stars.

I found it!
And now when the storms wail
and the face of the sun is masked in clouds,
when my shining fate revolves to dark,

my light will never be extinguished!
Everything that shadowed my life
wrapping it with night after night
has disappeared, lain down
in memory's grave,
since the day
my soul found
my soul.

Translated by Patricia Alanah Byrne with the help of the editor, and Naomi Shihab Nye

——The Aging City: the poet is speaking here of London, where she was on a visit.

——Nablus: the largest city in the West Bank and the poet's home town. Nablus was also known for its struggle, during the time of the British Mandate (1920–1948), against British rule and Zionist plans to take over Palestine from its Arab inhabitants.

Mamdouh ʿUdwan (b. 1941)

Syrian poet and playwright from Hama. Educated in Damascus, he worked as a journalist for many years. He has published eight collections of poetry, seven plays (four of which have been staged), four dramatic adaptations, five books translated from Western literature, and one novelette. Some of his work has been translated into several languages. Since 1979, he has worked for the translation department of the Ministry of Information. Among his collections of poetry are *The Green Shadows* (1962), *The Impossible Time Has Come* (1982), *My Mother Chases Her Murderer* (1982), *The Waving of the Tired Hands* (1982), and several others.

ELEGY FOR A MAN WHO DIED AND DIED

To al-Fasikh

He's still among us
    Fill his empty cup
Repeat the songs he raised
in chanting to the sky,
recall how wine and grief
could never weaken him—
Hand firm on the trigger,
Legs straight under the load,
A man of unfurling history,
he faced the ferocious motion of his time.
For him, the world had a solid core.

Naked, he dreamed death would be
the final shining cloak.
Humming the sad *maijana,*
he swam in the sorrow of its tune.
    "*Maijana,* oh *maijana,*
      death is a mantle that covers us,
      just spare us the shame of defeat."

When hunger dulled his sword,
he changed it to a sickle.
When sorrow bent the branches of his heart,
they drooped low with fruits.
When his basin filled with grief,
he transformed it to food
and the wind enveloped him
with compassionate sighs.

He's still among us
    He has drunk his wine
      so raise the glass!
He has consumed his whole life
in order to renew the living.
An unbreakable man—
When hunger raked
sharp streaks across the land,
he'd charge at his people,
sweep their constant invocations
to God's mercy, clipping the backbone
of prayer, and sweeping the pride of the tribes.

But days came when the enemy wore many colors,
famine impersonated faith,
fear begat sons and the clouds rained bombs.
The age of the metal bird surprised him
locked as he was on the land.
    "This new thing in the sky,
      My God, what power have I against it?
      No horse can run this fast,
      nor rifle shoot as far."

He reeled with hidden pain:
wrenching off old traditions,
facing a new generation
with' new weapons for the field.

His life grew scattered . . .
but watch how he'll come back
wrapped in his mighty songs!
    Fill his empty cup

and toast his *ʿataba* singing voice—
You'll sense him returning
like the scent of fire on a flowing breeze.

He shed his disjointed life,
depending again on his shoulders, his arms,
never disguising the shreds of his days.
He pretended to be full
and the sickle in his hand
grew strong again.

Now he stands gloriously,
gleaming sword to one side,
a vibrant image framed on the wall.
In his eyes the lost legends still shine.

We remember his sigh—
        "To drink to intoxication
        is to drink the dregs.
        I tasted wine's bitterness
        but time moved on to surprise me.
        I traversed the wilderness
        from the first lisps of childhood
        to these precious white locks."

A knock at the door—
My family is alarmed,
but Grandfather smiles through his wrinkles
(we think he is crying)—
A stronger knock at the door!
        He smiles again
        "Open the door, fear not
        these violent raps.
        Open—your father perfects
        the art of hospitality
        and with a brave heart
        meets his guests.
        Courage has two faces:
        One vanquishes enemies
        and the other, clear and unmasked,
        welcomes the visitor.

Open the door: I know his footsteps well.
I've chased him all my youth
in the raids and hunts.
Now he comes when I'm
exhausted from rushing after him.
Open and let him gaze into my eyes,
let him face his own weakness."

The wind settled like a tamed creature
while storms muffled their blows—
Against the sky, his body stretched,
was lifted by light.
    And the horizon
    opened up toward the bedouin desert
while the pine trees knelt
on the aging hills.

Translated by May Jayyusi and Naomi Shihab Nye

THE CASBAH

Between the ghetto's slumber,
the silence of its old folks
and curiosity of tourists,
the children grew up.
Poverty has ample place for the poor.
The women remained pregnant,
gave birth and remained pregnant,
kids grew up lazy and devilish,
became their own hungry homeland,
its price dipped in blood.
For the poor die twice, defending two countries:
    poverty and their masters' land,
    The poor are crowds marching unguided
    behind poverty and their masters' lies.

In the Arab ghetto
faces tightened,
harsh voices rose like knives
over the corrupt cities.

In the Arab ghetto
rivers of blood poured
from unlocked doors.
When cruel dreams coupled
with cruel bread,
the "War of Liberation" meant
lives seared with pain,
and the poor became the fence.
They broke the silence of their cells
    carried secret weapons
    dug up their wrath
    discovered their dignity
    and rushed forth naked into the world.
Indifferent to destruction,
they colored the earth with their blood.

Later they returned
    to discover their blood had turned to words,
    garlands for tyrants.

In the Casbah
blood dried over charred staircases,
heaped-up houses that had never seen light
were still stamped with their old poverty
and still unfortunate!
Night threw its mantle again on the Casbah
and found it moaning, trying to catch its breath
while ancient smells of poverty hung in the air.
Lazy men returned to cafes and the love of God,
the unemployed returned to theft,
children returned to smoking and picking
the pockets of strangers,
and the women?
They who had once cut off their braids
and thrown bombs on the enemy
now returned as slaves
or became whores together
with martyrs' wives.
The names of martyrs moved
to the glittering city quarters

and in the houses of the poor,
all names were put out.

The masters said,
 "God bless the poor—
 They gave us glory on this earth
 for theirs is the kingdom of heaven."

Translated by May Jayyusi and Naomi Shihab Nye

———*Maijana:* Like *'ataba*, it is a folk song often expressive of longing, but it can be more bouncy than *'ataba* and can embody a merrier content.

———*'Ataba:* like *maijana*, a folk song often expressive of longing, but rather sadder than the *maijana*.

Ahmad al-Mushari al-ʿUdwani (b. 1923)

Kuwaiti poet. After an Islamic education at the University of al-Azhar in Cairo, al-ʿUdwani occupied many responsible positions in his country, including director general of the National Council for Culture, Arts, and Literature in Kuwait, a post which he still occupies. His poetry is one of the strong expressions in the Gulf area of social and political dissent, revealing a skeptical mind and a critical vision that has never been reconciled to his traditional education. He has published one *diwan*, *Wings of the Storm* (1980).

AN ANSWER

The stranger asked me what my country was
My country knows no exile, no "abroad"
I told her: "My country is anywhere I meet
a stranger I can share friendship and love with
My country is an idea flowing with light
It is not bound to a flag, or a piece of earth
I've left behind the tranquil motherlands
to those grown used to a settled life
I've raced the winds on every horizon
The winds and I have sworn companionship

Translated by Hilary Kilpatrick and Charles Doria

FROM: PERSONAL REFLECTIONS

I asked the grave-digger, "Do you have
a treasure in your hand?"
"I'm the centuries' mortician,
all I have is the graveyard."
"Who rebels against the captive time?"
"We commit crimes in an age in which
the turbaned shaikhs and the military

hold sway.
And who are you?" he asked
"I am the pawn
locked in yesterday's vaults."
"Then here's your shroud," he said,
"Die any time you like
you'll find me here, mattock in hand
showing every corpse that's lost its way
how to get to the tomb."

Translated by Hilary Kilpatrick and Charles Doria

FROM: SIGNS

3
You I give no name to
The mysterious things within you
are an untrodden bower
over whose earthen orbit
planets move harboring
constellations of beauty.

4
You I give no name to
The mysterious things within you
are fragrance, light and melody
housed in flesh and blood
a sacred beacon that reveals
God's shadow.

6
The mysterious things within you
are a legend in my heart
With them I've built my castle
In them I've dug my grave
Drunk or sober I've loved them
They've comforted me
on my lonely way
hard as rock

If the mysterious things within you
were not strings for me to play on
I'd still have been their song.

Translated by Hilary Kilpatrick and Charles Doria

Al-Munsif al-Wahaybi (b. 1929)

Tunisian poet. Born in the city of Qairwan, which has been a center for Islamic learning for many centuries, he completed his early education in his home town before going to study Islamic philosophy and literature at the University of Tunis. After graduation, he became a teacher in Qairwan and went to teach for three years in Libya. He published his first collection, *Tablets*, in 1982, and is preparing his second. His poetry reflects his Islamic and mystical interests as well as his deep rootedness in Arabic culture, which he frequently celebrates. He uses vibrant imagery and a diction rich in mystical allusions, free of contemporary poetic gloom and anger. He is interested in translating poetry from other languages and among his translations are selections from the poetry of the Swedish poet, Östend Sjöstrand, which he did with Muhammad al-Ghuzzi and Sigrid Kahle.

THE DESERT

In the beginning the desert
was the ashes of a woman
inhabited by a storm.
Hidden secrets echoed,
and the silent poet
lay down on its grasses alone
or sat between its light
and shade, looking for something
that had disappeared
in its endless, rust-colored mirrors.

At the beginning, the language of the desert
was grass blooming against the wall of wind,
tall palms swaying in the season of seeding
and cinders carried by air
to the blue welcome of warm sand.
She was our first fountain, our mother,

who held us, then gave us away
to the age of waiting cities.

Translated by Salma Khadra Jayyusi and Naomi Shihab Nye

IN THE ARAB HOUSE

The deep blue of the earth
tempted me, and I came.
It was an Arab house
dedicated by wind to eloquent silence.
      I wished goodnight to the grasses of the garden,
then went away.

A woman awaits me.
She has fixed a spear at the threshold of the tent,
completed her beauty rituals, lain down
on the sands, and slept.
      As I move toward her in the dream,
  the star of the guest will see me
and follow my steps.

"Sir, oh Sir,
you who stealthily came to me in the dream,
      spread out in my body—
the morning star has entered our tent
and alighted in the mirror of frothing days."

Translated by Salma Khadra Jayyusi and Naomi Shihab Nye

CEREMONY

Embarrassed, you reach God's door.
Your face is pale, your spirit aflame.
This difficult love, Lord, has set me astray in the land,
won't you stretch a compassionate hand to save me?
He says, are you only a wayward desire
clamoring like wind when its routes are blocked?
If you should crave the fire of the Beloved,

do not alight,
they've lost their way who have come down before you.
And silence your hands when you approach my Kingdom,
only your foolhardy heart shall give the knock.

But I left my camel at His banks,
until sheets of rain enveloped it.
Solitary at last, God revealed Himself in my words,
a river following His waters.
The bathed spirit kindled for passion of Him
but His old love tempted it away.

Translated by Salma Khadra Jayyusi and Naomi Shihab Nye

THE CAMEL

Like rain falling
on barren land are your steps.
Camel of the *houdaj*, of journeying,
are you now only a wounded finger?

Protecting mountain for rebels,
most patient waiter,
are you a bitter frond
that's shriveled up
without clouds or wind?

To the ship of the desert,
the bridge that joins
the barren land with green,
I raise this praise.

Translated by Salma Khadra Jayyusi and Naomi Shihab Nye

A MAN RISES FROM THE CAVE OF ḤIRAʾ

A man, obsessed by people
and the weddings of the poor,
is called forth by night leaves and palm fronds
and he rises from the Cave of Ḥiraʾ.

Master of this desert,
take us to your Father who inhabits the mouth of rivers.
Grant us what the season's wind grants
when it wraps itself around the trees.

A pregnant land, we had watered it
till it shook and grew like a woman in labor.
Rains brought out the pasturing grass,
but we turned it into black scum
scattered by winds.

And the man rising from the Cave of Ḥira'
walks among people,
alone—
a single star glitters on the eastern horizon,
the pregnant earth turns its Arab circle,
and man is.

Translated by Salma Khadra Jayyusi and Naomi Shihab Nye

——*Houdaj:* a seat, usually canopied, on the back of a camel in which women rode.

——Ḥira': see note to M. M. al-Majdhoub.

Khalifa al-Wugayyan (b. 1941)

Kuwaiti poet. He completed his early education in Kuwait and his higher education in Cairo, where he obtained a Ph.D. from 'Ain Shams University in 1980, specializing in Arabic literature. He is now a high-ranking official at the National Council for Culture, Arts, and Literature in Kuwait. He has published two collections of poetry, *Those Sailing with the Winds* (1974) and *Metamorphosis of Time* (1983).

LETTER TO A BEDOUIN INFORMER

My friend! Miserable grass
You who suffer whenever you sneak a word

Everyone here has got his eye on you
And sees you for a thief
You have left your comrades and your children
The good Arab coffee
Your tumbledown hut
To suffer among hard-faced strangers
Who do not honor the guest
Who know nothing of you.
But in the desert
There are those
Who know your true worth
The lineage of your great forbears.

You linger here like a shadow, like a blank wall
Not comprehending what we say
It seems to me you don't know
If you are at a wedding or a wake!

My friend, son of our forefather Qahtan,
You are a palace in ruins
The tatters of a shining chronicle
The saddened song of the camel driver
A festering wound

The wasted fragrance of the wild jonquil
A scowling child
The remnants of the proud desert
Whose angry winds
Have scarred your cheeks
So that your face looks
Uncouth and lost.

My friend! Estranged spirit!
Heaped-up grief
Eloquent silence
Pure sands stained with oil
We loath remarking each evening your scowling face
We'd rather see you among your children
Living at ease
So go and sleep now
Dream of vernal greenness, of rain,
Of the moon smiling on the horizon
Of sweet conversation with friends
And if you should come tomorrow
To deliver your wicked report
Tell them whatever you like,
Or whatever they want to hear
What you know
Or what you don't know
And go on talking and talking
Until you see within you
Homes ruined,
Children dead,
The desert defiled.
But when remorse grips you
Tell them that beyond the sea
There is an alien dragon
Who wants to swallow the sun
To rob my child
Of his food
Tell them that beyond
The sea
An ogre is marching on!

Translated by Lena Jayyusi and John Heath-Stubbs

ELEGY

In Memory of Yusuf al-Babtain

The newspaper appears in the morning
with your name in it
It announces the unbelievable
Then goes on to tell
of the wedding of Fahd,
the birth of Zayd,
a tea party for a much liked guest,
It relates the usual trivia.

I read your obituary
once, twice, and then once more.
Perhaps they've got the name wrong,
that name that pulses in my veins
I know your name so well, your father's,
your grandfather's too, the whole family.
I go on looking for a printer's error
to preserve you alive
to have someone else dead
not checking my murderous fancy.

The minutes pass like an eternity
No news of you, no telephone call
to dismantle fear or grief
and the moment of terror.
The newspaper goes on screaming your name
in every corner
The name expands to cover all distances
I see nothing except that obituary
pounding at my ears
and locking all exits.
I dream about the telephone ringing
and of your voice, dear laughter, flowing through it
with gossip and small talk
and of sharing in your laughter
of throwing the newspaper away
and rushing to you
like an innocent child.

Have you really . . . left us?
What barren days lie ahead!
To come to you with our troubles
To seek your large spirit when we feel diminished
Your strength when we feel weak
All this . . . never again?

Translated by Lena Jayyusi and John Heath-Stubbs

——Qahtan: one of the two major tribes that constituted the ancient Arabs, the other being 'Adnan. Qahtan was composed of the southern (including the Yemenite) Arabs, part of whom emigrated north in the middle of the sixth century when the famous Ma'rib Dam (near the present capital, San'aa) burst, and formed the Ghassanid kingdom in Damascus, just before Islam.

Sa'di Yusuf (b. 1943)

Iraqi poet. He completed his higher education in Iraq, subsequently occupying responsible positions in various cultural institutions in Iraq. He has also taught in Algeria and worked in journalism in several Arab countries. Sa'di Yusuf's greatest attribute as a poet has been his capacity to speak in direct and simple yet highly poetic terms about life's constant routine and day-to-day experiences, subjects which so many other Arab poets shun. His poetry abounds with the sights, smells, colors, and movement of life around him, depicting scenes of great familiarity and intimacy. This is a great achievement in the face of the rage and fury and technical complexities of much of the other poetry written by his contemporaries. He has published several volumes, including the large one, *Collected Works* (1979), which contains all his former *diwans*.

THE WOODS

Twice I ended up in a forest.
Once, when I let myself go
with the other children
whose eyes spelled
mystery and age, the thin palm fronds,
the hands I had touched
and clothes soiled with mud,
a few songs.
But then I ended up in a forest . . .
The eyes I read
were closed to the sky of childhood now.
The hands I touched
carried sticks to strike with
and branches were rifles.
What happened to the muddy clothes?
Did the songs abandon us when anthems
advanced? Forest of childhood:

how did we come to you
free of care
to end up alone
seeking a spot between
the fingers for quarrel,
one for the trees?

Twice I entered a forest.
Once, when I let myself go
with the other children
and again, with myself.

Translated by Sargon Boulus and Naomi Shihab Nye

DEPARTURE OF ʼ82

In a while, all the rooms will be sealed.
Starting with the basement
we shall leave this place
chamber
by chamber
till we arrive at the roof
where the anti-aircraft cannons stand.
We will leave them standing there like that,
like the rooms,
and depart
to search in our blood, our own geography,
for other rooms!

Translated by Lena Jayyusi and Naomi Shihab Nye

SENTIMENT

Close to a tape shop,
he suddenly heard the song . . .
A woman threw a stone into a lake.
The drizzle was
warm
evaporating silently from the window glass.

The cypress trees near the lake
were dripping.
Did the street hear the song?

Translated by Lena Jayyusi and Naomi Shihab Nye

THREE DISPOSITIONS REGARDING ONE WOMAN

1

Why does your name continue
to be remembered?
In jail, while letters are forgotten
the meaning remains.
I try to remember
lining the letters up together
and every meaning

But they are obscure,
like your eyes, lady—
absent, like your visit when it ends—
and pale, like the smoothness
of your tiny oval face.
You could come then,
spoiled, desired, innocent,
a season of budding within your clothes.
Then I would forget your name
that wavers
between distraction
and imminence

2

The last train to Barcelona
hooted a final whistle
at the station.
You were pale
among morning branches that sipped
the wind, last murmurings, and cold.
So you are leaving
to seek a job as housekeeper
in a kingdom up north?

You, the gypsy restaurant mistress!
Will you remember how
you were encircled by singers
who took us for bride and groom
amid flowers, copper plates,
and shadow boughs?
A night . . .
                    and then you're off
          pale
                    on the last train to Barcelona

3
As though you never lived
at the pension in the narrow square
and never left on a chair
in your room—your dress, some sand
and the lily.
As though you never soaked in
the salt that tasted of seas
and narrowing waves.
As though, when we went down
to dawn's coffeeshop in a hurry,
you were not exhausted, very exhausted.

Translated by Sargon Boulus and Naomi Shihab Nye

A WOMAN

How should I direct my steps to her now?
In which land might I find her,
on what streets of which city should I ask?
Suppose I were to locate the path to her house,
even imagining it,
would I press the doorbell?
And what would I say?
How would I greet her,
would I stare into her face,
press the glistening wine of her fingers . . .
Would I unload
the pain of my years?

Once
twenty years ago
in the air-conditioned train
I kissed her the whole night long . . .

Translated by Lena Jayyusi and Naomi Shihab Nye

A HOT EVENING

In the air that limps between seashells . . .
tatters of a slain bird,
the fishes of sailors who will not return.
Air of fragrances:
an Indian woman brushing her hair
beneath the washline,
lobsters smoking on the grill—
and this damp shirt.

Translated by Lena Jayyusi and Naomi Shihab Nye

A STATE OF FEVER

It has been days, and still this wind
keeps coming to me from the sea.
All night long, this raving wind
delivers lobsters and jellyfish
in the rope-baskets of sunken ships,
and shirts printed with a laughing tiger . . .
All night long, this raving wind
moans, a cat scratches at the door,
and from under my bed,
I hear approaching footsteps . . .

Why have these lobsters
donned canvas shoes?
Who told them I was here,
trembling with fever?
And this cat . . .
will he jump, kangaroolike,
through the window?

Translated by Lena Jayyusi and Naomi Shihab Nye

Tawfiq Zayyad (b. 1932)

Palestinian poet and political writer. Educated in Nazareth and later in Moscow, where he studied Russian literature, he has worked in public life and struggled for the rights of the Palestinians in Israel through the Communist organization, Rakah. For several years he has been the elected mayor of Nazareth, where he has been very influential. Apart from his translations from Russian literature and his translation of Nazim Hikmat's major works, he has himself published several collections of poetry, among which *Warmly I Shake Your Hands* (1966) is regarded as a landmark in the history of the Palestinian struggle against Israel. It includes many poems of courage and resistance, some of which have been adapted to music and have become part of the lively tradition of Palestinian songs of struggle.

PASSING REMARK

When they ran over her,
the mulberry tree said:
"Do what you wish,
but remember
my right to bear fruit
will never die."

Translated by Sharif Elmusa and Charles Doria

BEFORE THEIR TANKS

On my window sill
rose petals bloomed
From the grapevine sprang
an arbor, a green
ladder
And my house leaned
against a bundle
of sunrays and bathed.

That was before their tanks
came.

Translated by Sharif Elmusa and Charles Doria

HERE WE WILL STAY

In Lidda, in Ramla, in the Galilee,
we shall remain
like a wall upon your chest,
and in your throat
like a shard of glass,
a cactus thorn,
and in your eyes
a sandstorm.

We shall remain
a wall upon your chest,
clean dishes in your restaurants,
serve drinks in your bars,
sweep the floors of your kitchens
to snatch a bite for our children
from your blue fangs.

Here we shall stay,
sing our songs,
take to the angry streets,
fill prisons with dignity.

In Lidda, in Ramla, in the Galilee,
we shall remain,
guard the shade of the fig
and olive trees,
ferment rebellion in our children
as yeast in the dough.

Translated by Sharif Elmusa and Charles Doria

THEY KNOW

But they know that my country
has known a thousand conquerors

and they know
that the thousand
have all melted away
like driven snow.

Translated by Sharif Elmusa and Charles Doria

SALMAN

Before a bomb buried
him in his courtyard
Salman told us:

"Loved ones,
for a long time we did not live
the way we wanted:
    now we do!"

Translated by Sharif Elmusa and Charles Doria

PAGAN FIRES

At our ease
we take the thread of light
from the knots of darkness,
tend the nursery of dreams,
cool the burning sand
with shadows of palm trees, and
for the bastards prepare a platter
like the moon. If one day we stumble
our roots will stand us straight.

At our ease
we learn the industry
of ants!

We do not flicker briefly
like matches; we burn
perpetually
like pagan fires
Our breath is as large
as the horizon.

And at our ease
we lead the capricious horse
of History.

Translated by Sharif Elmusa and Charles Doria

——Note: the first translator, Sharif Elmusa, would like to acknowledge his indebtedness to Sulafa Hijjawi's translations in her book, *A Lover from Palestine,* for the poems "Here we Will Stay" and "Pagan Fires," printed above.

TRANSLITERATED ARABIC NAMES OF POETS

Part I

Īlyā Abū Māḍi
ʿUmar Abū Rīsha
Ilyās Abū Shabaka
Al-Akhṭal al-Ṣaghīr
Saʿīd ʿAql
Badawi al-Jabal
Al-Tijāni Yūsuf Bashīr
Ilyās Farḥāt
Gibran Kahlil Gibran
Ḥāfiẓ Ibrāhīm
Muḥummad M. al-Jawāhiri
Muṭrān Khalīl Muṭrān
Aḥmad al-Ṣāfi al-Najafi
Ibrāhīm Nāji
Amīn Nakhla
Mīkhāʾīl Nuʿaima
Maʿrūf al-Raṣāfi
Abū al-Qāsim al-Shābbi
Aḥmad Shauqi
ʿAlī Maḥmūd Ṭāhā
Ibrāhīm Ṭūqān
Jamīl Ṣ. al-Zahāwi

Part II

Ḥasan ʿAbdallah
Muḥammad ʿAbd al-Ḥayy
Ṣalāḥ ʿAbd al-Ṣabūr
ʿAbd al-Razzāq ʿAbd al-Wāḥid
Shauqi Abī Shaqra
Adūnīs (ʿAli Aḥmad Saʿīd)
ʿAli Jaʿfar al-ʿAllāq
Muḥammad al-Asʿad
ʿAbdallah al-Baradūni
Salīm Barakāt
ʿAbd al-Wahhāb al-Bayyāti
Muḥammad Bannīs

Sargūn Būlus
Maḥmūd al-Buraikān
Aḥmad Daḥbūr
Maḥmūd Darwīsh
Zuhūr Dixon
Amal Dunqul
Ṣalāḥ Fāʾiq
Muḥammad al-Faitūri
Muḥammad al-Ghuzzi
Qāsim Ḥaddād
Yāsīn Ṭāhā Ḥāfiẓ
Buland al-Ḥaidari
Unsi al-Ḥāj
Khalīl Ḥāwi
Aḥmad ʿAbd al-Muʿṭi Ḥijāzi
Rāshid Ḥusain
Ḥasab al-Shaikh Jaʿfar
Salma al-Khadrāʾ al-Jayyūsi
Shafīq al-Kamāli
ʿAbd al-Karīm Kāṣid
Yūsuf al-Khāl
ʿAli ʿAbdallah Khalīfa
Khalīl Khūri
Muḥammad al-Māghūṭ
Sāmi Mahdi
ʿIṣām Maḥfūẓ
Muḥammad al-Mahdi al-Majdhūb
Nāzik al-Malāʾika
Khairi Manṣūr
ʿAbd al-ʿAzīz al-Maqāliḥ
Muḥammad ʿAfīfi Maṭar
Orkhān Muyassar
Huda Nuʿmāni
Amjad Nāṣir
Ṣalāḥ Niyāzi
Nizār Qabbāni
Samīḥ al-Qāsim
Ghāzi al-Goṣaibi

Sayf al-Raḥabi
Fuʾād Rifqa
Suʿād al-Mubārak al-Ṣabāḥ
Kamāl al-Sabti
Ḥamīd Saʿīd
Yūsuf al-Ṣāʾigh
Laila al-Sāʾiḥ
Saniyya Ṣāliḥ
Mai Ṣāyigh
Tawfīq Ṣāyigh
Badr Shākir al-Sayyāb

ʿAli al-Sharqāwi
ʿAbdallah al-Ṭayyib
Khalīl Tūma
Fadwa Ṭūqān
Mamdūḥ ʿUdwān
Aḥmad al-ʿUdwāni
Al-Munṣif al-Wahāybi
Khalīfa al-Wugayyān
Saʿdi Yūsuf
Tawfīq Zayyād

MUHAMMAD MUSTAFA BADAWI—Born in Egypt, he teaches now at Oxford University, where he has been a Fellow of St. Anthony's College since 1967. He has been a member of the Committee of Correspondence for the Annual Bibliography of *Shakespeare Quarterly* (1961–1980); founder and coeditor of *Journal of Arabic Studies*; and the author of several books and many articles on literature. Some of his main publications are *Coleridge: Critic of Shakespeare*; *A Critical Introduction to Modern Arabic Poetry*; and *Background to Shakespeare*, all in English. His collection of poems in Arabic, *Letters from London*, appeared in 1952. He has also translated many works from Arabic, including an *Anthology of Modern Arabic Poetry*. He is at present editing the fourth volume of the *Cambridge History of Arabic Literature*, dedicated to modern Arabic literature.

ISSA J. BOULLATA—Born in Jerusalem, Palestine, he graduated with a Ph.D. in Arabic Literature from the University of London in 1969. He taught at the Hartford Seminary in Connecticut, then joined McGill University, where he is now Professor of Arabic Literature and Language. His publications include *Outlines of Romanticism in Modern Arabic Poetry*; *Badr Shakir al-Sayyab: His Life and Poetry*, both in Arabic; *Modern Arab Poets 1950–1975*, an anthology of poetry in English translation; and, as editor, *Critical Perspectives on Modern Arabic Literature*. He is a member of the Editorial Board of PROTA.

SARGON BOULUS—See p. 183.

SHARIF ELMUSA—Born in Palestine, Sharif Elmusa came to the United States in 1971, and obtained a Ph.D. in urban studies and planning from M.I.T. in 1986. His poems in English have been published in several periodicals and will soon appear in *An Anthology of Arab-American Poetry*. He is one of PROTA's readers and reviewers, and has reviewed, among others, the final versions of the novels, *The Secret Life of Saeed, the Ill-Fated Pessoptimist*, by Emile Habiby (1983), and *Wild Thorns*, by Sahar Khalifa (1985). He has participated widely in the initial selections for the *Anthology of the Literature of the Arabian Peninsula*, prepared under PROTA. He lives with his wife and daughter in Washington, D.C.

FERIAL GHAZOUL—Born in Iraq, Ferial Ghazoul studied in Lebanon, Europe, and America, completing her doctorate in comparative literature at

Columbia University. Widely read in Russian Formalism and structuralism, she has written many articles, both in Arabic and English, on literary criticism. Her first book, *The Arabian Nights: A Structural Analysis* was published in 1980. She is now associate professor of English and comparative literature at the American University of Cairo, and is coeditor of *Alif: Journal of Comparative Poetics*.

ADNAN HAYDAR—Before taking up his appointment as associate professor of Arabic at the University of Massachusetts in Amherst, he taught Arabic language and literature at the American University in Beirut, at the University of California at Berkeley, and, for six years, at the University of Pennsylvania. His training is in critical theory and poetics, and he has written several articles on modern and classical Arabic poetry. Recently he has written a book, prepared with Michael Beard, titled *Naked in Exile*, which consists of a translation and interpretation of Khalil Hawi's *The Threshing Floor of Hunger*. He is interested in folk poetry and has now finished a book on the metrics of Lebanese *zajal*. He is a member of the editorial board of PROTA.

LENA JAYYUSI—Born in Amman, Jordan, to Palestinian parents, Lena Jayyusi was educated first in England where she obtained a Ph.D. in sociology from the University of Manchester, then at Boston University, where she obtained an M.S. in Film Studies. Her first book on sociology, *Categorization and the Moral Order*, was published by Routledge and Kegan Paul in 1984. She also writes on cine-semiotics, and her writings include a study on the "Socio-Logic of the Film Text," *Semiotica*, in press. She was assistant to the producer on three documentary films about women in the Middle East in 1981. Lena Jayyusi is one of PROTA's readers and reviewers and has translated, with Naomi Shihab Nye, selections from the poetry of the Tunisian poet, Abu al-Qasim al-Shabbi (forthcoming). She has worked as an assistant professor of sociology at Wellesley College and is now preparing an English language version of the well-known epic folktale, *Sayf ibn Dhi Yazin* (part translation, part retelling), with an introduction. She lives with her husband and daughter in greater Boston.

MAY JAYYUSI—Born in Amman, Jordan, May Jayyusi was educated in London, and studied philosophy at University College of the University of London. She later did graduate film studies at Boston University. Widely read in European thought and literature, especially the novel, she is one of

PROTA's readers. She has worked as a production assistant on *Wedding in Galilee*, a film made by Michael Khleifi, and has been working on a translation of selections from Ghassan Kanafani's works for PROTA. She lives with her husband and two children in Jerusalem.

HILARY KILPATRICK—Of Canadian origin, she was educated at Oxford University, specializing in Arabic. She has taught at several universities and is now senior lecturer in Arabic literature at the Catholic University of Nijmegen, Netherlands. Her publications include *The Modern Egyptian Novel* and a translation of Ghassan Kanafani's novella, *Men in the Sun* and other stories, as well as several articles on modern and medieval Arabic literature. She is currently doing research on *Kitab al-Aghani*.

ANNE ROYAL—She was a research assistant in the Asian studies program at Dartmouth College. Her doctoral thesis for the linguistics department of the University of Texas at Austin examined the interaction of sex and social class in the pronunciation of Cairo Arabic. Before her death in 1985 she was translating Mikha'il Mishaqah's nineteenth-century memoir, *The Answer Address'd to the Loved Ones' Request*, with the support of a grant from the National Endowment for the Humanities. Her untimely and tragic death put an end to a most promising career in Arabic studies and translation.

MATTHEW SORENSON—He is the son of an anthropologist and an artist. He studied linguistics and Arabic at the universities of Utah and Texas at Austin. While working on a doctoral dissertation on language interaction in a psychiatric hospital, he is developing educational software. He lives with his wife and four children in Utah.

MICHAEL BEARD—He is an associate professor of English and peace studies at the University of North Dakota. He is the author, with Adnan Haydar, of *Naked in Exile*, a study (and translation) of Khalil Hawi. He has recently finished *A Blind Owl Companion*, which examines the Iranian writer Sadeq Hedayat in the context of world literature.

ALAN BROWNJOHN—He obtained his college degree at Merton College in Oxford. He has taught at various schools and is now a full-time writer. He has published several volumes of poetry, and his *Collected Poems* appeared in 1983. In 1979 he received the Cholmondeley Award for Poetry. His translation, with his wife Sandy Brownjohn, of Goethe's play *Torquato* was broadcast by Britain's Radio 3 in 1982.

PATRICIA ALANAH BYRNE—Born in Massachusetts, Patricia Alanah Byrne has an M.A. from Regis College, Weston, Mass. Her poetry has been published in the United States, Alaska, Britain, Canada, France, and Italy. *Cat in the Mirror*, her first book, was published by Mitre Press, London (1970) under her married name, Patricia Alanah Rosenfield. Her second book, *Whetstone*, is soon to be published. She teaches English at Wellesley High School in Wellesley, Mass. She is a volunteer post-translation reviewer for PROTA.

DIANA DER HOVANESSIAN—An award-winning American poet, she is the translator and coeditor (with Marzbed Margossian) of *Anthology of Armenian Poetry; Sacred Wrath, Selected Poems of Vahan Tekeyan; The Arc, Poems of Shen-Mah;* and *Land of Fire, Poems of Charents*. She has also translated the works of the medieval poet Nahabet Koutchag *(Come Sit Beside Me and Listen to Koutchag)*; and Gevorg Emin *(For You on New Year's Day)*; as well as the poems of Vahan Derian *(Coming to Terms*, forthcoming). Her own work, which has appeared in various literary periodicals, is collected in *How to Choose Your Past*, and has been translated into Armenian and published in the Soviet Union. She has worked as a visiting lecturer and writer-in-residence at many universities, and has been president of the New England Poetry Club since 1979. She has recently become a member of the national board of the Columbia University Translation Center.

CHARLES DORIA—American poet and translator. He did his graduate studies at Harvard and SUNY, Buffalo, in classics and comparative literature. At present he teaches art at Rutgers University and is editor and publisher of *Assembling Press* in New York. Aside from his many scholarly articles on literature, particularly on classical literature, he has published three books of poetry, *The Game of Europe; Short;* and *Short r.* His translations include *Origins: Creation Texts from the Ancient Mediterranean, The Tenth Muse: Classical Drama in Translation,* and eight poems of Salma Khadra Jayyusi published in *Women of the Fertile Crescent,* ed. by Kamal Boullata (1977).

ALISTAIR ELLIOT—Born in Liverpool, England, he lived in America during World War II, was later educated at Edinburgh and Oxford, and lived for two years in Iran. He has worked in the professional theatre and as a librarian. In 1982 he took an early retirement from his job as special collections librarian at Newcastle University, and is now a full-time poet. Among his collections are *Contentions; Talking Back;* and *On the Appian Way.* He has also translated Heine's *The Lazarus Poems* and Verlaine's *Femme/ Hombre, Women/Men,* and has edited John Dryden's translation of Vergil's *The Georgics.*

THOMAS G. EZZY—A dual (U.S.-Canada) national, he was born to a Lebanese-American father and a French-Canadian mother, and received an M.A. in English from the University of Toronto. A poet and writer of fiction, he has so far published two poetry chapbooks, *Parings* and *Arctic Char in Grecian Waters,* but is now working exclusively in fiction. Currently he resides in Montreal, where he teaches English at Dawson College. He has cotranslated, with Michael Young as first translator, Bechir Ben Slama's novel, *Aisha,* for PROTA (forthcoming).

SAMUEL HAZO—An American of Palestinian and Lebanese origin, S. Hazo is the founder and director of the International Poetry Forum in Pittsburgh, and a professor of English at Duquesne University. He is a poet, fiction writer, critic, and translator. His most recent works are *The Wanton Summer Air,* a novel; *Transformations of the Lover,* a translation of poetry by the Arab poet, Adunis; and *Thank a Bored Angel,* a collection of poetry.

JOHN HEATH-STUBBS—An English poet, critic, and translator, he obtained a degree in English from Queen's College, Oxford, in 1942 and lectured at the universities of Alexandria and Michigan and at the College of St. Mark and St. John in London. He now lectures at Oxford University. Among his many writings is his long poem, *Artorius,* for which he won the

Queen's Gold Medal for poetry in 1972. In 1978 he won the Oscar Williams and Geane Derwood Poetry Award in New York. He has published criticism, plays, and poetry collections, the last of which is *Naming the Beasts* (1983). He has also translated *Selected Poems and Prose of Giacomo Leopardi* with Iris Origo; and, with Peter Avery, has translated *Hafiz of Shiraz* and *The Rubaiyat of Omar Khayyam*. He has worked extensively with Salma Khadra Jayyusi on the *Anthology of the Literature of the Arabian Peninsula*, prepared by PROTA (forthcoming).

W. S. MERWIN—American poet, playwright, and translator, he is the author of several volumes of poetry, including *A Mask for Janus*, *The Dancing Bears*, *The Moving Target*, the Pulitzer Prize-winning *The Carrier of Ladders*, and *The Compass Flower*. His many translations include *Spanish Ballads*, *The Satires of Persius*, *Products of the Perfected Civilization* (selected writings of Chamfort), *Twenty Love Poems and a Song of Despair* (poems by Pablo Neruda), and *Sanskrit Love Poetry*. He lives in Hawaii.

CHRISTOPHER MIDDLETON—English poet and translator. His most recent works include a book of poems, *111 Poems* (Manchester and New York, 1983), and a book of essays, *The Pursuit of the Kingfisher* (Manchester and New York, 1983). His translations include Goethe's *Selected Poems* (Boston, 1983), and Gert Hofmann's *The Spectacle at the Tower* (New York, 1984). Forthcoming from Oasis Press, London, is *Serpentine*, a book of short prose. He teaches German literature and comparative literature at the University of Texas, Austin.

NAOMI SHIHAB NYE—Poet and musician. Born in St. Louis to a Palestinian father and an American mother, she graduated from Trinity University, San Antonio. Between 1966 and 1967 she lived in Jerusalem. She worked as a poet-in-the-school for ten years in Texas, as Holloway lecturer at the University of California, Berkeley, and as lecturer in poetry at the University of Texas at San Antonio. Her publications include *Hugging the Jukebox* and *Different Ways to Pray*, as well as poems published in numerous journals and anthologies. Her next book, *Yellow Glove*, is due to appear in the spring of 1987. She has cotranslated, with Lena Jayyusi, selections from the poetry of the Tunisian poet, *Abu al-Qasim al-Shabbi*, and participated widely in the translations of both poetry and fiction for the *Anthology of the Literature of the Arabian Peninsula*. She lives with her husband and son in San Antonio, Texas.

DESMOND O'GRADY—Born in Limerick, Ireland, in 1935, he studied at Catholic schools in his hometown, then at the Cistercian College in Roscrea. Later on he went to Harvard, where he received his M.A. in comparative Celtic studies. He taught at the Berlitz School in Paris for a year in 1955, then went to Rome where he was senior English master at the Overseas School for several years. In 1975–76 he was poet-in-residence at the American University in Cairo and in 1978 he became a lecturer in English literature there. These experiences enhanced his cultural relations with the Arab world and aroused his interest in Arabic literature. In the eighties he was back at Harvard, where he lectured for some time before returning to Ireland. He has many publications, among which are several collections of poetry and some verse translations, including the famous ode of the pre-Islamic poet, Umru'u al-Qais.

PETER PORTER—Born in Brisbane, Australia, he is of English and Scottish extraction. He came to England in 1951 and has lived and worked in London ever since. He is a freelance poet, reviewer, and broadcaster, specializing in contemporary verse and in musical forms allied to poetry. His *Collected Poems*, which brought together his eight original collections of verse plus his translation of the first-century Latin poet, Martial, was published in 1983. His latest collection is titled *Fast Forward*.

ANTHONY THWAITE—English poet and writer. He was educated at Oxford University, taught English at the universities of Tokyo and Libya, was literary editor of the *Listener* and the *New Statesman*, and is now coeditor of *Encounter*. He is widely traveled and has published eight books of poetry, the most recent of which is *Poems 1953–1983*. He has also published criticism, anthologies, and books on travel and topography. He is a Fellow of the Royal Society of Literature in Britain.

CHRISTOPHER TINGLEY—Born in Brighton, England, he received his education at the universities of London and Leeds. Following initial teaching experience in Germany and Britain, he lectured on English and linguistics at the University of Constantine, Algeria, the University of Ghana, and the National University of Rwanda. He collaborated with S. K. Jayyusi on the translation of the extracts of Arabic poetry in her two-volume work, *Trends and Movements in Modern Arabic Poetry*. With Elizabeth Hodgkin, he has translated from the French Mohamed Mzali's *La Parole de l'Action* (forthcoming), and with Olive and Lorne Kenny as first translators he has cotranslated Muhammad Yusuf al-Qaʿid's novel, *War in the Land of Egypt* (1986), for PROTA.

RICHARD WILBUR—Born in New York City, he did his graduate studies at Harvard, where he was a Junior Fellow of the Society of Fellows. He taught English at Harvard, Wellesley, and Wesleyan. At present, he is writer-in-residence at Smith College. He has published many collections of poetry, including *Things of This World, Walking to Sleep, The Mind Reader*, and *Seven Poems*. He has also published *Responses*, a book of criticism. He has translated widely, and his *The Whale* includes poems from Old and Middle English, Russian, Italian, Spanish, Portuguese, and Hungarian. His translation of four verse plays of Molière was republished in 1982 in one volume, *Molière: Four Comedies*. The same year he published his verse translation of Racine's *Andromache*. At present he is working on a verse translation of Racine's *Phèdra*.